MultiMate Advantage on the IBM PC

Other Books by Leo J. Scanlon

Assembly Language Programming with the IBM PC AT
80286 Assembly Language on MS-DOS Computers
8086/88 Assembly Language Programming
IBM PC & XT Assembly Language: A Guide for Programmers.
  Enhanced and Enlarged Edition.
MultiMate on the IBM PC

MultiMate Advantage on the IBM PC

Leo J. Scanlon

A Brady Book
Published by Prentice Hall Press
New York, New York 10023

MultiMate Advantage on the IBM PC

A Brady Book
Published by Prentice Hall Press
A Division of Simon & Schuster, Inc.
Gulf + Western Building
One Gulf + Western Plaza
New York, New York   10023

PRENTICE HALL PRESS is a trademark of Simon & Schuster, Inc.

Designed by Michael O'Brien
Cover design copyright © 1986 by Robert Anthony, Inc.
Cover photo by Robert Stevens, courtesy of THE WORKBOOK
   California Edition
Manufactured in the United States of America

1 2 3 4 5 6 7 8 9 10

Library of Congress Cataloging-in-Publication Data

Scanlon, Leo J.
   MultiMate Advantage on the IBM PC.

   "A Brady book."
   Includes index.
   1. Word processing.   2. MultiMate Advantage
(Computer program)   3. IBM Personal Computer—
Programming.   I. Title.
Z52.5.M85S28   1986   652'.5   86-91486
ISBN 0-89303-676-5

Contents

Preface

This book is a practical guide to the *MultiMate Advantage Professional Word Processor*. By "practical" we mean that it shows you how to use MultiMate Advantage (hereafter called Advantage) to perform everyday tasks. It describes Advantage from the user's point of view, with an emphasis on composing informal and formal correspondence, reports, and form letters, and revising text.

The discussion is illustrated with simple yet realistic examples. Each chapter ends with practical hints and warnings and a key point summary. Most chapters include a series of questions and answers addressing common problems.

Intended Audience

This book assumes no prior word processing or computer experience beyond the simple ability to start up your computer. With this in mind, we explain everything in plain English and use technical terms only when absolutely necessary. Furthermore, we move at a relaxed pace and introduce new topics as required to do useful work. We assume that you are primarily concerned with using Advantage to simplify your writing tasks, not with learning every possible command or nuance.

What Kind of Computer Should You Have?

Advantage requires an IBM Personal Computer—regular, extended (XT), or advanced (AT)—with at least 320K memory and either two double-sided floppy disk drives or a floppy disk drive and a hard (fixed) disk. Owners of IBM PC-compatibles and other MS-DOS computers should consult their dealers or Multimate International to determine whether Advantage will run on their machines as well.

What This Book Contains

This book has 13 chapters. Chapter 1 is a general overview of word processing, and then it describes the features, applications, and requirements of Advantage. It also discusses how Advantage differs from ordinary typing.

Chapter 2 launches into the actual use of Advantage. It describes the methods required for casual jobs such as personal correspondence and household lists. Here you learn how to correct typing errors, divide text into paragraphs, print documents, and save your work on disk.

Chapter 3 discusses preparing formal correspondence with stricter and more precise formats. This involves setting margins and tabs, right-justifying, handling multipage letters, underlining, and centering. We also show you how to set up tables and use abbreviations for material you refer to often.

Chapter 4 explains how to locate and correct spelling errors. It also discusses using Advantage's Thesaurus to obtain a list of synonyms for a word, and replacing the word with a synonym if you choose to do so.

Chapter 5 describes the composition of reports and other longer documents. This involves learning about double-spacing, page numbering, headers and footers, bold print, subscripts and superscripts, and footnotes. We also discuss managing disk space and disk files.

Chapter 6 discusses revising text. It explains how to move and copy material, and how to use search and replace operations to correct and update documents.

Chapter 7 describes how to save text and commands you use often in "key procedures." Chapter 8 shows you how to produce form letters.

Chapter 9 discusses tailoring Advantage to your specific needs. Chapter 10 discusses using Advantage with other programs such as spreadsheets (e.g., Lotus's *1-2-3*) and databases (e.g., Ashton-Tate's *dBASE II*).

Chapter 11 introduces *MultiMate On-File*, an information management program included with Advantage. On-File is a computerized version of the ordinary index card filing system found in offices. Like the office filing system, On-File lets you create card boxes and the cards that go in them, except here both the boxes and cards are stored on computer disks. This chapter also explains how to edit, print, cross-reference, and delete cards, as well as how to search for similar cards to form a "deck."

Chapter 12 discusses some advanced On-File operations, such as sorting card decks and printing labels. Chapter 13 describes using On-File with Advantage and other programs. It discusses how to merge the information on cards with Advantage documents to produce form letters or reports. It also describes how to transfer data between On-File cards and a spreadsheet or database program.

Appendices A and B summarize Advantage and MultiMate On-File commands, respectively.

What You Will Learn

This book will give you a firm grasp on using Advantage to prepare letters, reports, term papers, contracts, legal documents, forms, lists, and memoranda. You will learn how to correct typing errors quickly and easily, set up different page formats, produce special features such as underlining and bold print, and handle tables, equations, quotations, references, and footnotes. You will also learn how to use the versatile index card features of MultiMate On-File. To sum up, this book will teach you how to use Advantage and On-File to simplify a wide range of everyday writing jobs.

Leo J. Scanlon
Inverness, FL

Limits of Liability and Disclaimer of Warranty

Trademarks

1

Introduction

What Is Word Processing?

Word processing is the electronic creation of letters, reports, memoranda, articles, books, and other documents without erasures, misspellings, or unsightly corrections. It lets you deal with words as you do in your mind rather than on paper. That is, you can replace them, erase them, insert them, move them, change their appearance, or rearrange them quickly and easily without any fuss or mess. It is as great an advance over even the most elaborate correcting typewriter as that typewriter is over the quill pen.

Even at its simplest level, word processing is a tremendous convenience. You can turn out professional-quality letters, reports, articles, term papers, and manuscripts even if you can't type very well. You don't need special correction tape or fluid, cutting and pasting, or trying to insert typing into copies. Instead, you simply enter your material, make your corrections and changes on a display screen, and print the final copy.

Not only is word processing faster and more convenient than regular typing, but it also gives you much more freedom to change and improve your work. You can correct mistakes easily, even in a nearly final draft that you would never change by hand. You can reorder your ideas, improve your explanations, remove or change repetitive words or phrases, or insert material at the last minute. In short, word processing lets you concentrate on what to say rather than on making it look right. It's even better than having someone type for you, since it's faster, more accurate, and more convenient.

You can do more things with word processing than you could even consider doing manually. For example, you can

1. Build a library of standard letters, paragraphs, clauses, or other material that you can have ready for immediate use.
2. Insert material from other sources (e.g., contracts, invoices, or financial statements) without retyping.
3. Merge materials to create longer documents.
4. Produce special formats such as underlining, bold print, subscripts, and superscripts.
5. Check an entire document for misspellings, incorrect or obsolete material, and repetitions of words and phrases. You can also make all the required changes or corrections with simple commands.
6. Automatically add features such as headings, wider or narrower margins, and page numbers.
7. Copy and change documents without destroying the originals or producing work that looks sloppy or unprofessional.
8. Produce customized or personalized form letters, notices, and memoranda that look like original typing.

All these features can dramatically increase both the quantity and quality of your work. Once you have worked with a word processor, going back to an ordinary typewriter is comparable to living without your automobile, television set, or refrigerator. Word processing is a tremendous advance in convenience, speed, and ease of use.

"But," you may ask, "isn't it difficult to learn? Don't I have to be a computer expert?" The answer to both questions is *no*. You can become a competent word processor in a relatively short time. You need not understand computers or computer programming any more than you would to operate an automatic teller machine, an electronic cash register, or a calculator.

One of the nicest features of word processing is that you can learn gradually. You don't have to master every aspect of it to do useful work. You can start by simply using the word processor as a correcting typewriter. Then, as you gain experience and confidence, you can learn the more advanced functions. The more you learn, the more you can do, but each new step is worthwhile. This step-by-step approach is the one we use in this book.

What Is MultiMate Advantage?

The MultiMate Advantage Professional Word Processor is a word processing program designed by Multimate International (East Hartford, Connecticut) for use on an IBM Personal Computer (PC) or a compatible. Advantage is an enhanced version of the company's popular *MultiMate* word processing program.

Major Features of Advantage

Advantage can perform the following tasks:

- Insert or delete characters, words, lines, sentences, or pages of text. A *character* is any letter, number, punctuation mark, or other symbol on the keyboard.
- Replace characters.
- Automatically rearrange text after insertions or deletions to produce lines of the proper length.
- Control the format and appearance of a printed document.
- Justify text to create an even right-hand margin.
- Move blocks of text (anything ranging from a word to many pages) anywhere in a document, or even from one document to another.
- Search an entire document for characters, words, or phrases.
- Produce underlining, double underlining, bold print, subscripts, and superscripts.
- Allow you to abbreviate lengthy phrases, names, addresses, titles, or even entire paragraphs. Advantage expands the abbreviations at your request.
- Number the pages in a document.
- Number section titles in either Roman (e.g., I, I.A, I.B) or Numeric (e.g., 1, 1.1, 1.2) style, and generate a table of contents based on numbered titles.
- Keep track of footnotes, so that they always remain on the same page as their references.
- Add rows or columns of numbers in tables.
- Draw lines or boxes within a document. This lets you construct borders around titles and create bar charts.
- Save documents for later use and read them back when needed.
- Check a document for, and correct, spelling errors.

- Allow you to create templates for commonly-used formats or for forms that can be filled in later by someone else.
- Produce "personalized" form letters from a mailing list.
- Convert files created by other programs for use in Advantage documents.

Version 3.6 or later of Advantage can perform these additional tasks:

- Arrange text in columnar format. You can choose between columns that contain related material running side by side or columns in which text runs continuously, in newspaper fashion.
- Look up definitions and synonyms for words or phrases in a built-in thesaurus.
- Print the current page from within a document.
- Produce form letters using variable information supplied from the keyboard.
- Allow you to specify how fast keys repeat when you hold them down.

MultiMate Advantage comes with a computerized index card package called *MultiMate On-File.* Information in On-File cards can be searched, sorted, edited, cross-referenced, printed, or merged with Advantage documents to produce form letters or reports.

Typical Applications

Advantage has many applications to many people. Typical users include:

- Managers, business people, and government or other professional workers who want to produce memoranda, reports, notices, price lists, schedules, mailings, and formal correspondence.
- Students who want to write assignments, term papers, theses, and dissertations.
- Researchers who want to prepare proposals, articles, studies, forecasts, talks or presentations, and status reports.
- Writers who want to produce articles, essays, scripts, stories, poems, and books.
- Lawyers, bankers, accountants, and other professionals who want to generate contracts, notices, briefs, wills, transcripts, financial statements, and reports.

- Teachers who want to prepare lectures, class rosters, assignments, notes, and tests.

You can also use Advantage at home for letters, invitations, club or organizational mailings, rosters, and other lists, schedules, bulletins, newsletters, notices, and creative or nonfiction writing.

The MultiMate On-File index card package is convenient for writers who want to create an index or bibliography for a book, researchers who want to organize their notes, businesspeople who want to maintain customer and inventory lists or generate mailing lists, and anyone who needs the data-managing capabilities of an index card system.

Differences between Advantage and MultiMate

As mentioned earlier, Advantage is an enhanced version of the MultiMate word processing program. New features include footnoting, automatic section numbering (which lets you generate a table of contents), line and box drawing, double underscore, and, of course, the MultiMate On-File program.

Advantage also offers easier ways to perform some existing MultiMate operations. For example, Advantage's Merge Print Utility lets you create a Data File that displays a blank form called a *Template* into which you enter data for form letters. The Data File is also convenient for filling in forms. Other notable improvements include:

- When inserting text, you can tell Advantage to "push" new material onto the screen (by moving existing text to the right) instead of clearing the rest of the screen.
- Advantage spell-checks about three times faster than MultiMate.
- During spell-editing, you can now type in a replacement word manually without leaving the spell-edit mode.
- During spell-editing, once you add a word to the custom dictionary or clear its place mark, Advantage automatically unmarks subsequent occurrences of the word. Similarly, if you correct a word manually, Advantage makes the same change to subsequent mentions of that word.
- Advantage provides a command that replays the last key procedure you executed.

Required Equipment

To use MultiMate Advantage, you need an IBM Personal Computer or compatible with two double-sided floppy disk drives, at least 320K of memory, and a printer. You may also use a computer that has one floppy disk drive and a hard disk drive such as an IBM PC XT or AT.

Floppy disk drives record and play thin, flexible magnetic media called *diskettes* or *disks.* These are available in computer stores and most office supply stores. A *hard disk* is a recording mechanism capable of holding much more information than a floppy disk. Disks serve the same purpose as tapes used to record and play back music, language lessons, or dictation.

Differences from Regular Typing

If you are used to working on a standard typewriter, you may be intimidated by all the oddly-marked keys on the computer's keyboard. We will explain here what those keys do.

Figure 1-1 shows three groups of keys. The white keys in the center are like those on a typewriter. However, on the keyboard for the IBM PC and XT, there is a key marked \ and ¦ between Z and the left-hand Shift key. Shift is marked with a wide upward-pointing arrow. If you are a touch typist, be careful to avoid pressing this extra key instead of Shift. On the IBM PC AT keyboard the \ key is located at the upper right-hand corner of the central key group, so you will not have this problem.

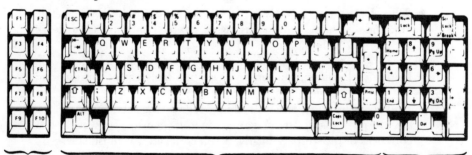

Function keys   Typewriter keyboard   Numeric keypad

Figure 1-1. IBM Personal Computer Keyboard.

The white keys also include some extra symbols. They are:

[   ]   {   }   `   ~   <   >

Control Keys

The dark keys on both sides of the central white ones are control keys. They affect other keys or make the computer do something other than just enter a character. Figure 1-2 shows the control keys you will use most often with Advantage.

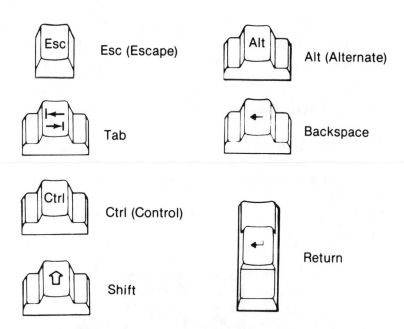

Figure 1-2. Frequently-used control keys.

We already mentioned the Shift key. The key with the bent left arrow is the Return key (the IBM manuals call it "Enter"). On a typewriter, you press Return at the end of each line. With Advantage, you press it only at the end of a paragraph or to skip a line. The computer divides normal text into lines automatically. The dark key with both left and right arrows (left of Q) is the Tab key; it is used to move right, just as on a typewriter.

Caps Lock is a handy variation of a shift lock key; it locks in capital letters but *leaves the nonletter keys in lowercase.* Be careful with Caps Lock. Pressing it once locks in capital letters, but pressing it again returns the keyboard to lowercase. The IBM PC AT keyboard has a special green light that indicates whether Caps Lock is on or off, but the PC and XT keyboards do not. Fortunately, Advantage provides its own indicator: it puts *S:* (for Shift) and a vertical arrow at the bottom of the screen. A down arrow means Shift and Caps Lock are off; an up arrow means one of them is on.

Of course, you can always press a letter key and see what appears on the screen. One added feature is that when Caps Lock is on, you can press Shift to enter lowercase letters. Nonletter keys always work normally.

Among the other control keys, you will only use Esc (Escape), Ctrl (Control), and Alt (Alternate) with Advantage. We will describe their functions later.

Numeric Keypad

The keys on the right in Figure 1-3 are like the keys on a calculator. We call them a *numeric keypad* because they can be used to enter long sequences of numbers, such as item prices, grades, and population figures. The regular number keys in the typewriter section are also available, but they are rather hard to reach. These keys are used like a normal calculator.

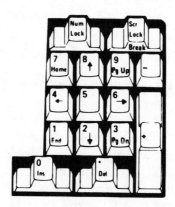

Figure 1-3. Numeric keypad.

Note that four of the white keys are marked with arrows. They provide you with a way to move from one place to another on the screen. Home, End, PgUp (Page Up), and PgDn (Page Down) are also movement keys, but they let you move greater distances than the arrow keys do.

Ins (Insert) and Del (Delete) at the bottom on the keypad, as well as + and − at the right, are used to insert material into existing text or remove material from it. We describe how Ins and Del differ from + and − later.

Note that the keys in the numeric keypad have both lowercase and uppercase markings. Pressing the Num Lock key changes these keys from one case to the other. As with Caps Lock, the IBM PC AT has a special green light that indicates which case is active, but the PC and XT keyboards do not. Advantage does provide an indicator. It puts N: and a vertical arrow on the bottom line of the screen. A down arrow means Num Lock is off; an up arrow means it is on.

Function Keys

The dark keys at the far left are *function keys,* labeled F1 through F10. With Advantage, use these keys to give the computer special commands such as start a new page, indent, and combine pages.

Keyboard Hints

The following hints will help you use the PC keyboard effectively. Be particularly careful if you are an experienced typist; some keys are not where you would expect, and blind reaching will result in a lot of errors. Watch the screen closely until you become accustomed to the keyboard.

1. Note the difference between the space bar on the PC and on a typewriter. Pressing the space bar on the PC actually enters a space; that is, it blanks the current position on the screen. This is different from a typewriter, where the space bar moves the carriage or typing element right without affecting the text. The right-arrow key on the PC's numeric keypad is equivalent to the space bar on a typewriter.
2. Always be sure you have Caps Lock and Num Lock off. Fortunately, as we noted, Advantage indicates when they are on by showing up arrows

marked *S:* and *N:* on the bottom line. If you are getting all capital letters, or getting numbers when you meant to move somewhere on the screen, check the display and turn the lock off. The usual problem is pressing a lock key by accident, particularly pressing Caps Lock when you meant to press Shift.

3. Be careful when you reach for the Shift keys. Not only is there an extra key between Z and the left-hand shift, but there are also extra keys at the ends of the space bar (Alt on the left and Caps Lock on the right). Be careful to press Shift, not one of the other nearby keys.

4. Note that Caps Lock is below the right-hand Shift key, not above the left-hand Shift key, as Shift Lock is on most typewriters.

5. Don't reach too far when you intend to press Return. It's a large key, but there are keys to its right, unlike the situation on most typewriter keyboards.

6. Type symbols carefully. Particularly watch the locations of common ones such as ", - (a lowercase character), and '.

7. Watch what you're doing when you press control keys (Alt, Ctrl, or Tab) and function keys. It's easy to hit the wrong key, and the effects are often very different.

Differences between Word Processing and Typing

Although word processing is similar to typing, there are some differences that affect everyday work. They include:

1. A long list of commands. More capabilities usually mean more commands (as well as more potential errors). Don't try to memorize commands. The common ones will become habits, and you can always look up the lesser ones in the appendix of this book or in the Advantage manual.

   The keyboard layout, quick reference card, and stick-on color key labels that come with Advantage are also valuable aids, as is the optional keyboard template offered by Multimate International. Finally, Advantage can also display a description of the commands (called a *Help function*) you can see at any time.

2. What you see on the screen is not necessarily what comes out on the printer. Your printer may not be able to produce subscripts, superscripts, or boldface, even though Advantage can produce them. It may, on the other hand, have special typefaces and features such as compressed print that you cannot see on the screen. Furthermore, the

printer's letters and spacing may look different from the computer's, and your printer may not even be able to produce certain characters. You will become familiar with the differences after a while, but this distinction can create problems.

3. Disks require special treatment. Save them in their paper jackets when not using them, label them carefully (using only a felt-tip pen), and store them upright in a box or special container. You may turn off the PC with disks in the drives, but *never remove a disk when the computer is using it.* Disks need not be handled like precious jewels, but handle them as carefully as you do your best records or tapes.

Preparing Your Word Processing System

The Advantage *Beginner's Guide* contains a detailed description of how to set up Advantage for day-to-day work. For a computer with floppy disk drives, the Guide tells you:

1. How to make working copies of the Boot, System, Advanced Utilities, Speller/Dictionary, and Thesaurus disks.
2. How to customize the System disk for your printer. This involves copying onto it the appropriate Printer Action Table (PAT) program from the Printer Tables Diskette.
3. How to create a data disk (the *Guide* calls this a "non-bootable diskette") to store the documents you will create with Advantage. In this book, we refer to this as your Learning Disk.

For a computer with a hard disk drive, such as an IBM PC XT or PC AT, the *Beginner's Guide* tells you:

1. How to create a *path* to the Disk Operating System (DOS) programs on the hard disk. Advantage, and most other programs, must use DOS features from time to time.
2. How to create a control program that points the computer at the DOS programs whenever you switch the power on. This program is called AUTOEXEC.BAT.
3. How to copy DOS into its own area, or *subdirectory,* on the hard disk. (Note: Unless you just bought your computer, somebody has probably already done steps 1, 2, and 3.)

4. How to copy the programs on the Advantage disks into a separate sub-directory. The *Beginner's Guide* suggests that you name this subdirectory **MM.**

5. How to make Advantage use the hard disk for all of its work. This is necessary because the Advantage disks assume you have a floppy disk system.

If your computer has a hard disk, you have to enter two commands every time you use Advantage. When the C> prompt appears, do the following:

- To put the computer into the Advantage subdirectory (MM), enter **cd \mm**, then press the Return key.
- To start Advantage, enter either **mm** or **wp** and press Return again. (We discuss the differences between typing **mm** and **wp** shortly.)

To avoid this, you can create start-up files that perform *both* steps when you type **mm** or **wp**.

Creating Start-Up Files for Advantage

Here are the procedures for creating two start-up files. The computer uses one file when you type **mm** and uses the other when you type **wp**. To create the *mm* start-up file:

1. Type **copy con: mm.bat** and press Return.
2. Type **cd \mm** and press Return.
3. Type **mm**
4. Press the F6 key.

To create the *wp* start-up file:

1. Type **copy con: wp.bat** and press Return.
2. Type **cd \ad** and press Return.
3. Type **wp %1**
4. Press the F6 key.

Disk Drive Names

Your computer recognizes its disk drives by specific one-letter names. You must know these names for some Advantage operations. For a computer with two floppy disk drives, the left-hand drive is called drive *A* and the right-hand drive is called drive *B*. (This assumes that you have an IBM PC or PC XT, in which the drives are side-by-side. On an IBM PC AT, the drives are installed vertically; here, the top drive is A and the bottom drive is B.) If your computer has a hard disk, it is called drive *C*.

Note to Hard Disk Users

From time to time within this book, I direct you to insert a disk in drive A or B. If your PC has a hard disk, ignore these instructions. All the programs you need are on the hard disk (drive C), and Advantage automatically puts the documents you create onto the hard disk. Therefore, *you only have to insert a floppy disk into the computer when you are copying information to it to create a backup.*

2

Informal Writing

Advantage lets you quickly do informal writing such as notes, personal letters, or shopping lists. In this kind of writing you use the PC much like an ordinary typewriter.

Notes, personal letters, and shopping lists come and go. Most people don't keep copies or use the same thing twice. Other informal documents are worth keeping, such as lists of names and telephone numbers, Christmas card lists, class rosters, or an inventory of your household effects or insured valuables. This chapter shows you how to use Advantage for both temporary and permanent documents.

Getting Started

The procedure for starting Advantage depends on what kind of computer you have. If it has only floppy disk drives, put your System disk in drive A and your Learning Disk in drive B, then switch the power on. Otherwise, if your computer has a hard disk, simply switch the power on.

When the computer asks for the date, enter it in the form *month-day-year,* then press Return. For example, on May 29, 1986, enter **5-29-86,** then press Return. When the computer asks for the time, press Return.

When you see A>—or C>, if you have a hard disk—type **wp** (**WP** or **Wp** will also do—the computer is not particular in this case) and press Return. This makes Advantage display its *Main Menu* (see Figure 2-1).

```
┌─────────────────────────────────────────────────────┐
│                                                       │
│            ┌─────────────────────────────┐            │
│            │     MultiMate Advantage      │           │
│            │        Version 3.60          │           │
│            └─────────────────────────────┘            │
│                                                       │
│          1) Edit an Old Document                      │
│          2) Create a New Document                     │
│                                                       │
│          3) Print Document Utility                    │
│          4) Printer Control Utilities                 │
│          5) Merge Print Utility                       │
│                                                       │
│          6) Document Handling Utilities               │
│          7) Other Utilities                           │
│          8) Spell Check a Document                    │
│          9) Return to DOS                             │
│                                                       │
│              DESIRED FUNCTION:                        │
│                                                       │
│                                                       │
│       Enter the number of the function; press RETURN  │
│        Hold down Shift and press F1 for HELP menu     │
│                                                  S:1 N:1│
└─────────────────────────────────────────────────────┘
```

Figure 2-1. Advantage's Main Menu.
Courtesy of Multimate International Corp.

The blinking rectangle after DESIRED FUNCTION: is the *cursor*. It indicates where you are working and tells you that the computer wants some information. In this case, the computer wants you to choose from the nine different tasks in the Main Menu. The first thing we want to do is enter new material, so press **2** to select "Create a New Document," then press Return.

Creating a New Document

Pressing Return makes Advantage display a "Create a New Document" form (Figure 2-2) asking you for the document's name. We want to write a letter to John, so enter **John** then press Return.

CREATE A NEW DOCUMENT

Enter the Name of the New Document

Drive: __   Document: _____

Approximately _____ **characters [** _____ **Page(s)] available on** __

Figure 2-2. Create a New Document form.
Courtesy of Multimate International Corp.

Advantage displays a "Document Summary Screen" with your document's name (*John*) at the top. This form is handy for keeping track of documents. We discuss it later; for now, press F10 to advance past it.

The next form, "Modify Document Defaults," lets you change some of Advantage's assumptions about how you want your text handled. This is another form we discuss later, so press F10 once again.

Status and Format Lines

Pressing F10 a final time clears the screen and puts two lines of information at the top and a blinking underline (the cursor) below them.

The top line, the *status line,* tells you where the cursor is located. It is currently at Page 1, Line 1, Column 1 of Document *JOHN.* These numbers change as you enter text.

The second line, the *format line,* tells you how Advantage spaces the document when it prints it (the *1* here indicates single-spacing) and shows where various markers are located. The ≫ symbols are tab markers; Advantage has set tabs at columns 5, 10, and 15.

Advantage uses ≪ to indicate the end of the line. If you type a word that extends beyond the ≪, the computer automatically brings it down to the next line.

Entering a Letter

Now it's time for you to type something. Figure 2-3 contains a sample letter. Don't worry about typing errors; you will soon learn how to correct them.

```
May 11, 1986

Dear John:

Believe it or not, I'm writing this letter on my IBM Personal Computer!  I
bought a word processing program called MultiMate Advantage that lets me
use the PC just like a typewriter.  Since this is my first try at using
it, I can't tell you how easy it actually is, but so far so good.

Pat and I want to invite you, Sandra, and Robby to our new cabin by Bender
Lake.  To paraphrase an old joke, when can you drop in?  Write soon.

All the best,



(Type your name here)
```

Figure 2-3. Sample letter to a friend.

Start by typing the date. The first letter will appear at the cursor's location in the upper left-hand corner of the screen. The cursor moves right automatically as you type. Now press Return. The computer's Return key is like the Return key on a typewriter; that is, it moves the typing location indicator (cursor) to the beginning of the next line. (When you press Return, Advantage marks it with a ≪ symbol.)

Since the salutation starts two lines below the date, press Return again, then type **Dear John:**. Now press Return twice more to reach the line where the body of the letter begins.

Type the body, but *do not press Return at the end of each line.* This is a major benefit of word processing over ordinary typing. Advantage keeps track of how long each line is and automatically brings the cursor down to the next line. Press Return only when you reach the end of a paragraph or want to skip a line.

After you type the close (**All the best,**), press Return four times to reach the line for your name, then type it and press Return once more.

Correcting Errors

You probably made some mistakes when you typed the letter. Fortunately, correcting errors is easy with word processing. After all, the errors are on the screen, not on paper.

To correct an error, first move the cursor to it. Use the arrow keys and the other keys on the numeric keypad. Remember that you can't use the space bar to move over material, because that will *erase* the material!

Moving the Cursor

As you may have guessed, the arrow keys on the numeric keypad move the cursor in the direction they point; that is, right (6), left (4), up (8), and down (2). The Home and End keys move the cursor to the beginning or end of the text on the screen, while PgUp and PgDn move it up or down a whole screen—that is, 18 lines at a time. Finally, holding Ctrl (Control) down while you press Home or End moves the cursor to the top or bottom of the *page,* which may be past the area the screen shows.

Figure 2-4 shows how these cursor-moving keys are arranged. Be sure Num Lock is off when you use these keys. If Num Lock is on, Advantage displays an up arrow just after *N:* at the bottom right-hand corner of the screen. In that case, press Num Lock to turn it off.

Figure 2-4. Cursor-moving keys.

Not only do the arrow keys have directions marked on them, they are also placed according to the way they point. The up-arrow key is above the others, the left-arrow key is to the left, and so on. These keys *repeat*—they keep the cursor moving as long as you hold them down. (It may, in fact, move *too* fast to suit you. We show how to change the speed later in this chapter.)

If you have followed directions so far, the letter is on the screen and the cursor is on the line below your name. Press the up-arrow key. It will move the cursor up one line each time you press it. Move up a line or two, then keep your finger on the key until the cursor reaches the top (date) line. The cursor will not move any higher. In fact, if you attempt to move it higher, Advantage will display *THIS IS THE FIRST PAGE* at the bottom of the screen.

Now press the down-arrow key until the cursor is on the first line of the second paragraph—the line that starts with "Pat and I." If the cursor moves too far, use the up-arrow key to backtrack.

Suppose we really want to type Pam instead of Pat. Here's how to correct this mistake.

Changing Characters

Changing a character is easy: move the cursor to it and type the new character. Advantage automatically replaces the old character with the new one.

Therefore, to change *Pat* to *Pam*, use the arrow keys to move the cursor to the *t* in *Pat*. Now type **m**. The *t* is replaced by *m*. (Note that you don't have to erase the *t* first, as you would on a correcting type-writer.) If you made any other one-character mistakes, correct them now using the method just described.

It is just as easy to change several characters. Simply move the cursor to where the changes begin, then type the new characters.

Inserting and Deleting Characters

To insert or delete characters, use the dark + (plus) and − (minus) keys at the far right of the numeric keypad. The Advantage manual calls the + key "Insert Character" and the − key "Delete Character."

To insert a character, move the cursor to where you want to make the insertion, then press the + key. This opens a gap in which you can type the new character. If the additional character makes the line too long, Advantage moves the excess to the next line and rearranges the paragraph to make every line the proper length.

To erase or delete a character, move the cursor to it, then press the — key. The gap created by the deletion closes automatically.

To see how insertion and deletion work, let's try them on our example letter. Specifically, let's change Sandra's name to *Saundra* and back to *Sandra* again.

Move the cursor to the first line of the second paragraph, then right to the *n* in *Sandra.* Now press **+** once (Advantage opens a one-character gap), then press **u**. The extra letter makes the line too long, so Advantage automatically moves the word *Bender* to the next line and rearranges the rest of the paragraph as follows:

```
Pam and I want to invite you, Saundra, and Robby to our new cabin by
Bender Lake.  To paraphrase an old joke, when can you drop in?  Write
soon.
```

Now let's delete the *u.* The cursor is under *n,* so press the left-arrow key once (the cursor moves to *u*), then press the — key. Saundra returns to its original spelling. If you see other words that have too many or too few characters, make the appropriate insertions and deletions similarly.

Working on Groups of Characters

You can also use the **+** (Insert Character) and **—** (Delete Character) keys to insert or delete groups of characters, but this is inconvenient. For example, suppose you want to change Pam (second paragraph) to Pamela. One way to do this is to move the cursor to the space between *Pam* and *and,* then type

+ e + l + a

Not only does this double the number of keystrokes, but if you forget to press **+**, the letter you type replaces the character in the text. Fortunately, Advantage provides ways to work with entire groups of characters rather than just single characters. To insert or delete groups of characters, use the Ins (Insert) and Del (Delete) keys at the bottom of the numeric keypad, just to the right of Caps Lock.

To insert text, move the cursor to where you want to make the insertion, then press Ins. Advantage clears the rest of the screen and displays *INSERT WHAT?* on the top (status) line. Don't worry, the extra material is still in the computer. Advantage shows the first 35

characters at the bottom of the screen, just to the left of the *S:* and *N:* indicators.) Type the insertion, then press Ins again to retrieve the rest of the text. As before, if the insertion makes the line too long, Advantage automatically rearranges the paragraph.

To delete text, move the cursor to the beginning of it, then press Del. Advantage highlights the character where the cursor is and displays *DELETE WHAT?* on the status line. Move the cursor to the last character you want to delete, then press Del again. Note that since deleting is a drastic act, Advantage highlights everything it will delete. This gives you a chance to change your mind before you press Del.

To see how Ins and Del work, let us change the first sentence of our letter to John. Let's insert the word *new* before IBM, changing *I'm writing this letter on my IBM Personal Computer!* to *I'm writing this letter on my **new** IBM Personal Computer!*.

To make the change, move the cursor to the *I* in *IBM* and press Ins. When you do this, the rest of the letter (from *IBM Personal Computer* on) disappears and the cursor is where *IBM* used to be. Further, to let you know that it is still holding on to the old text, Advantage shows

```
IBM Personal Computer.  I bought a
```

at the bottom of the screen. Type the word **new**, then press the space bar (to put a space after it) and Ins.

Let's delete the clause *Believe it or not,* from the first line. Move the cursor to the *B* in *Believe,* then press Del. *B* is highlighted (although you may have to adjust the contrast and brightness controls on your display to see the highlighting). Now move the cursor to the space between *not,* and *I'm* and press Del again to complete the operation. The rearranged paragraph looks like this:

```
I'm writing this letter on my new IBM Personal Computer.  I bought a word
processing program called MultiMate Advantage that lets me use the PC just
like a typewriter.  Since this is my first try at using it, I can't tell
you how easy it actually is, but so far so good.
```

Ins is also convenient when you want to make words longer. For instance, earlier we showed how you could use character insertions with + to change *Pam* to *Pamela*. To make this change with Ins, move the cursor to the space between *Pam* and *and,* then press Ins.

The text starting at *and* disappears, so you simply enter **ela** (with *no Return* and *no space*), then press Ins again.

Canceling Ins and Del

Because the Ins and Del keys are located directly below the numeric keypad, you may sometimes press one of them when you mean to press a cursor-moving key. Fortunately, Advantage lets you cancel the insert or delete operation by pressing Esc (Escape). Esc is a dark key. On an IBM PC or XT, it is located just left of the 1 key at the top of the regular keyboard; on a PC AT, it is located just above the 7 key on the numeric keypad. Pressing Esc clears the status line prompt (*INSERT WHAT?* or *DELETE WHAT?*) and restores the screen to its original form.

Esc is Advantage's "panic button." You can press it to cancel just about any operation you started accidentally or absent-mindedly.

Selecting Words, Lines, and Sentences

To delete a group of characters, put the cursor at the first character and press Del. Then move the cursor to the last character and press Del again. This can be somewhat tedious when you want to delete a lot of text, because the arrow keys move the cursor rather slowly.

Fortunately, Advantage provides a way to quickly reach the last deletion character: simply type it! Advantage moves the cursor to the character you just typed and highlights everything in between. To complete the deletion operation, press Del again.

For example, once you put the cursor on the first character to be deleted, you can do any of the following:

- To delete a *word,* press Del, space, and Del.
- To delete a *line,* press Del, Alt-F6, and Del. Pressing the Alt (Alternate) and F6 keys simultaneously selects the entire line and moves the cursor to the end of it.
- To delete a *sentence,* press Del, period, space, space, and Del. Pressing the space bar twice here selects the spaces between this sentence and

the next one. (If your sentence ends with a question mark, exclamation point, or quotation mark, type that character instead of the period.)

For example, in the preceding section we inserted the word *new* in our letter to make an existing sentence read *I'm writing this letter on my new IBM Personal Computer!*. To delete *new* using the technique just described, move the cursor to the *n*, then press Del, space (to highlight the word), and Del again.

Selecting Consecutive Units

You can also extend the highlighting to select *consecutive* units (words, lines, or sentences) for deletion. After you select the first unit, simply use a similar approach to select the next one, and so on. When all of the units you want to delete are highlighted, press Del to complete the deletion operation.

Entering end characters to extend the highlighting is convenient if it doesn't involve too much work to reach them. However, if there are many such characters between where the cursor is and where you want it to end up, you should probably stick with using the arrow keys to extend the highlighting. For example, selecting the sentence

```
Dr. George R. Hardy of Adams Ave. Clinic in St. Louis, Mo. charges only
$2.50 for a house call.
```

requires you to press the period key seven times to reach the period at the end. It is faster and easier to move the cursor there directly using the arrow keys.

Working on Paragraphs

Advantage separates paragraphs with Returns. It also shows where you pressed Return by displaying ≪. You can use Returns to insert or delete a paragraph, to divide one, or to combine two paragraphs into one.

Inserting and Deleting Paragraphs

To insert a paragraph, put the cursor at the end of the line that precedes where you want the insertion, then press Ins. Advantage clears the rest of the screen. Press Return to begin the new paragraph, then enter it and press Return at the end. Finally, press Ins to retrieve the rest of the text.

To delete a paragraph, put the cursor at the beginning of it and press Del. Then press Return to select (highlight) the paragraph and Del to delete it.

To Advantage, a paragraph is everything from just after the last Return, up to and including the next Return. This will not be an entire paragraph if there are extra Returns because of equations, titles, lists, or quoted material. Thus, Advantage may well think of one paragraph as several, and will also think of each equation, title, list entry, quotation, or other material set off by Returns as a paragraph by itself.

Dividing Paragraphs

Pressing the Return key tells Advantage to begin a new paragraph. Therefore, to divide a paragraph, simply move the cursor just ahead of the sentence where you want the new paragraph to begin, then press Ins, Return twice, and Ins again. Advantage moves the rest of the paragraph down two lines and rearranges it to form a properly-spaced new paragraph.

For example, suppose you have accidentally combined two unrelated topics in a single paragraph. Perhaps you wrote

```
Jim and Ellen stopped over for bridge last night.  Jim is a mediocre
player, but Ellen plays like a professional.  Of course, they beat us
easily, as usual.  Tom had a cold, but he's almost totally recovered now.
We expect to send him back to school on Tuesday.«
```

To put the two subjects (bridge and Tom's cold) into separate paragraphs, move the cursor to the space preceding the *T* in *Tom*, then press Ins, Return, Return, and Ins. Your text now looks like this:

```
Jim and Ellen stopped over for bridge last night.  Jim is a mediocre
player, but Ellen plays like a professional.  Of course, they beat us
easily, as usual.«
«
Tom had a cold, but he's almost totally recovered now.  We expect to send
him back to school on Tuesday.«
```

Combining Paragraphs

To combine two paragraphs, move the cursor to the Return after the final sentence of the first paragraph and press the space bar, then the + (Insert Character) key on the numeric keypad. The two paragraphs are now one.

Note that pressing the space bar replaces the Return mark with a space (and combines the paragraphs), while pressing + inserts another space. Their net effect is to put two spaces between the sentence that ended the first paragraph and the one that began the second paragraph.

Saving a Document on Disk

At this point, the letter you entered should still be on the screen. Now that you are done editing, you will want to print it. To do that, you must first save it on disk.

To save the letter on disk, press the F10 key. When you do, the red light on drive B comes on and the drive makes a whirring sound. When Advantage finishes saving the letter, the Main Menu reappears.

Printing the Letter

Now you can print the letter. Well . . . almost. Since this is the first time you are printing, you must tell Advantage which kind of printer is attached to your computer. (You only have to do this once. Advantage will remember which printer you chose, and automatically use it in the future.)

Specifying the Printer

In Chapter 1 we suggested that you use the instructions in the *Advantage Beginner's Guide* to copy a Printer Action Table (PAT) program for your printer onto your working copy of the System disk. (With a hard disk, simply copy *all* of the PAT programs into your Advantage subdirectory.) However, copying a printer program to the System disk is not sufficient; you must also tell Advantage to *use* it. To do this:

1. Type **4** to select "Printer Control Utilities" in the Main Menu, then press Return. This makes Advantage display its *Printer Control Utilities* menu.
2. Type **2** to select "Edit Printer Defaults", then press Return. Advantage displays its *Modify Printer Defaults* form (see Figure 2-5). In this array of options, we want to change only those that select the printer and sheet feeder. These are: "Printer Action Table", "Sheet Feeder Action Table", and "P(arallel)/S(erial)".

```
                      MODIFY PRINTER DEFAULTS


   Start Print At Page Number        001    Lines Per Inch [6 or 8]                6
   Stop Print After Page Number      999    Justification: [N or Y or M(icro)]     N
   Left Margin                       000    Proportional Spacing: [N or Y]         N
   Top Margin                        000    Char Translate / Width Table      _____
   Pause Between Pages: [N or Y]       N    Header / Footer First Page Number    001
   Draft print: [N or Y]               N    Starting Footnote Number [1-871]     001
   Default pitch [4 = 10 CPI]          4    Number of Original Copies            001
                                            Document Page Length                 066
   Printer Action Table           TTYCRLF   Sheet Feeder Action Table         _____
   Sheet Feeder Bin Numbers [0 - 3]:        First page: 0  Middle: 0  Last page:   0
   P(arallel) / S(erial) / L(ist) / A(uxiliary) / F(ile)                           P
                                            Device Number                        001


   Print Doc. Summary Screen:  [N or Y]  N  Print Printer Parameters: [N or Y]     N
   Background / Foreground:  [B or F]    B  Remove Queue Entry When Done: [Y or N] Y



   Press F1 for Printers, F2 for Sheet Feeders - only the first 16 are displayed

                    (Printer types are listed here.)

          Press F10 to Continue, Press ESC to Abort              S:1 N:1
```

Figure 2-5. Modify Printer Defaults form.
Courtesy of Multimate International Corp.

3. Press the down-arrow key until the cursor reaches *TTYCRLF* on the "Printer Action Table" line.
4. Enter the name of your printer. If it has fewer than seven characters, press the space bar to erase any characters left over from *TTYCRLF*. For example, if you have an Integral Data Systems Prism printer, type **prism,** then press the space bar twice to erase *LF*.
5. If your printer has an electronic sheet feeder attached, press the right-arrow key until the cursor reaches "Sheet Feeder Action Table." Then enter the name of the feeder's SAT program.
6. Press the down-arrow key to reach the "P(arallel)/S(erial)..." line.

   The terms Parallel and Serial refer to the two ways a printer may be connected to a computer. Advantage assumes your printer uses a parallel connection. If it uses a serial connection instead (consult your printer manual or ask your dealer), type **s.**
7. Press F10 twice to return to the Main Menu.

Print Procedure

To begin the print operation:

1. Turn your printer on and, if necessary, switch it "on-line" (i.e., ready to communicate with the computer).
2. Type **3** and Return to select "Print Document Utility" from the Main Menu. Advantage displays a form titled *Print A Document*, with the cursor in the "Document" field and a list of available documents at the bottom. For the moment, we have only one document (*JOHN*), but this list will increase as you add additional documents to the Learning disk.
3. Enter **john** then press Return. This brings on a new form, *Print Parameters for Document* (see Figure 2-6). This is the same as the Modify Printer Defaults form (Figure 2-5), except it has date and time information at the bottom. Here, you may specify print parameters for this document that are different than those Advantage assumes you want.

Print Parameters for Document   B:DOCNAME

Start Print At Page Number	001	Lines Per Inch [6 or 8]	6
Stop Print After Page Number	001	Justification: [N or Y or M(icro)]	N
Left Margin	000	Proportional Spacing: [N or Y]	N
Top Margin	000	Char Translate / Width Table	
Pause Between Pages: [N or Y]	N	Header / Footer First Page Number	001
Draft print: [N or Y]	N	Starting Footnote Number [1-871]	001
Default pitch [4 = 10 CPI]	4	Number of Original Copies	001
		Document Page Length	066
Printer Action Table	TTYCRLF	Sheet Feeder Action Table	
Sheet Feeder Bin Numbers [0 - 3]:		First page: 0 Middle: 0 Last page:	0
P(arallel) / S(erial) / L(ist) / A(uxiliary) / F(ile)			P
		Device Number	001
Print Doc. Summary Screen: [N or Y]	N	Print Printer Parameters: [N or Y]	N
Background / Foreground: [B or F]	B	Remove Queue Entry When Done: [Y or N]	Y
Current Time is HH:MM:SS		Delay Print Until Time is HH:MM:SS	
Current Date is MM/DD/YYYY		Delay Print Until Date is MM/DD/YYYY	

Press F1 for Printers, F2 for Sheet Feeders - only the first 16 are displayed

(Printer types are listed here.)

Press F10 to Continue, Press ESC to Abort   S:1 N:1

Figure 2-6. Print Parameters for Document form.
Courtesy of Multimate International Corp.

4. Press F10 to start printing. Advantage puts the Main Menu back on the screen while it is printing the letter.

If Advantage cannot perform the print operation for some reason (e.g., printer out of paper, not on-line, cable connected incorrectly), it will display

```
PRINTER NEEDS ATTENTION. PRESS <ESCAPE> TO CONTINUE.
```

Correct the problem then press Esc.

Setting Print Margins

Depending on how your printer is set up, the printed copy may or may not be to your liking. For one thing, Advantage assumes that you have adjusted the paper to allow for a left margin, and so it starts printing at the leftmost position. It also assumes that you have provided for a top margin, so it begins printing on the current line.

Suppose your printer's print head sits at the leftmost position of the top edge of the paper, and you want Advantage to provide one-inch margins on the left and at the top. To make it do this:

1. Type **4** and Return to select "Printer Control Utilities" in the Main Menu.
2. Type **2** and Return to select "Edit Printer Defaults" in the Printer Control Utilities menu.
3. When the "Modify Printer Defaults" form appears, press the down-arrow key to reach the "Left Margin" field. The left margin value is measured in *characters*. Advantage is set up for 10 pitch (that is, 10 characters per inch) type, so we need *10* to get a one-inch left margin.
4. For "Left margin", enter **010**, then move to the "Top margin" field. The top margin is measured in *lines*. Advantage is set up to print six lines per inch, so we need *6* to get a one-inch top margin.
5. Enter **006** for "Top margin", then press F10 twice to return to the Main Menu.

Now print your letter to John again to see the effects of the new margin settings. As before, select 3 (Print Document Utility) from the Main Menu. When the Print a Document form appears, press Return ("Document:" already shows *JOHN*), then press F10 to bypass the Print Parameters for Document form.

Editing a Disk Document

Once you have documents on the disk, you will probably spend more time working on them than creating new ones. To retrieve a document from disk, select "Edit an Old Document" from the Main Menu, by typing **1** and Return. Advantage displays an *Edit an Old Document* form that asks you for the document's name. It also provides a list of the available documents.

If you have just turned the computer on, you must enter the name of the document and press Return. Otherwise, Advantage suggests the document you last worked on. If you want that one, press Return; if you want another, enter its name and press Return. Pressing

Return makes the Document Summary Screen appear. Press F10 to bypass it and get to your document.

To see how this works, let's edit our letter to John. Suppose you remember that John and Sandra recently had a baby girl named Teri, and you want to include her in the invitation. To change *invite you, Sandra, and Robby* to *invite you, Sandra, Teri, and Robby*, proceed as follows:

1. Type **1** and Return to select "Edit an Old Document" from the Main Menu.
2. When the "Edit an Old Document" form appears, enter **john** in the "Document" field (if it is not already there) and press Return.
3. When the "Document Summary Screen" appears, press F10. Advantage puts the letter on the screen.
4. Move the cursor down to the second paragraph, then right to the *a* in *and*.
5. Press Ins (the rest of the letter disappears) type **Teri,** and press the space bar and Ins again. Advantage displays the revised paragraph.
6. Press F10 to save the letter on disk and get back to the Main Menu.

Now you can print the new version using the same procedure as before.

Canceling Changes

If you are editing a disk document and make some major mistake (such as accidentally deleting a line or sentence), you can cancel all changes to that page by pressing Esc. When the screen shows

```
Do you wish to escape without saving this page? (Y/N)
```

press **y**. Advantage will return to the Main Menu, but leave the page as it was when you retrieved or *loaded* it from the disk.

Loading at Start-Up

If you know what disk document you want to work on (and remember its name), you can tell Advantage to load it when you start. Type **wp** and the document name when the A> prompt appears.

For example, you can start with the letter to John by typing **wp john**. Advantage bypasses the Main Menu and displays the Document Summary Screen. Press F10 to obtain the document itself.

Leaving Advantage

To leave Advantage, type **9** and Return to select "Return to DOS". When the DOS prompt appears (A> for floppy disks, C> for hard disks), you may do one of two things. If you are finished working on the computer, switch the power off. If you want to format a new data disk, copy an existing one, or do something else that involves disks, you need to use the functions provided on the DOS disk.

Using the DOS Disk

To use the DOS disk, put it in the left-hand drive in place of the Advantage disk. At this point, the computer is waiting for you to enter a DOS command.

If you want to format a new disk, replace the Learning Disk in the right-hand drive with the disk to be formatted. For the procedure to format a disk, refer to the *Advantage Beginner's Guide* or to the FORMAT command in the IBM *DOS* manual.

Returning to Advantage

To leave DOS and return to Advantage, replace the DOS disk with the Advantage System disk, then type **wp** and press Return.

Changing the Line Length

We described earlier how you can change the size of the margins that Advantage uses for printing. You may also want to change the way it arranges text.

Note that for our example letter, Advantage assumes you want to print 75 characters on each line. Hence, if your printer uses 10-character-per-inch type on standard 8 1/2-inch paper, Advantage leaves only one inch for side margins (say, 1/2 inch on each side).

Here we describe how to change Advantage so that it puts *65* characters on a line. Once you change the line length, Advantage will use it automatically for every new document you create.

With the Main Menu on the screen, press **7** to select "Other Utilities", then press Return. When the *Other Utilities Menu* appears, press **1** to select "Edit System Format Line", then Return. This makes Advantage display its "System Format Line Modification" form (see Figure 2-7).

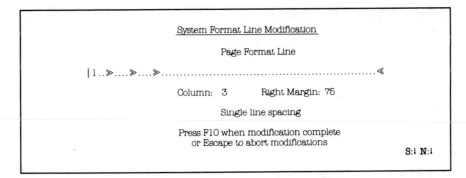

Figure 2-7. System Format Line Modification form.
Courtesy of Multimate International Corp.

The line with the dots is the *system format line.* Like the format line that appears at the top of documents, it shows you what line spacing Advantage will use and where the tabs and right margin are located. To change the line length (that is, the right margin) to 65:

1. Move the cursor right by pressing the right-arrow key on the numeric keypad. Note that the *COL* (column) number changes as the cursor moves.
2. When the screen shows *COL: 65,* press Return. (If you accidentally go past column 65, press the left-arrow key to move the cursor left.) Note that Advantage has automatically updated the form to show *Right Margin: 65.*

3. Press the F10 key to return to the Other Utilities Menu, then press F10 again to return to the Main Menu.

Now Advantage will use the revised system format whenever you create a new document. Figure 2-8 shows how our letter to John will look if you change the right margin setting to 65 before you enter it.

```
May 11, 1986

Dear John:

Believe it or not, I'm writing this letter on my IBM Personal
Computer!  I bought a word processing program called Advantage
that lets me use the PC just like a typewriter.  Since this is
my first try at using it, I can't tell you how easy it actually
is, but so far so good.

Pat and I want to invite you, Sandra, and Robby to our new cabin
by Bender Lake.  To paraphrase an old joke, when can you drop
in?  Write soon.

All the best,


(Type your name here)
```

Figure 2-8. Letter prepared with right margin set to 65.

Deleting Documents

Because you must save a document on disk before you can print it, your data disks may end up containing temporary documents—those you want to print once then discard. To discard or *delete* a document, put its disk in drive B when you start Advantage. When the Main Menu appears, press **6** and Return to select "Document Handling Utilities." Advantage displays its *Document Handling Utilities Menu* (see Figure 2-9).

DOCUMENT HANDLING UTILITIES MENU

1. Copy a Document

2. Move a Document

3. Delete a Document

4. Rename a Document

5. Print Document Summary Screens

6. Search Document Summary Screens

7. Restore a Backed-up Document

Function:

Enter function number, Press return
Press F10 to return to Main Menu

S:1 N:1

Figure 2-9. Document Handling Utilities Menu.
Courtesy of Multimate International Corp.

To delete a document, press **3** and Return. When Advantage displays its *DELETE* form, enter the document's name and press F10 (or Esc, if you got to this form by accident). Once you delete a document, it's gone forever; you can never get it back. For this reason, when you press F10, Advantage asks if you're really sure you want to delete the document. It displays

```
<ESCAPE> to abort, any other key to continue
```

To get back to the Document Handling Utilities Menu without deleting, press Esc. To proceed with the deletion, press the space bar.

If you have floppy disks, pressing the space bar makes Advantage prompt

```
INSERT DISKETTE(S), PRESS ANY KEY WHEN READY
```

Put the disk that contains the deletion victim into drive B (if it isn't already there), then press the space bar.

When Advantage finishes deleting a document, it displays

–OPERATION COMPLETE–

To delete another document, press the space bar to get the Delete form back; otherwise, press Esc twice to return to the Main Menu.

Insert, Backspace, and Cursor Speed Options

Advantage provides options that let you change how an insert (Ins key) operation affects text on the screen, what effect the Backspace key produces, and how fast the cursor moves when you hold an arrow key down. These three options are on Advantage's *Modify System Defaults* form. To obtain it, press **7** and then Return to select "Other Utilities" from the Main Menu. Then press **3** and Return to select "Edit System Defaults" from the Other Utilities menu. This makes Advantage display its Modify System Defaults form (see Figure 2-10).

```
                        MODIFY SYSTEM DEFAULTS

    Insert Mode [(D)rop Down / (P)ush]?     D      Acceptable Decimal Tab [ . or , ]?        ‗
    Allow Widows And Orphans?               Y      Number Of Lines Per Page?                55
    Automatic Page Breaks?                  N      Display Spaces As Dots [.]?               N
    Destructive Backspace?                  N      Keep Document Closed For Safety?          Y
    Backup Before Editing Document?         N      Strikeout Character?                      /
    Display Directory?                      Y
    (T)ext Or (P)age Associated Headers And Footers?                                        T

    System Date Standard [(U)SA,(E)urope,(J)apan, Or (D)OS]?                                D
    Print Date Standard [(U)SA,(E)urope,(J)apan, Or (D)OS]?                                 D

    Section Numbering Style [(R)oman Or (N)umeric]?                                         R

    Acceleration Rate [0 - 9]?              5      Acceleration Responsiveness [0 - 9]?      5
    Main Dictionary?                  WEBSTER      Custom Dictionary?                   CLAMFL

                   Press F10 to Continue, Press ESC to Abort                      S:1 N:1
```

Figure 2-10. Modify System Defaults form.
Courtesy of Multimate International Corp.

Changing the Insert Option

As you saw earlier, pressing Ins (Insert) key causes Advantage to clear the rest of the screen and display *INSERT WHAT?* at the top. However, seeing all of that text disappear can be distracting to some users. Therefore, the people who designed Advantage let you change what happens when you press Ins. Specifically, you can make Advantage keep the text on the screen, and simply move it to the right as you insert new material.

To make Advantage "push" insertion text onto the screen, type **p** (for Push) in the "Insert Mode" field of the Modify System Defaults form. Then press F10 twice to get back to the Main Menu.

Once you make that change, Advantage displays *INSERT* (rather than *INSERT WHAT?*) at the top of the screen whenever you press Ins. Then it "pushes" everything you type in front of the existing text until you press Ins again.

Activating the Backspace Key

The dark key marked with a left-arrow above Return is the *Backspace* key. When you get Advantage, Backspace does the same thing as the left-arrow key on the numeric keypad—it moves the cursor to the left. However, by changing one of Advantage's system default settings, you can make Backspace operate as a "delete previous character" key. That is, you can make it move the cursor left to the preceding character and *delete* that character. This feature is valuable for correcting mistakes that you just typed.

To activate the Backspace key, obtain the Modify System Defaults form and press the down-arrow key three times to reach the "Destructive Backspace?" field. Then type **y** and Return to change this field from *N* (No) to *Y* (Yes). Finally, press F10 twice to get back to the Main Menu.

Changing the Cursor Speed

As we mentioned earlier, most keys on the keyboard *repeat* if you hold them down. This is especially handy for moving the cursor around on the screen. However, Advantage repeats so quickly that you can easily pass the place where you meant to stop. Fortunately, you can change the repetition rate to suit yourself.

To increase or decrease the speed at which keys repeat, obtain the Modify System Defaults form and press the down-arrow key until the cursor reaches the "Acceleration Responsiveness [0-9]?" field on the next-to-last line. Then press the left-arrow key to reach the "Acceleration Rate [0-9]?" field. Advantage sets this field to *5* automatically. To increase the speed, type a number between **6** and **9**; to decrease it, type a number between **0** and **4**. Then press F10 twice to return to the Main Menu.

Questions and Answers

By now you probably have many questions, so let's stop and answer some.

Question: How can I make something appear on a line all by itself?
Answer: Press Return before and after typing it. It will then always have a line to itself.

Question: Everything I type is appears in capital letters. Why?
Answer: You probably pressed Caps Lock by accident. Check the bottom line to see if the arrow just right of *S:* is pointing upward. If so, press the Caps Lock key to turn the lock off.

Question: When I try to move the cursor, the computer puts a number on the screen. What's wrong?
Answer: You pressed Num Lock by accident. Check the bottom line to see if an up-arrow appears just right of *N:*. If so, press Num Lock to turn the lock off.

Question: Why does the text disappear when I move the cursor right?
Answer: You're using the space bar instead of the right-arrow key. The space bar enters a space in place of whatever is at the cursor position.

Question: I just typed *rum* instead of *run*. How do I correct it?
Answer: Press Backspace, then **n**. Note that the — (Delete Character) key won't do the job, since the cursor is already to the right of *rum*.

Question: I was reaching for the Ins key, but accidentally pressed Del. Now Advantage is demanding *DELETE WHAT?* I don't want to delete anything! What do I do?

Answer: Press the Esc key. This makes Advantage forget about deleting and gets you back to editing.

Hints and Warnings

Always be aware of the following features of Advantage:

1. When you make changes, the new characters you enter will replace old characters. They will not be added to the text (unless you first pressed Ins).
2. Note that inserting or deleting involves pressing Ins or Del twice—once to start the operation and once again to end it. This procedure of repeating key commands is a personality trait of Advantage. You must often press the same keys at the beginning and end of an operation.
3. Be particularly careful when deleting. Always check to see what Advantage has highlighted before you press Del the second time.
4. If you have activated the Backspace key, use it, not Del, to delete what you just typed.
5. When you are entering information into one of Advantage's forms, press the right-arrow key to reach the next field or the down-arrow key to reach the next line. You can also use the left-arrow or up-arrow key to go back to the previous field or previous line.
6. Remember that you can press Esc to cancel most operations. For example, pressing Esc during an insert or delete operation clears the prompt and restores the text to its original form. Pressing Esc while a form or menu is on the screen returns you to the previous form or menu. Pressing Esc with text on the screen tells Advantage to discard all changes made since you last saved that page.
7. Always give your disk documents reasonable names that suggest what they contain. It is difficult to remember what "D1" or "X" contains, but not "FINRPT86" or "RESUME".

Key Point Summary

Here are the key points you learned in this chapter. Table 2-1 summarizes the keys and functions introduced.

Table 2-1. Keys and functions introduced in Chapter 2.

Key(s)	Function
Alt-F6	*In delete mode:* Select line
F10	Complete current operation
− (minus)	Delete character
+ (plus)	Insert character
Backspace	Delete previous character
Del	Delete text
Esc	Cancel current operation
Ins	Insert text
Cursor-moving keys	
End	End of screen
Ctrl-End	End of page
Home	Top of screen
Ctrl-Home	Top of page
PgDn	Next screen (18 lines)
PgUp	Previous screen (18 lines)

1. To start Advantage, put the System disk in drive A and a data disk in drive B, then switch the power on. When the computer asks for the date, enter it and press Return. Press Return when it asks for the time. When you see A>, type **wp**. Advantage displays its Main Menu.
2. Advantage's Main Menu lets you select from several activities by entering a number and pressing Return. The activities include editing an old document, creating a new document, and printing a disk document.
3. To start a new document, select "Create a New Document" from the Main Menu and enter the document's name when requested. When the Document Summary Screen appears, press F10. Press F10 again when the Modify Document Defaults form appears.
4. You can move the cursor by pressing keys on the numeric keypad. An arrow key moves the cursor in the direction it points. Holding it down keeps the cursor moving in that direction. The Home and End keys move the cursor to the beginning or end of the screen; PgUp and PgDn move it up or down one screen (18 lines); Ctrl-Home and Ctrl-End move it to the beginning or end of the current page.

    Advantage always indicates the cursor's current line and column position on the status line at the top of the screen.

5. Advantage keeps track of the length of text lines and starts a new line automatically when necessary. Press Return only when you reach the end of a paragraph or want to skip a line.

6. To replace characters, move the cursor to where the replacement should start and type the new characters. You do not have to erase (delete) the old characters.

7. To insert text, move the cursor to where you want the first new character to appear and press Ins (Insert). Advantage clears the screen from the cursor position onward. Enter the insertion and press Ins again. You may also insert a single character by pressing the + key on the numeric keypad, then typing the character in the gap Advantage provides.

8. To delete text, move the cursor to the first character and press Del (Delete). Then move the cursor to where the deletion ends (Advantage highlights the affected text) and press Del again. You may enter a space, Alt-F6, a punctuation mark, or Return to select the current word, line, sentence, or paragraph for deletion.

   You may also delete a single character by pressing either the − key on the numeric keypad (deletes the character at the cursor position) or the Backspace key (deletes the previous character).

9. To quit editing and return to the Main Menu, press the F10 key. This makes Advantage save the document on the data disk. To return to the Main Menu without saving changes to the current page, press the Esc key, then enter **y** in response to the prompt.

10. To print a document, select "Print Document Utility" from the Main Menu and enter the document's name when requested. When the Print Parameters for Document form appears, press F10.

11. To load a document from a data disk, select "Edit an Old Document" from the Main Menu and enter the document's name when requested. When the Document Summary Screen form appears, press F10.

    You can also load a document when you start Advantage. When the A> prompt appears type **wp** and the document's name (e.g., type **wp john**), then press Return. When the Document Summary Screen appears, press F10.

12. To leave Advantage, select "Return to DOS" from the Main Menu.

13. Advantage's system format line determines the line spacing, tabs, and line length for new documents. To change it, select "Other Utilities" from the Main Menu, then "Edit System Format Line" from the Other Utilities Menu.

14. You must save a document on disk before you can print it. However, you can discard a temporary document after printing it. To do this, select "Document Handling Utilities" from the Main Menu,

then "Delete a Document" from the Document Handling Utilities Menu. Enter the document's name when requested and press F10. When the prompt appears, press the space bar.

15. By changing three parameters on the Modify System Defaults form, you can activate the PC's Backspace key (make it delete characters as the cursor moves left), change how an insert operation affects text on the screen (add insertions to existing text rather than clear the rest of the screen), and increase or decrease the rate at which the cursor moves.

3

Formal Correspondence

This chapter describes how to use Advantage to prepare formal business correspondence, such as requests for payment, order confirmations, and memoranda. Such correspondence usually has strict, standardized formats with precise margins and other special requirements. Furthermore, formal correspondence is often several pages long and may include repetitive names, addresses, or phrases.

We begin by preparing the business letter shown in Figure 3-1.

Restarting Advantage

To enter the letter, you must restart Advantage. Put the System disk in drive A and the Learning Disk in drive B, then turn the power on. The first thing the computer does is ask you for the date. Enter it (e.g., type **7-20-86**), then press Return. Press Return when the computer asks for the time.

When A> appears, type **wp** and press Return. When Advantage's copyright information appears, press the space bar. Then select "Create a New Document" from the Main Menu, name the document **thompson**, and press Return. Pressing Return makes Advantage display its *Document Summary Screen* (see Figure 3-2).

```
                              211 Washington Street
                              San Diego, CA 92121
                              July 3, 1986

Mr. Samuel Thompson
Gospel Island Computer Co.
146 Moonrise Drive
Inverness, FL 32650

Dear Mr. Thompson:

As of the close of business on 30 June 1986, your company has
outstanding invoices over 30 days old totaling $7,350.00.  We
must request immediate payment of these invoices or we will be
forced to add a 1 1/2% monthly service charge.

Until we receive payment, we cannot extend credit to your
company or process further orders.  Please remit this payment to
my attention as soon as possible.

                              Sincerely yours,



                              Marie F. Gerard
                              Assistant Credit Manager
```

Figure 3-1. Business letter.

Document Summary Screen

The Document Summary Screen is a convenient log form. It shows the name and length of the document (in keystrokes), when it was created, and when it was last modified (edited). It also provides space for you to enter such details as the name of the author, addressee, and operator (the person who typed the letter), and comments about the document.

Advantage displays this form whenever you edit a document. As you will see later, Advantage also lets you search all of the forms for a specific item (e.g., a certain addressee's name or a creation date). Hence, the Document Summary Screen is a valuable aid for filing and retrieving information. Let's fill it out for our example letter.

```
                    DOCUMENT SUMMARY SCREEN


      Document     docname          Total pages    0
      Author     _____
      Addressee  _____
      Operator   _____

      Identification key words:
                 _____
                 _____
                 _____


      Comments:
               _____
               _____
               _____
               _____


      Creation Date     01/01/80   Modification Date      01/01/80
      Total Editing Time 00:00:00  Editing Time Last Session 00:00:00
      Total Keystrokes         0   Keystrokes Last Session       0

          Use tab keys to change fields - Press F10 when finished

    To create: LIBRARY-Leave Screen empty Press F5, DATA FILE-Press Shift F10    8:1 N:1
```

Figure 3-2. Document Summary Screen.
Courtesy of Multimate International Corp.

In the Document Summary Screen for the letter to Mr. Thompson, we want to enter the names of the author and the addressee, some key words that we might want to search for later (*invoice* and *overdue* are appropriate here), and an appropriate comment.

Advantage starts in the "Author" field, so that's where we'll begin filling out the form. Proceed as follows:

1. Type **Gerard** and press the Tab key to reach the "Addressee" field. Tab is the dark key with both left and right arrows; it is located between F4 and Q.
2. Type **Thompson** and press Tab twice to reach "Identification key words:".
3. For the key words, type **invoice, overdue,** and then press Tab to reach "Comments:".
4. For the comment, type **Cancel credit to Gospel Island Computer due to outstanding invoices.**
5. If you made any mistakes, press Shift and Tab to backtrack, then correct the offending entry. When you finish, press F10. This tells Advantage to accept the form.

Pressing F10 makes Advantage display its Modify Document Defaults form. Press F10 to bypass it.

Setting Tabs

In our one-page business letter, the return address, complimentary close, and the writer's name and title all start at the center of the page. The easiest way to place this material is by using a tab. Here we describe how to change the *format line*, the second line of the screen, to fix the tab.

Changing the Format Line

To start modifying the format line, press F9. When you do this, Advantage moves the cursor to the dot that follows *1* (the single-spacing indicator). The status line tells you that this is column 3.

Advantage provides tabs at columns 5, 10, and 15, and marks them with ≫. We want to clear these built-in tabs and fix a new one at column 32. To clear the first tab, use the right-arrow key to move the cursor to it, then press the space bar to erase it. Do the same thing to clear the other two tabs. Finally, move the cursor to column 32 and press the Tab key; Advantage puts a tab marker there. We don't want to make any more format changes, so press F9 to get back to editing.

Spacing and Line Length

The format line also controls the line spacing and the line length. Therefore, we could have easily changed those settings when we changed tabs. We left them alone because:

- The number *1* on the format line produces single-spacing.
- The right margin marker (≪) is at column 65, which makes Advantage put 65 characters on a line. Because we are using 10-pitch type and have set the left margin value to one inch (see Chapter 2), the right margin will be one inch.

We want single-spacing and one-inch side margins for formal correspondence. You can change these values if you want to.

Changing the spacing involves changing the number at the beginning of the format line. We will discuss this in Chapter 5. *Changing the line length* involves moving the right-hand margin marker. Once you put the cursor on the format line (by pressing F9), move it to where you want the line to end. To shorten the line, press Return and F9. To widen it, press F9.

Entering the Business Letter

After you set the tabs, you can enter the letter in Figure 3-1. Press Tab before typing the return address, since it must start at the center. Enter the body of the letter normally, but press Tab before typing *Sincerely yours* and the writer's name and title. Remember to enter an extra Return to skip a line.

Saving and Printing the Letter

To save the completed letter on disk, press the F10 key. To print it, switch your printer "on-line," then select "Print Document Utility" from the Main Menu. When the Print a Document form appears, press F10. Press F10 again to bypass the Print Parameters for Document form.

Proportional Spacing

Advantage lets you print documents with proportional spacing. With this feature, the printer gives each character the amount of space equal to its width. For example, it gives an "i" less space than an "m."

Of course, your printer must be able to produce proportional spacing; not all printers can. The "Printer Information" appendix in the *Advantage Reference Manual* lists printers that can produce proportional spacing. It marks their *Prop space* entry with "h," "ps," or "pm."

To get proportional spacing, start the print operation as usual, but when the Print Parameters for Document form appears, move the cursor to the "Proportional Spacing: N/Y" field and enter **y** (for yes). Then press F10 to start printing.

Justifying Text

Many people like correspondence to have an even (or *justified*) right margin. Advantage cannot justify text as you enter it, but it can *print* a document in justified form. To produce this, Advantage inserts spaces between words so that the final character of each word on a line is printed at the right margin.

However, the extra spaces between words can result in wide gaps that make the text look somewhat unprofessional. Advantage provides a "micro-justification" option that inserts small amounts of space *inside* words (as well as character-size spaces between them) to achieve a cleaner effect.

Every printer can produce regular justification, but not all can produce micro-justification. The "Printer Information" appendix in the *Advantage Reference Manual* shows which printers can micro-justify; it marks their *Prop space* entry with "h" or "pm." (These models can also produce proportional spacing. Printers marked with "ps" can proportional-space, but cannot micro-justify.)

Justification

To produce justified text, start the print operation as usual, but when the Print Parameters for Document form appears, move the cursor to the "Justification [N or Y or M(icro)]" field and enter **y**. Then press F10 to start printing.

Figure 3-3 shows how our example business letter looks if you print it with the justification option.

```
                              211 Washington Street
                              San Diego, CA 92121
                              July 3, 1986

Mr. Samuel Thompson
Gospel Island Computer Co.
146 Moonrise Drive
Inverness, FL 32650

Dear Mr. Thompson:

As  of  the  close  of business on 30 June 1986, your company has
outstanding  invoices  over  30  days old totaling $7,350.00.  We
must  request  immediate  payment of these invoices or we will be
forced to add a 1 1/2% monthly service charge.

Until  we  receive  payment,  we  cannot  extend  credit  to your
company  or process further orders.  Please remit this payment to
my attention as soon as possible.

                              Sincerely yours,



                              Marie F. Gerard
                              Assistant Credit Manager
```

Figure 3-3. A justified business letter.

Micro-Justification

To produce micro-justified text, start the print operation as usual, but when the Print Parameters for Document form appears, move the cursor to the "Justification [N or Y or M(icro)]" field and enter **m**. Then press F10 to start printing.

By combining micro-justification with proportional spacing, you can produce documents that almost look typeset.

Multi-Page Letters

So far, we have prepared only one-page letters. Formal correspondence is often longer—sometimes *much* longer. Figure 3-4 shows a two-page memorandum summarizing a company's regional sales for the second quarter of 1986.

This material is on the first page:

Date: July 15, 1986

To: Gloria A. Powell, National Sales Manager

From: Frank P. Hall, Southeast Regional Sales Manager

Subject: Second Quarter Sales

Attached are the second quarter sales figures for my region. As
you can see, Cynthia Chamber continues to lead, but Jerry
Leonard is gaining ground on her. Dick Morris is still at the
bottom of the list; he blames that on the recent cancellation by
the Wilson & Sons account.

In all, second quarter sales are 15 percent higher than those of
last quarter.

Enclosure

This material is on the second page:

Southeast Region Sales, Second Quarter, 1986

State	Sales Rep.	Units Sold	Revenues ($)
Alabama	Adams, Jason	500	215,000
N. Carolina	Holmes, James	550	236,500
S. Carolina	Jackson, Charles	490	210,700
Florida	Chamber, Cynthia	640	275,200
Georgia	Grogan, Phyllis	420	180,600
Louisiana	Leonard, Jerome	610	262,300
Mississippi	Morris, Richard	320	137,600
Tennessee	Baker, Thomas	540	232,200
Virginia	Nelson, Patricia	480	206,400
Totals		4,550	1,956,500

Figure 3-4. Two-page memorandum.

To enter this memorandum, create a new document and name it
salesq2. When Advantage's blank screen appears, enter the first
page. After typing the final word (*Enclosure*), press Return.

Starting a New Page

To start a new page, press the F2 key. The light on drive B comes
on and the bottom of the screen shows

```
<<< PLEASE WAIT >>>
```

When that message disappears, the cursor is at the top of a new, blank page (note that the top line shows *PAGE: 2*).

Setting Tabs for a Table

Before entering the sales table, set tabs for it. First, we must decide where the tabs go. The easiest way to do this is to enter the table headings and the longest line of data (the *S. Carolina* line, in this case), then adjust the spacing. We can then see where to put the tabs.

To begin, enter the headings with three spaces between columns as shown here:

```
State    Sales Rep.    Units Sold    Revenues ($)
```

When you finish, press Return twice to reach the line where the data starts. Then enter the *S. Carolina* line:

```
S. Carolina    Jackson, Charles    490    210,700
```

Now that we have entered the headings and the longest data line, we must adjust the spacing. To begin, move the cursor to the *S* in *Sales* and press the + (Insert Character) key until the S is directly over the *J* in *Jackson*. (Note that we use + instead of Ins to insert the spaces. We do this because Ins clears the bottom of the screen, which would make it impossible to visually align the heading with the data.)

Now move the cursor to the *U* in *Units Sold* and align it with the *4* in *490*; this puts three spaces between the sales representative's name and the *Units Sold* heading.

Next we must center the last two data columns underneath their headings. To do this, put the cursor on the *4* in *490* and align it with the *t* in *Units*. Finally, put the cursor on the *2* in *210,700* and align it with the *v* in *Revenues*. When you are done, the screen should show:

```
State          Sales Rep.        Units Sold    Revenues ($)

S. Carolina    Jackson, Charles      490         210,700
```

The tabs belong at the left edges of the data columns. To find out where these columns start, move the cursor to the data line, then right to the beginning of each column. Note what *COL:* value appears on the status line each time; it tells you where to set the tab. If you have followed directions, you should find that the data columns start at columns 15, 37, and 49, respectively.

To set the tabs, press F9 to reach the format line, then move the cursor right to column 5 and press the space bar to delete the automatic tab there. Delete the tab at column 10 similarly. Column 15 already has a tab (coincidentally), so we leave it alone. Move the cursor to column 37 and press the Tab key; then move it to column 49 and press Tab again.

You should now have tabs at columns 15, 37, and 49. Move the cursor to those positions to ensure that they are correct. If, by chance, you have misplaced a tab, clear it by pressing the space bar. Then move the cursor to where this tab belongs and press Tab. When you finish setting tabs, press F9 to return to editing.

Completing the Table

The table contains eight more lines—two above the one we entered and six below it. To make room for the first two lines, move the cursor to the beginning of the *S. Carolina* line and press Ins.

Enter the *Alabama* columns using Tab to move the cursor and press Return at the end of the line. Enter the *N. Carolina* line in the same way and press Ins to leave the insert mode. Now press End (the 1 key on the numeric keypad) to move the cursor to the blank line following the table and enter the remaining six data lines. When you finish, save the memorandum on disk by pressing F10.

Paging

In the preceding memorandum, we knew exactly where to end the first page and begin the second. However, we usually don't know ahead of time where page breaks will occur.

If you are using standard 11-inch paper, one page can hold 55 single-spaced lines. When you reach line 56, Advantage beeps the computer and makes the LINE number flash at the top of the screen. These are warnings that you have filled the page. Before printing, you will have to adjust the text; we will discuss *how* to adjust it shortly.

Changing the Automatic Page Breaks Setting

Advantage lets you specify the paging technique for either a selected document or for all new documents. In both cases, the paging technique is controlled by a parameter called "Automatic page breaks?". If "Automatic page breaks?" is set to N (for no), Advantage beeps the computer and makes the line number flash when you exceed the page capacity. Otherwise, if it is set to Y (for yes), Advantage starts a new page when the current page is full.

To alter the paging technique for a document, change the "Automatic page breaks?" setting on the Modify Document Defaults form. This form appears whenever you create a new document. To change the *default* paging technique (i.e., the technique that Advantage assumes you want for every new document), change "Automatic page breaks?" on the Modify System Defaults form.

Since most people want Advantage to apply their preference to every new document, we will describe only the procedure for changing "Automatic page breaks?" on the Modify System Defaults form. The procedure is:

1. Select "Other Utilities" from the Main Menu.
2. Select "Edit System Defaults" from the Other Utilities Menu. Advantage displays its Modify System Defaults form.
3. Move the cursor to "Automatic page breaks?" and enter **y** (to make Advantage start new pages automatically) or **n** (to make the computer beep when a page is full).
4. Press F10 to return to the Other Utilities Menu.
5. Press F10 again to return to the Main Menu.

Moving between Pages

Sometimes changes or corrections on one page will require changes on another page. Or you may suddenly think of an error or omission on some other page. Advantage lets you move quickly to any page in a document.

Moving is simplest if the other page is the next one up or down from where you are working. Then all you do is press Ctrl and PgUp to move it back a page or Ctrl and PgDn to move it ahead a page. Better yet, if the cursor is on the first or last line of a page, press the up-arrow key or down-arrow key to move it back a page or ahead a page, respectively.

To move to some other page, press F1. Advantage will display

```
GO TO PAGE?   [    ]
```

at the bottom of the screen. Enter the number of the page you want to work on and press Return. If, for example, you are working on page 4 and want to move to page 2, press F1, type **2**, and press Return. The computer will put page 2 on the screen with the cursor at the top left-hand corner.

Further, you can move to the first or last page in a document without entering its page number. Just press F1, then either Home (for first page) or End (for last page).

Pages in Memory and on the Disk

An important aspect of paging is that Advantage keeps only the current page of a document in memory; it keeps the rest on disk. Thus, only the changes to the current page are ever in a vulnerable state. They are the *only* thing you will lose if the power goes off or you absent-mindedly switch the computer off without saving your work on disk!

Repaginating

If changes make a page too long, you must move the excess to the next page. Similarly, if they make a page too short, you may want to fill the space with something from the next page. In either case, you can make Advantage divide the text into even-sized pages by giving it a *repaginate* command.

To repaginate a document, move the cursor to where the changes start (or to the beginning of the document), then hold Ctrl down and press F2. Advantage displays a *Repagination* form at the bottom of the screen that lets you choose from three options:

- Repaginate Document
- Generate a Table of Contents
- Reassign Section Numbers

It assumes that you want to repaginate a document ("Repaginate Document" is set to *Y*) and put 55 lines on each page (for standard 11-inch paper). Since this is indeed what we want, press F10 to start the repagination.

Advantage spends some time repaginating (the message *Repaginating—PLEASE WAIT* appears at the bottom of the screen); then puts the cursor at the beginning of the current page.

Changing Page Boundaries

If you don't like the way Advantage has paginated your letter, you can change the page boundaries manually. To do this, put the cursor where you want to split a page, press + (the Insert Character), and then press F2. Advantage will move the rest of the current page to a new page.

Of course, the new page will be only partially full. To fill the space, press Ctrl-End to reach the end of the page, then press Shift and F2. Pressing Shift-F2 makes Advantage move the contents of the next page to this one. If combining pages makes the current page too full (the LINE number at the top is flashing), either move the cursor to the top and repaginate or insert additional page breaks until you get what you want.

Preventing Widow and Orphan Lines

A possible disadvantage of repaginating is that Advantage doesn't care how it arranges the text; it simply fills each page to capacity. Unlike a good typist, it may leave the first line of a paragraph alone at the bottom of a page (a *widow*) or leave the last line at the top of a new page (an *orphan*). Fortunately, you can break it of this sloppy habit.

To make Advantage keep the first and last two lines of a paragraph together on a page, do the following:

1. Select "Other Utilities" from the Main Menu.
2. Select "Edit System Defaults" from the Other Utilities Menu.
3. For "Allow widows and orphans?" in the Modify System Defaults form, enter **n** (for no).
4. Press F10 twice to return to the Main Menu.

Note that this change only affects how Advantage repaginates, not how it arranges text on the screen. Hence, if you are using the automatic page break option and start a paragraph on line 55, Advantage still breaks the page at line 56 (leaving the first line at the bottom of the previous page).

Similarly, if you start the last line of a paragraph on line 56, Advantage still moves it to the top of the next page. To eliminate the widow and orphan lines, you must repaginate the document.

Printing the Current Page

Sometimes you want to print the page you're working on without returning to the Main Menu. You can do this by using Advantage's so-called "hot print" feature. To print a page, put the cursor anywhere in it and turn your printer on. Then hold Ctrl down and press the PrtSc key. (PrtSc, short for Print Screen, is the dark key to the right of the right-hand Shift key.) Advantage displays *HOTPRINT-ING* at the top right-hand corner of the screen and prints the page.

Underlining

Writers use underlining for emphasis or to indicate a new term, a book title, or a magazine name. You can also use it to create mathematical symbols such as $\geq$ or $\pm$.

To underline material, move the cursor to it, then hold Shift down and press the underscore key (_). Underscore is the uppercase symbol on the key to the right of 0 (zero) on the main keyboard. For example, if your sales letter says

```
We must reduce the inventories of bedspreads this
month.
```

you may want to underline *must* for emphasis. To do this, move the cursor to *m*, then press Shift and underscore. Hold both keys down until Advantage has underlined the *t*.

Automatic Underlining

You can also make Advantage underline material as you type it. When you get to where the underlining should begin, press Alt and underscore (rather than Shift and underscore). After that, Advantage will underline everything—even spaces—until you press Alt-underscore again. Suppose you want to enter

```
Our company's name is Frank O. Gold, Inc., not Franco
Goldink, as in your recent article.
```

To produce it, type normally up to the *F* in *Frank*, then press Alt-underscore. Type **Frank O. Gold, Inc.** (Advantage underlines it), press Alt-underscore again, and finish the sentence.

If you don't want spaces and punctuation underlined, press *Alt-+*, instead of Alt-underscore, to turn underlining on and off. (To enter $+$, type the uppercase symbol on the $=$ key, not the $+$ key on the numeric keypad.) If you used Alt-$+$ for our preceding example, Advantage would produce

```
Our company's name is Frank O. Gold, Inc., not Franco
Goldink, as in your recent article.
```

Removing Underlining

You can also *remove* underlining with Shift-underscore. To do this, move the cursor to where the underlining starts, and then hold Shift and underscore down until the cursor gets past the underlined material.

Be careful when removing underlining that you have produced with Alt-+. If you simply hold down Shift-underscore, Advantage will underline the spaces and punctuation marks that previously had no underlining! To avoid this, you must erase underlining word by word, and use the right-arrow key to skip spaces and punctuation.

Centering

Tables usually require centered titles. You can produce one by pressing the F3 key, or you can center an existing title by pressing + (Insert Character) on the numeric keypad, then F3.

Let's center the title on page 2 of the memorandum in Figure 3-4. Load *salesq2* into the computer from disk using the Main Menu's "Edit an Old Document" option. Move the cursor to page 2 by pressing Ctrl-PgDn, then move it to the beginning of the title. Center the title by pressing + and F3. (Note that Advantage puts a ↔ symbol ahead of the title; this is the "centered" marker.) Finally, press F10 to save the memorandum with the centered title.

Using Abbreviations

One way to save on typing and reduce the number of errors is by abbreviating common names, addresses, or phrases. For example, a letter might have many references to the Department of Defense, United States Steel Corporation, or the law firm of Rosencrantz, Guildenstern, and Hamlet. You might also be constantly mentioning "the party of the first part," "the cooperating investigative agencies," or "the three major television networks."

Wouldn't it be nice if you could use simple abbreviations such as DoD for Department of Defense, USS for United States Steel Corporation, and pfp for "party of the first part"? You can do this by defining abbreviations in a *library*.

A library is a document whose pages contain text that corresponds to one abbreviation or *entry*. Hence, a single abbreviation can represent up to an entire page of text.

Creating a Library

To create a library:

1. Select "Create a New Document" from the Main Menu.
2. When the Create a New Document form appears, enter the name of the library and press Return. For example, if the library is to contain abbreviations for Acme International Corporation and your name, enter **names** as the library name.
3. When the Document Summary Screen appears, press F5. As the message at the bottom indicates, F5 tells Advantage that this is a library rather than a regular document. Pressing F5 makes Advantage clear the screen and display

```
Library Entry Name? [   ] -- Press Shift F1 for a list of entries.
```

Advantage is asking for the first abbreviation you want to use in your documents.

4. Enter an abbreviation of up to three characters, then press Return. For example, to abbreviate Acme International Corporation as *aic,* enter **aic**.

    Advantage displays the first page of the library. On the status line, *LIBRARY:* has replaced *DOCUMENT:* and *ENTRY:* and your abbreviation has replaced *PAGE:* and the page number.
5. Enter the text for the entry. For example, enter **Acme International Corporation** for the *aic* entry.
6. When you finish, you have two choices: to return to the Main Menu, press F10; to enter another abbreviation, press F2 (New Page) key.

Using a Library

To use a library with a document, you must first *attach* it. To do this, load the document into memory and then press Shift and F5. Advantage shows

```
What Library? Drive B Name: _____   Press Shift F1 for directory.
```

Enter the library's name (e.g., **names**) and press Return. If you don't remember its name, press Shift-F1. Advantage will list all the files on your data disk; it's up to you to know which ones are libraries.

Inserting Library Entries

Whenever you reach a place where you want a library entry, press the F5 key. Advantage displays the prompt

```
Library Entry Name? [   ] -- Press Shift F1 for a list of entries
```

Enter the abbreviation of the entry you want and press Return. For example, to insert "Acme International Corporation" from the *names* library, enter **aic** and press Return. As with the library name, if you don't remember the abbreviation, press Shift-F1 for a list of them.

Switching Libraries

Advantage can attach only one library at a time to a document. However, you can switch libraries by pressing Shift-F5 and giving the new library's name.

Editing and Adding Entries

You can change the contents of a library in much the same way you change a regular document. To begin, select "Edit an Old Document" from the Main Menu, then enter the name of the library and press Return. Advantage displays the first page in the library; that is, the text for the first abbreviation you entered. Now you can either edit an existing entry or add a new one to the library.

To edit an existing library entry, you must move to its page (if you're not already there). As with a document, Ctrl-PgUp and Ctrl-PgDn move the cursor up or down a page, while F1-Home and F1-End move it to the first or last page of the library. To reach any other page, press F1, enter the abbreviation you want to change, and press Return. When you are done making changes, press F10 to save the revised library.

To add a new entry to the library, press F1 and End to move the cursor to the last page. Then press Ctrl-End to reach the end of the page and F2 to start a new page for the entry. When Advantage asks for the entry name, enter the abbreviation and press Return. Now you can enter the text for your new entry. To add another new entry, press F2 to start another new page; to save the changes, press F10.

Using Document Summary Screens

When you tell Advantage to create a new document or edit an old one, it first displays a *Document Summary Screen* form. On it, Advantage shows the document's name, length, and the dates when you created it and last edited it. It also provides space for you to enter the name of the author, addressee, and operator, plus key words and comments.

Advantage can display or print Document Summary Screens; it can also search through them for specific entries. For example, you can search for documents . . .

- Whose names start with the word "sales".
- Prepared by a particular author.
- Addressed to a particular customer.
- Prepared during October of 1986.
- Having the key word "invoice".

Hence, Advantage's Document Summary Screen facilities can be a tremendous help in keeping track of documents on your disks. The search feature is particularly useful to people who have a hard disk, which can store *hundreds* of documents.

Displaying Document Summary Screens

To display the Document Summary Screens for the documents on a disk:

1. Select "Document Handling Utilities" from the Main Menu and then "Print Document Summary Screens". Advantage displays a *Print Document Summary Screens* form.
2. To display the Document Summary Screens, press F10. To print them, turn your printer on and switch it "on-line." Then press Return to reach "(S)creen or (P)rinter," type **p,** and press F10.
3. If you are displaying the screens, press the space bar to move to the next one. If you are printing them, Advantage produces two per page. In either case, pressing Esc twice returns you to the Document Handling Utilities Menu; pressing it a third time returns you to the Main Menu.

Searching Document Summary Screens

Searching the Document Summary Screens on a disk requires a procedure similar to the one we just described for displaying them. Specifically, select "Document Handling Utilities" from the Main Menu and then "Search Document Summary Screens". When Advantage displays its *Search Document Summary Screens* form, press F10 to send the results to the screen or set "(S)creen or (P)rinter" to *P* and press F10 to print them.

Advantage then displays a *Search Document Summary Screens* form. Figure 3-5 shows that this is essentially a blank Document Summary Screens form. To tell Advantage what to search for, fill in the appropriate fields (use the arrow keys to move between them), then press F10. Possibilities include:

1. To search for documents whose names start with *sales,* enter **sales** for "Document". This will find *sales85, salesq2, salesrpt,* and so on.
2. To search for documents written by Harry Jones, enter **Jones** for "Author".
3. To search for correspondence to George Thompson, enter **Thompson** for "Addressee".
4. To search for documents that contain the key word *Account #1238-B,* enter **#1238-B** for "Identification key words".
5. To search for documents created during May of 1986, enter **05/01/86** to **05/31/86** for "Creation Date".

SEARCH DOCUMENT SUMMARY SCREENS

This utility will search Document Summary Screens
and output the names of the matching documents
to either the SCREEN or the PRINTER

Drive   : <u>B</u>
Directory   : <u>   </u>
(S)creen or (P)rinter   : <u>S</u>

NOTE: If you are going to output to the Printer, then
the Printer MUST BE ON and NOT IN USE.

Press F10 when done or ESCAPE to Abort
Press Ctrl Home to select default directory, Ctrl End to select next directory

S:l N:l

Figure 3-5. Search Document Summary Screens form.
Courtesy of Multimate International Corp.

When you finish entering items in the form, press F10 to start the search operation. Advantage clears the screen and shows *SEARCH DOCUMENT SUMMARY SCREENS* at the top and *Any key to pause, <ESCAPE> to abort.* at the bottom.

Advantage searches each Document Summary Screen for an entry that matches one in your list. If a screen has a matching entry, Advantage displays the document's name. This eventually produces a list of every document whose Document Summary Screen contains one or more of your search items.

When the search operation finishes, *PRESS ANY KEY TO EXIT* appears at the bottom of the screen. Press the space bar to return to the Document Handling Utilities Menu or F10 to return to the Main Menu.

Questions and Answers

Question: I keep reaching for the Tab key and nothing happens. What's the problem?

Answer: Look where you're reaching. You're probably pressing Ctrl instead of Tab.

Question: How can I make Advantage start a new page?

Answer: Put the cursor at the end of the current page (pressing Ctrl-End will do this) and press the F2 key.

Question: While working on page 7 of a long letter, I decided to change some terms that I mentioned on page 2. How do I get back and forth?

Answer: Give Advantage a Go to Page command by pressing F1, then typing **2** and Return. Make your changes, then do another Go to Page to return to page 7. If page 7 is as far as you have typed, you can use F1 and End to return to it.

Question: I only want to underline words, not the spaces between them. How can I do this?

Answer: Press Alt and + on the top row. Advantage will underline everything you type except spaces and punctuation. When you finish, press Alt and + to turn the underlining off.

Question: I entered a table, then decided to center the title. But when I pressed F3, Advantage centered it, but erased the first letter. What did I do wrong?

Answer: By pressing F3 alone, you make Advantage *replace* the first letter of your title with the centering mark (↔), rather than *insert* the mark. You should press + (Insert Character) on the numeric keypad, then F3. (You can also use this one-character insertion procedure to restore your missing letter.)

Question: I work for Johnson Tool Company, so I put an abbreviation for it in a library. But when I try to insert the name, Advantage displays *ENTRY NOT FOUND*. What's wrong?

Answer: You probably entered a wrong form of the abbreviation. Advantage only recognizes the form you entered when you defined the entry. Hence, if you defined it with *jtc,* Advantage will not accept *JTC* or *Jtc.* To obtain a list of abbreviations in the library, press Shift-F1 when Advantage asks for the entry name.

Question: There is an entry in my library that I never use. How can I delete it?

Answer: To delete an entry from a library, move the cursor to the beginning of it and press Del. Then press Ctrl-End to reach the end of the page and press Del again. Since you have deleted the entire definition, Advantage removes its name from the library.

Hints and Warnings

1. Advantage does not automatically rearrange the document when additions or deletions make pages longer or shorter. To adjust the page boundaries, you must press F2 to start a new page, Shift-F2 to combine pages, or Ctrl-F2 to repaginate.

2. Combining pages using Shift-F2 usually produces a page that is too full. You must repaginate (or get rid of the excess otherwise) before you print that page.

3. Advantage always starts repaginating on the same page as the cursor. To make it repaginate the entire document, move the cursor to the first page (press F1, then Home on the numeric keypad).

4. Advantage keeps only one page of a document in memory at a time; it keeps the rest on disk. Hence, if the power goes off or you absent-mindedly switch the computer off without saving your work on disk, you will lose only the changes to the current page.

5. The simplest way to remove underlining from a single character is to put the cursor on it, then type the character again.

6. When naming or using library entries, remember that Advantage differentiates between lowercase and capital letters. Thus, if you abbreviate "First National Bank" as *fnb,* you cannot refer to it using *FNB.* You can, however, use names differing only in case as separate abbreviations, but this is confusing. Don't do that if you can avoid it.

7. If you forget which libraries are on a disk, press Shift-F1 when Advantage asks for the library name. Similarly, if you forget which library entries are in memory, press Shift-F1 when Advantage asks for the entry name.

Key Point Summary

Table 3-1 summarizes the keys and functions we introduced in this chapter.

Table 3-1. Keys and functions introduced in Chapter 3.

Key(s)	Function
Alt-+	Turn underlining on; skip spaces and punctuation
Alt-underscore	Turn underlining on or off
Shift-underscore	Underline (or de-underline) character at cursor position
Ctrl-PgDn	Move cursor to next page
Ctrl-PgUp	Move cursor to previous page
Ctrl-PrtSc	Hot print (print the current page)
F1, then number	Move to specified page
F1, then End	Move to last page
F1, then Home	Move to first page
F2	Start a new page
Ctrl-F2	Repaginate
Shift-F2	Combine pages
F3	Center line
F5	*With library attached:* Insert library entry *From a Document Summary Screen:* Create a library
Shift-F5	Attach library
F9	Change or accept format line

1. Advantage's Document Summary Screen form shows the dates a document was created and last edited. It also has spaces for the names of the author, addressee, operator, and key words comments.
2. Advantage displays the current tab settings on the format line—the second line on the screen. To change tabs, press F9 to move the cursor to the format line. To set a tab, move the cursor to where you want it and press Tab. To clear a tab, put the cursor on its ≫ marker and press the space bar.
3. Advantage can print text with proportional spacing on printers that can produce it. To obtain this feature, make the "Proportional Spacing: N/Y" option Y in the Print Parameters for Document form.
4. Advantage normally prints text with a ragged right margin. To print it with an even right margin, make the "Justification" option Y in the Print Parameters for Document form.

Advantage can also produce micro-justification, in which it inserts space inside words as well as between them. To obtain this, set "Justification" to *M*.

5. Advantage automatically divides single-spaced text into 55-line pages. When you start the 56th line, it beeps the computer and makes the line number at the top of the screen flash. To make it start a new page automatically, change "Automatic page breaks?" on the Modify System Defaults form to *Y*.

6. To force Advantage to start a new page anywhere, press + (Insert Character), then F2. To combine two pages, put the cursor at the end of the first page, then press Shift and F2.

7. To move the cursor to the previous page or the next page, press Ctrl-PgUp or Ctrl-PgDn. To move it to any other page, press F1. In response to the prompt, enter a page number and Return, or press Home or End to reach the first or last page.

8. If additions or deletions make pages too long or too short, adjust them by repaginating. To repaginate, move the cursor to the page where you want to start and press Ctrl and F2.

9. By changing "Allow widows and orphans?" to *N* on the Modify System Defaults form, Advantage will no longer leave the first line or last line of a paragraph alone on a page. However, you must repaginate to make it enforce this rule.

10. To print the current page, put the cursor anywhere in the page and turn your printer on. Then press Ctrl and PrtSc.

11. To underline existing material, move the cursor to where it is to start and press Shift-underscore. To underline new material, press either Alt-underscore (to underline everything) or Alt-+ (to exclude spaces and punctuation).

12. To center an existing line, move the cursor to the start of it, then press + on the numeric keypad and function key F3. To center a new line, press F3 before you type it.

13. You can use abbreviations for frequently-used text (up to one page long) by putting the text in a library. Create a library just as you create a document, but when the Document Summary Screen appears, press F5. When requested, enter an abbreviation (up to three characters), then press Return. Advantage presents a blank page on which you enter the corresponding text. To create another entry, press F2 to change pages; to save the library, press F10.

14. To use (attach) a library, move the cursor to the place in a document where you want to refer to it, then press Shift and F5. Give Advantage the library's name and press Return.

15. To insert a library entry in a document, press F5, then enter the abbreviation and press Return.

16. To edit a library entry, move to the page where it is defined. To add a new entry to a library, press F1 and End to reach its last page, then press Ctrl and End to reach the end of that page. Press F2 to start a new page, then create the entry as described in point #11.

17. Options in the Document Handling Utilities Menu allow you to display the Document Summary Screens for documents on a disk or search them for specific entries.

4

Spelling Checker and Thesaurus

Advantage can check a document, or a portion of one, for spelling errors. It does this by looking for each word in its dictionary. If a word is not there, Advantage marks it. Then, when you next edit the document, you can correct an individual word by moving the cursor to it and entering the correct spelling directly, or correct all of the words in sequence by telling Advantage to "spell-edit" the document.

During spell-editing, Advantage stops on each marked word and asks whether you want to ignore it (e.g., is it a proper name or part of a book title), leave it marked for later correction, add it to a user dictionary (e.g., is it a technical term not found in most dictionaries), choose from a list of close words from the dictionary, correct it manually, or return to editing.

Advantage also has a *Thesaurus* (new with Version 3.6). This is similar to the popular book version, but much faster because the synonyms appear almost instantly. To obtain a list of synonyms, simply move the cursor to the word or phrase in question, then start the Thesaurus. Advantage displays a definition for the word and its synonyms. These may be nouns, verbs, or adjectives, whatever is appropriate. You may then either choose a replacement from the list or return to editing.

Spell-Checking Procedure

To spell-check a document:

1. Select "Spell Check a Document" from the Main Menu.
2. When Advantage asks you to *Enter the Name of the Document to be checked,* type it (the screen shows the available document names), and press Return. The screen now shows the additional prompt

```
Start page [1  ]  End page [999]
```

3. To spell-check the entire document, press F10. To spell-check a selected range of pages, enter the starting page number (and, if you want it to stop before the end, an ending page number), and press F10.
4. If your computer has floppy disks, Advantage shows

```
Insert Dictionary Disk into Drive A - Press
Any Key.
```

Replace the System disk with your Dictionary disk and press the space bar.

During the checking operation, Advantage displays the following at the bottom of the screen:

```
              OPERATION IN PROGRESS
[nnnnn] WORDS MISSPELLED   [mmmmm] WORDS TOTAL
```

where *nnnnn* and *mmmmm* are running totals of the words it can't find and the number of words it has checked. When the computer beeps and shows

```
OPERATION COMPLETE - PRESS ANY KEY TO CONTINUE
```

press the space bar to return to the Main Menu.

When spell-checking, Advantage marks each word that is not in its dictionary by making the first letter flash on the screen. Your job now is to find the flashing words and correct them, if necessary. Do this using Advantage's spell-editing feature.

Spell-Editing Procedure

To spell-edit a document, leave the Dictionary disk in drive A and proceed as follows:

1. Select "Edit an Old Document" from the Main Menu.
2. When requested, enter the document's name and press Return, then F10.
3. When the first page appears, press Alt and F10. Advantage finds the first marked word and puts the cursor on it. At the bottom, it displays the Spell Edit menu (see Figure 4-1). We will discuss this menu shortly.

Please enter desired function

    0)   Add this word to the Custom Dictionary
    1)   Ignore this place mark and find the next mark
    2)   Clear this place mark and find the next mark
    3)   List possible correct spellings
    4)   Type replacement spelling
    5)   Delete a word from the Custom Dictionary
    Esc) End Spell Edit and resume Document Edit

Figure 4-1. Spell Edit menu.
Courtesy of Multimate International Corp.

4. Press the key to select the option you want.
5. Advantage continues finding marked words and presenting the Spell Edit menu. Finally, when there are no more marked words, it displays

```
UNABLE TO FIND NEXT MISSPELLING - PRESS ANY KEY
```

6. Press the space bar to return to editing.

Spell Edit Menu

Here is an explanation of each option in the Spell Edit menu:

- *0—Add this word to the Custom Dictionary*   This makes Advantage create a "custom" dictionary (if it doesn't already exist) and add this word to it. In future spell-check operations, Advantage will automatically search the custom dictionary as well as the standard one.
- *1—Ignore this place mark and find the next mark*   This leaves the word marked, so you can find it later. It is useful if you aren't immediately sure how to deal with the word.
- *2—Clear this place mark and find the next mark*   This lets you skip a word you don't use often enough to want to add to the dictionary.
- *3—List possible correct spellings*   This makes Advantage provide a list of possible replacement words from its dictionary. This option works for a minor error such as a transposition or a single incorrect vowel or consonant, and it also works for phonetic misspellings (e.g., "Shikawgo" for "Chicago").
- *4—Type replacement spelling*   This lets you correct a word manually. When Advantage tells you to type the correct spelling, enter it and press F10.
- *Esc—End Spell Edit and resume Document Edit*   This allows you to leave the spell-editing procedure and return to regular editing. You might do this if you spot something you intended to change earlier. To resume spell-editing from that point, press Alt and F10 again.

Options 0, 2, 3, and 4 operate not only on the current word, but on every occurrence of that word throughout your document. That is, if you add a word to the custom dictionary (0) or clear its place mark (2), Advantage automatically unmarks subsequent occurrences as it encounters them. Similarly, if you change a word either from a list (3) or manually (4), Advantage will make the same correction to all later occurrences.

Spelling Correction Example

As an example of using the spell-checking and spell-editing features, consider the letter in Figure 4-2. With the aid of *Webster's New World Misspeller's Dictionary,* a few typing mistakes, and our

own ingenuity, we have introduced several spelling errors. If you try
this example on your own, don't be restricted by our mistakes;
surely you can make bigger, better, or different ones.

```
                              2211 Washington Street
                              San Diego, CA 92121
                              May 16, 1986

Mr. Carl Johnson
1236 Summit Drive
San Diego, CA 92121

Dear Mr. Johnson:

In response to your recent rikwest, we need the following
information to cunsider a credit applivdation:

     1) Name and adddress of your bank, along with your account
        number.
     2) Three credit references.
     3) A signed corprate resullution indicating trepponsabillity
        for payment.

You may either use our enclosed form or sumbit a standard one of
your own.  Please indicate any ratings you may have from credit
burows.

                              Sincerely yours,



                              Marie F. Gerard
                              Assistant Credit Manager

Enclosure
```

Figure 4-2. Credit application letter with misspellings.

After you enter the letter (call it *spelsamp*) and save it on disk,
proceed as follows to correct the spelling:

1. Select "Spell Check a Document" from the Main Menu.
2. When asked for the name of the document, type **spelsamp** and press
   Return.
3. Insert the Dictionary disk in drive A, and press the space bar.
4. When Advantage displays starting and ending page numbers, press
   F10 to accept its suggestions.
     The program proceeds to search the document for words that it
   cannot find in its dictionary. Besides misspellings, these may include

proper names, abbreviations, and technical terms. In our case, it reports 21 unmatched words.

5. When spell-checking is finished, press the space bar to return to the Main Menu.

6. Load the *spelsamp* letter into memory using "Edit an Old Document". The letter appears on the screen, flashing like a Christmas tree. (Note that Advantage includes repeated words in figuring the unmatched word count. For example, it counts the two occurrences of "San" as two unmatched words.)

7. Press Alt and F10 to begin spell-editing. Advantage puts the cursor on the first marked word ("San" in the return address) and displays the Spell Edit menu at the bottom of the screen.

Dealing with Unmatched Words

In our case, we deal with the 21 unmatched words using the following:

- Press **0** to add *San, Diego, CA, Carl, Johnson, Marie, F.,* and *Gerard* to the dictionary. In each case, Advantage asks

```
Is capitalization required? Enter 'Y' for yes, 'N' for no
```

Enter **y** so that future spell-checking will mark one of these words if we accidentally type the capital letter as lowercase. For *F.,* Advantage also asks

```
Is the ending period required? Enter 'Y' for yes, 'N' for no
```

Enter **y** to make the dictionary contain "F." rather than just "F".

After Advantage adds a word to the dictionary, press the space bar to advance to the next marked word.

- Press **3** to obtain a list of possible corrections for *rikwest, corprate, resullution,* and *burows.* In each case, Advantage presents nine numbered choices. For *rikwest,* it shows

```
      Enter the number of the word to replace the misspelled word
                or press Esc to return to Document Edit.
   1) request        4) requests       7) retrials
   2) waitress       5) redress        8) requisite
   3) retries        6) regress        9) retires
```

Press 1 for *request.*

- Press **4** to correct *cunsider, applivdation, adddress, sumbit,* and *trepponsabillity* directly from the keyboard. Specifically, we changed *cunsider* to *consider, applivdation* to *application, adddress* to *address, sumbit* to *submit,* and *trepponsabillity* to *responsabillity.*

After one spell-editing pass, the letter looks like Figure 4-3.

```
                              2211 Washington Street
                              San Diego, CA 92121
                              May 16, 1986

Mr. Carl Johnson
1236 Summit Drive
San Diego, CA 92121

Dear Mr. Johnson:

In response to your recent request, we need the following
information to consider a credit application:

     1) Name and address of your bank, along with your account
        number.
     2) Three credit references.
     3) A signed corporate resolution indicating responsabillity
        for payment.

You may either use our enclosed form or submit a standard one of
your own.  Please indicate any ratings you may have from credit
bureaus.

                              Sincerely yours,



                              Marie F. Gerard
                              Assistant Credit Manager

Enclosure
```

Figure 4-3. Credit application letter after a spell-edit pass.

Another spell-editing pass shows that *responsabillity* is still misspelled. However, the Spell Edit menu's 3 option gave us the correct form, *responsibility,* so we are home free.

Spell-Checking a Portion of a Document

You can spell-check a word, paragraph, or any other selected portion of a document without returning to the Main Menu. To do this, put the cursor where you want to start and press Ctrl and F10. Advantage shows

`CHECK WHAT?`

in the upper right-hand corner. Move the cursor just past the last word you want to check (Advantage highlights everything in between) and press Ctrl and F10 again. When requested, replace the System disk with the Dictionary disk and press the space bar.

When Advantage finishes Advantage spell-checking, it puts the cursor back where you started. Now you can either correct the mistakes directly or press Alt-F10 to start spell-editing. Suppose you type

`You could file before June 21, but we don't reccomend it.`

To check *reccomend*, put the cursor on the *r* and press Ctrl-F10. When *CHECK WHAT?* appears, move the cursor to the space between *reccomend* and *it* and press Ctrl-F10 again.

Insert the Dictionary disk and press the space bar. When *SPELL CHECK COMPLETE* appears, press Alt-F10 to obtain the Spell Edit menu, and then press 3 to request a list of possible replacements. Press 1 to select *recommend* and then press Esc to return to your text.

Clearing Place Marks

If you exit spell-editing without dealing with one or more marked words, they will remain marked (i.e., flashing) when you next edit the document. Advantage has a command that "unmarks" all marked words in a document. To use it, put the cursor anywhere in the document and press Alt and Y. Advantage displays

CLEARING PLACEMARKS

on the top line and shows each page as it searches for place marks. When it finishes, it puts the cursor at the top of the page where you started.

Starting the Thesaurus

To start the Thesaurus, move the cursor to the word you want to look up and press Alt and T. Advantage highlights the word and displays *LOOK UP WHAT?* at the top right-hand corner of the screen. To look up that word, press Alt-T again. To look up a phrase (e.g., "willy-nilly", "cater to", or "whether or not"), move the cursor to the end of it and press Alt-T. If your computer has floppy disk drives, replace the System disk with the Thesaurus disk when Advantage tells you to and press Return.

Advantage searches for the highlighted word and then does one of two things. If the Thesaurus does not contain that word, the screen shows *No information found, press any key to continue*; press Return to get back to editing. If the Thesaurus has synonyms, it lists up to nine of them, along with a definition for the word. It also puts the following message at the bottom of the screen.

```
Enter Number for Replacement, ESC - Exit Thesaurus,
Alt T - Look Up New Word
```

Your choices are:

1. To replace the word with one from the list, type its number.
2. To look up a word you haven't typed yet, press Alt-T again. When the screen shows *Enter new word:*, type it and press Alt-T again.
3. To return to editing, press Esc.

If there are more than nine synonyms, the prompt includes *Spacebar for more Synonyms*; press the space bar to see them. Similarly, if there are additional meanings, the prompt includes *PgDn— Next Meaning PgUp—Prior Meaning.*; press PgDn to obtain the next one or PgUp to obtain the previous one.

Questions and Answers

Question: I prepared a letter, put the cursor at the beginning and pressed Alt-F10 to locate the errors. After a moment, the computer showed *UNABLE TO FIND NEXT MISSPELLING—PRESS ANY KEY*. Does this mean my letter is perfect?

Answer: No, it simply means that Advantage couldn't find any *marked* words. Alt-F10 makes Advantage spell-edit the document, but you never spell-checked it. You *must* spell-check a document before you can spell-edit it.

Question: I corrected the spelling in a four-page letter, but have since made changes to page 2. How can I correct just that page?

Answer: Start the "Spell-Check a Document" procedure as usual, but when Advantage shows

```
Start page [1 ]   End page [999]
```

enter **2** and press Tab. Then enter **002** for *End page* and press F10.

Question: I accidentally spell-checked the wrong document, and now it's filled with flashing letters. How can I turn off the flashing?

Answer: Put the cursor anywhere in the document and press Alt-Y. This is Advantage's *Clear all place marks* command.

Question: Advantage marked the name of my company as misspelled, so I added it to the dictionary. However, there are more mentions of the company in my letter. Do I have to correct them as well?

Answer: No. Once you add a word to the dictionary (option 0 in the Spell Edit menu), clear its place mark (option 2), select a replacement from the dictionary (option 3), or change the spelling from the keyboard (option 4), Advantage will unmark all subsequent occurrences of the word throughout your document.

Hints and Warnings

1. Advantage acts as a proofreader as well as a spelling checker. Many of the errors it finds are really typing mistakes.
2. Even if you are reasonably sure of a correction, you might as well have Advantage look it up. This takes only a few seconds and verifies the spelling.
3. In practice, you should add abbreviations, proper names, and technical terms to the dictionary rather than just ignoring them. If you ig-

nore them, Advantage will find them every time it spell-checks the document. This is time-consuming and annoying.

4. Advantage checks spelling, but not grammar. It will not locate such errors as duplicated words (e.g., "I drove the the car.") or double punctuation (e.g., "Bill,, that's the best thing you ever said."). You must correct these yourself.

5. Advantage counts words as it spell-checks a document, and displays the total when it finishes. This is handy for writers and students who want to prepare an article, short story, report, or term paper of a specific length.

6. To stop a spell-check operation before it finishes, press Esc.

Key Point Summary

Table 4-1 summarizes the keys and functions we introduced in this chapter.

Table 4-1. Keys and functions introduced in Chapter 4.

Keys	Function
Alt-F10	Spell-edit
Ctrl-F10	Spell-check from within document
Al5-T	Thesaurus
Alt-Y	Clear all place marks

1. Correcting spelling with Advantage involves two operations. *Spell-checking* marks the words that Advantage cannot find in its dictionary, while *spell-editing* locates marked words and asks what you want to do with them. The dictionary is contained on the Dictionary disk; both operations will prompt you to put this disk in drive A, if necessary.

2. To spell-check a document, select "Spell Check a Document" from the Main Menu. When requested, enter the document's name and press Return. When Advantage asks for the range of pages you want to check, enter them and press F10; to check the entire document, just press F10.

3. When you load a spell-checked document from disk, the first letter of each unmatched word flashes on the screen. To spell-edit the document, press Alt-F10. Advantage stops on each marked word and displays a Spell Edit menu. Choices in the menu allow you to add the word to the dictionary, leave the word marked, remove the marking,

display a list of alternates from the dictionary, correct the word from the keyboard, or return to editing.

4. To spell-check text from within the document, put the cursor on the first character and press Ctrl-F10. Then move the cursor just past the text and press Ctrl and F10 again.

5. To clear all spell-checking place marks, put the cursor anywhere in the document and press Alt-Y.

6. Advantage's Thesaurus can look up synonyms for a word or phrase and replace it with a synonym. To begin, move the cursor to the word you want to look up and press Alt-T. Highlight the word and press Alt-T again.

7. If the Thesaurus does not contain the word you requested, the screen shows *No information found, press any key to continue.* Press Return to get back to editing.

8. If the Thesaurus has synonyms for your word, it lists them along with a definition for the word. At this point, you can replace the word with a synonym by typing the synonym's number. You can also press the space bar to view additional synonyms, press PgUp or PgDn to view additional meanings, or press Esc to return to editing.

5

Reports

To write a report with Advantage, you will need the features discussed in this chapter. For example, you will want the pages numbered. You may also want a heading on the top of each page and the chapter number, section title, or report title at the bottom.

Furthermore, you may want the report double-spaced, but with single-spaced lists or tables. You may also want titles in **bold print,** and you may want to use subscripts or superscripts in references, equations, and formulas.

A Sample Report

Figures 5-1A through 5-1E show a sample five-page report for a company's quarterly sales. It consists of a cover page, three summary tables, and accompanying descriptions. Note the following:

- All titles are in bold print.
- Descriptive text is double-spaced.
- Tables are centered.
- The page number and report title appear at the bottom of every page except the cover.

We will enter this report and discuss its features as we encounter them. To begin, create a new document as usual, and name it **rptq286**.

ACME CORPORATION

National Sales Report

Second Quarter, 1986

Gloria A. Powell
National Sales Manager
July 19, 1986

cc: P.M. Cornell, President
    J.R. Johnson, Vice-President
    Regional Sales Managers

Figure 5-1A. Sample report, cover page.

This report summarizes national sales for the second quarter of
1986.   Table 1 lists the sales figures for the six regions and
compares them to the second quarter of 1985.   As the table
shows, sales are moderately better than last year in every
region except the Southwest.

The Southeast region tops the list with a 9.9 percent gain, due
in part to large orders from Jenco in Florida and Symtech in
Georgia.   Although the Southwest region continues to lead in
volume, its sales are slightly below last year's.   This reflects
decreased orders from Winicon Corp. in Nevada, which has been
troubled by economic conditions.   In all, this quarter's sales
are 5.7 percent higher than those of the second quarter of 1985.

Table 2 lists the leading sales representatives in each region.
These are the same people listed on last year's report, with one
exception: Doris Kim, who joined Acme in January, closed a
290⇒unit order with Pacifico to put her on top in the
Northwest.   Our sales force continues to be among the best in
the business, but I am especially proud of the exceptional
individuals listed here.

⇒2⇒ (Second Quarter Report/1986)

Figure 5-1B. Sample report, second page.

Table 1. Second Quarter Sales

Region	Units Sold	Revenues ($)	% Change from 1985
Northeast	5,770	2,481,100	+6.7
Southeast	4,550	1,956,500	+9.9
Midwest	6,430	2,764,900	+8.8
Mountain	4,300	1,849,000	+4.7
Northwest	5,130	2,205,900	+7.4
Southwest	6,780	2,915,400	⇒0.3
Totals	32,960	14,172,800	+5.7

Table 2. Top Sales Representatives

Region	Sales Rep.	Units Sold	% Increase from 1985
Northeast	R. Roberts	790	22.4
Southeast	C. Chamber	640	16.3
Midwest	J. Wilkes	730	19.1
Mountain	P. Wallach	620	20.6
Northwest	D. Kim	590	⇥⇥
Southwest	B. Lloyd	710	17.7

⌐3⌐ (Second Quarter Report/1986)

Figure 5-1C. Sample report, third page.

Table 3 lists the orders that were placed by key accounts during the quarter. Most significant of these is the 510-unit order by Chicago Gear, whose orders appeared to have leveled off at about 400 units per quarter during the past two years. The Wilburg Sons and Storr Brothers accounts also show notable increases; both orders are about 19 percent higher than in recent quarters.

-4- (Second Quarter Report/1986)

Figure 5-1D. Sample report, fourth page.

Table 3.   Orders by Key Accounts

Region	Account	State	Sales Rep.	Order
Northeast	Wilburg Sons	New York	R. Roberts	430
Southeast	Jenco	Florida	C. Chamber	390
	Symtech	Georgia	P. Grogan	240
Midwest	Chicago Gear	Illinois	J. Wilkes	510
Mountain	Hart Foods	Montana	P. Wallach	420
Northwest	Pacifico	Oregon	D. Kim	290
Southwest	Storr Bros.	California	B. Lloyd	470

-5- (Second Quarter Report/1986)

Figure 5-1E. Sample report, fifth page.

Entering the Cover Page

Figure 5-1A shows that the cover has a centered, bold title and the author's name and title, date, and distribution list ("cc" means carbon copy) in the lower left-hand corner. In this figure, the title starts three inches from the top.

Assuming you have either adjusted your paper for a one-inch top margin, or have changed Advantage to provide it automatically (see "Printing the Letter" in Chapter 2), you must still move the cursor two inches down the page. To do this, press Return 12 times (Advantage's default spacing is six lines per inch) to reach line 13 and press F3 to prepare Advantage for centering.

Bold Print

To make something print in **bold type**, press Alt and Z. Advantage puts a rectangle (▌) on the screen; this means it will embolden everything you type until you enter Alt-Z again. (This can be a character, word, paragraph, or even an entire document.) Note the following about bold print:

- The ▌ mark that Alt-Z produces is a *control character*. It makes Advantage do something (embolden text, in this case), but does not show up when you print the document.
- Although the emboldening mark looks different from letters, numbers, punctuation marks, and other regular characters, it takes up a character position and can be treated as a character. That is, you can replace, insert, or delete an emboldening mark exactly as you can replace, insert, or delete a regular character.

Finishing the Cover Page

To embolden the title on the cover page:

1. Press Alt-Z to turn emboldening on.
2. Enter **ACME CORPORATION** and press Return twice.
3. Press F3 and enter **National Sales Report** and press Return twice.

4. Press F3 and enter **Second Quarter, 1986** and press Alt-Z (to turn emboldening off) and Return.

To complete the page, press Return to reach the line where the author's name goes. Since we want seven lines (including a blank line) at the bottom of a 55-line page, the author's name belongs on line 49. Press Return until the status line at the top shows *LINE: 49.* Then enter the author's name and title, the date, and the distribution list. Pressing Return after *Regional Sales Managers* makes Advantage start the second page.

Entering the Second Page

The second page has two features we have not used before; it is double-spaced and has a page number at the bottom.

Double-Spacing

To double-space the second page, you must change the line spacing value in the format line. To reach it, press F9. Advantage shows *FORMAT CHANGE* in the top right-hand corner and puts the cursor on the first dot in the format line.

As we mentioned earlier, line spacing is controlled by the number at the beginning of the format line; it is currently set to *1* for single-spacing. To switch to double-spacing, press the left-arrow key to put the cursor on the number, then enter **2** and press F9.

Advantage will now print text double-spaced, although it will still display it single-spaced on the screen. (Notice, however, that the LINE number at the top changes by 2 as you move the cursor up or down.)

Now enter the text for the second page as shown in Figure 5-1B. The next thing we want is to make Advantage print the following line at the bottom of this page and pages 3 through 5:

```
-n- (Second Quarter Report/1986)
```

where *n* is the page number.

Headers and Footers

Headers (as you might suspect) are lines printed at the top of a page, such as a section title. *Footers* are similar except they go at the bottom. Each can be up to five lines long.

Once you set up a header or footer, Advantage automatically puts it on every page until you delete or change it. Further, if you set up different headers or footers on consecutive pages, Advantage will alternate them. That is, it will print one on right-hand (odd-numbered) pages and the other on left-hand (even-numbered) pages.

Creating a Header

To create a header, move the cursor to the top of the first page where you want one, then press Alt-H (Advantage shows ⌗) and Return. Enter the header text, press Return, press Alt-H, and press Return once again. After that, enter the text for the page normally.

Creating a Footer

To create a footer, finish typing text on the first page where you want one, then press Return to reach the line where the footer is to appear. When you get there, press Alt-F (Advantage shows *f*) and Return. Now enter the footer text, press Return, press Alt-F, and press Return once more. To begin a new page, press F2.

Page Numbering

You can use *&PAGE&* in a header or footer to indicate the current page number. Advantage will automatically replace *&PAGE&* with the page number on each page. For example,

```
Page &PAGE&
```

becomes *Page 1* on the first page, *Page 2* on the second page, and so on. Similarly, you can indicate the last page number with *&LPAGE&*. For example,

```
Page &PAGE& of &LPAGE&
```

becomes *Page 1 of 20* on the first page, *Page 2 of 20* on the second page, and so on.

Advantage can also replace occurrences of &PAGE& and &LPAGE& in the text as well as in a header or footer. You can use this feature in an introduction where you say, "This report is &LPAGE& pages long." Advantage changes the value of &LPAGE& automatically as the report expands or shrinks due to editing or repaginating.

Although &PAGE& is convenient, there are some instances where you won't want to use it. For example, suppose your document has a title page and a one-page table of contents, and you want to number the first page of regular text *1*. &PAGE& won't work here because on this third page, its value is *3*, and you can't change it.

Fortunately, you may use an alternate symbol, #, in a header or footer (but not in text) to indicate the current page number. Advantage lets you specify the initial value of # when you print the document. We discuss this later under "Saving and Printing a Report."

Footer for the Sample Report

Our second quarter report has a footer but no headers. To set it up:

1. Press Return until the cursor reaches line 54.
2. Press Ins to put Advantage in insert mode. (This is necessary to prevent it from starting a new page when you cross line 55.)
3. Hold Alt down and press F, then press Return twice (this puts a blank line between the text and the footer).
4. Press F3 to center the line.
5. Type **-&PAGE&- (Second Quarter Report/1986)** and press Return.
6. Press AltF and Return.
7. Press Ins to get back to regular text mode, then press F2 to start a new page.

Entering the Third Page

Figure 5-1C shows the third page, which consists of two tables. Before entering them, note the following:

- We must change the line spacing back to single-spaced.
- We need different tabs for each table, because the columns are spaced differently.
- The tables and titles are centered.

To begin, use the same procedure as before to switch Advantage back to single-spacing. Press F3 to get centering, then enter the title for Table 1 and press Return twice to move the cursor to where the table begins.

Centering a Table

At this point we must create tabs for the table. To determine where they go, enter the table headings and the longest line of data, adjust the spacing, then center the headings and move the data under them. The starting points of the data tell us where to set tabs.

To begin, enter the headings and the first line of data, with three spaces between columns. Remember to press Alt-underscore before and after each heading to underline it. The two lines should look like this:

```
Region      Units Sold     Revenues ($)     % Change from 1984

Northeast   5,770   2,481,100   +6.7
```

To adjust the spacing, move the cursor to the "U" in "Units" on the first line, then press + on the numeric keypad three times to put the U directly above the 5 in *5,770*. This puts three spaces between the *Units Sold* heading and *Northeast* on the data line.

The insertion spaces the headings correctly. *Revenues ($)* and *% Change from 1984* do not need additional spacing, because they are longer than the entries below them.

Now move the cursor to the *R* in *Region* and press +, then F3 to center the headings. The screen should show:

```
Region      Units Sold   Revenues ($)   % Change from 1984

Northeast   5,770   2,481,100   +6.7
```

We must now put the data items underneath their headings. To do this, put the cursor at the beginning of the data line and press + until *Northeast* is below *Region*. Now adjust the other three data items in the same way. When you are done, the screen should show:

```
Region      Units Sold   Revenues ($)   % Change from 1984

Northeast      5,770      2,481,100        +6.7
```

The tabs belong in the leftmost character position in each data column; these are columns 5, 19, 31, and 52. Now you can set up the format line for Table 1. Press F9 to reach the format line, then erase the automatic tabs at columns 10 and 15 and add new ones at columns 19, 31, and 52. Finally, press F9 to return to editing.

After setting the tabs, you can use them on every line except the last two (*Southwest* and *Totals*). You shouldn't use them on the *Southwest* line because you must underline the spaces in front of the data columns. Advantage won't let you do that with tabbed material. Similarly, on the *Totals* line you can't use Tab because some data starts ahead of the tab positions.

You can enter Table 2 in much the same way as Table 1, except you must use a different format line for Table 2. The steps are:

1. Move the cursor to the line where the title goes.
2. Press Alt-Z for emboldening, then enter the title and press Alt-Z again and Return.
3. Move the cursor to the line where the headings belong.
4. Enter the headings (underlined) and the top line of data.
5. Insert spaces ahead of the *Sales Rep.* heading until there are two spaces between it and the first column of data.
6. Center the headings by inserting F3 at the beginning of the line.
7. Insert spaces in front of the data line until its first column is aligned with the headings.
8. Align the last three data columns under their headings.
9. Record the tab setting for each column; if you followed directions they will be at columns 4, 16, 32, and 50.

Now you must set up the tabs for Table 2. To do this, you must change the format.

Inserting a Format Line

To change the format within a page, insert a format line and make your changes to it. Advantage will use the new format settings until you change the format line again.

To insert a format line, move the cursor to where you want it, then do one of the following:

- Insert a copy of the *current* format line by pressing Shift and F9. You might do this to set a new tab for a table that has one more column than the preceding table.
- Insert a copy of the *page* format line (the one at the top of the page) by pressing Alt and F9. This is convenient for pages that have a table between two blocks of text. Pressing Alt-F9 after the table reactivates the format settings you need to enter more text.
- Insert a copy of the *system* format line (the one Advantage starts with) by pressing Ctrl-F9. This puts Advantage back in its normal format.

To delete a format line, put the cursor on any character that follows it, then press Del (for delete mode), F9, and Del again.

Changing Tabs between Tables

Since Table 2's tab positions are entirely different from Table 1's, we should insert a copy of the system format line. To do this, move the cursor to where the second data line belongs (if it isn't already there), then press Ctrl-F9. Advantage puts the cursor on the new format line. Erase the automatic tabs and set the tabs you just recorded. Then press F9 to return to editing. Now enter the rest of the table and press F2 to begin page 4.

Entering the Fourth Page

Like the second page of the report, the fourth page (shown in Figure 5-1D) is double-spaced. Therefore, use the F9 key to change the line spacing to 2. Now enter the text. When you finish, press F2 to begin the final page.

Entering the Fifth Page

Page 5 is much like page 3. Once again, you must change the line spacing back to 1. You must also create a centered table with new tabs.

Saving and Printing a Report

After entering the final page, press F10 to save the report on the disk. When the Main Menu reappears, you can print the report. However, you generally want more than just one copy of a report.

Printing Multiple Copies

To print multiple copies, you must change the "Print Parameters for Document" form. For example, we can get nine copies as follows. First, select "Print Document Utility" from the Main Menu, then enter **rptq286** on the "Print a Document" form and press Return. When the "Print Parameters for Document" form appears, move the cursor to the "Number of original copies" field in the right-hand column, enter **009** and press F10.

Controlling Page Numbering

For our sample report, we let Advantage number the pages from the beginning, with the title page 1, the second page 2, and so forth. However, some documents have a title page, table of contents, and an introduction or preface whose pages are to be unnumbered, so you want to start numbering on the first page of regular text. To do this, enter a header or footer that includes the symbol # on the first page to be numbered.

Advantage assumes you want to number the first header or footer page *1*. To start with some other number, enter it in the "Header/Footer First Page Number" field of the "Print Parameters for Document" form, then print. For example, if you intend to attach a custom-made title page to a document, put your header or footer on the first page and enter **002** for "Header/Footer First Page Number" when you print.

Printing Selected Pages

Advantage also lets you print selected pages. To do this, enter the first and last page numbers you want in the "Start print at page number" and "Stop print after page number" fields on the "Print Parameters for Document" form. Note that you must always enter three digits for the page numbers. For example, to specify page 6 you must enter **006,** not just **6**.

Advantage automatically sets the "Stop" page to the last page number. To print everything from some specific page onward, leave it alone.

Working during a Print Operation

As soon as Advantage starts printing, it restores the Main Menu. This means you can actually do other work *during* the print operation! For example, you can select an additional document, or a different portion of the same one, for printing. Doing this makes Advantage add the second document to its list of printing jobs or *print queue,* and print it immediately after the first one. You can also create a new document or edit an existing one, as long as it's not in the print queue.

Stopping a Print Operation

If you spot a mistake in a report or remember something you meant to add, you can stop the print operation by holding Ctrl down and pressing Break. Break is the dark key at the top right-hand corner of the keyboard; it is marked Scroll Lock on top and Break on the front edge.

Pressing Ctrl-Break makes the computer beep and display a "Printer Queue Control" form. This form includes a menu followed by a list of the documents in the print queue, with the first document name highlighted. To make Advantage stop printing, press **1** repeatedly until the document list disappears, then press F10 to return to the Main Menu. The printer will print whatever text remains in its internal memory (usually a page or two), then stop.

Required Page Breaks

In Chapter 3 we discussed repaginating, where Advantage divides pages into a specified number of lines. Repaginating is convenient if you want the maximum amount of material on each page. However, if you want page breaks to remain in certain places (to keep a figure or table on a page by itself, or to separate sections), you must enter *required page breaks* before repaginating. A required page break is a marker that tells Advantage to move to the next page, even if the current page is not full.

To set a required page break, put the cursor where you want the new page to begin, then press Alt-B. Advantage moves the remaining text (if any) to a new page. It also marks the required page break with a ⊥ symbol.

Now when you repaginate, Advantage will start a new page at the required page break marker. Of course, to keep an entire page intact (a page that contains a table or figure, for example), you must put a required page break at the end of both the current page and the preceding page.

Inserting Required Page Breaks

Sometimes you may want to insert a required page break in a document. This is common if, for example, repagination puts a section title at the bottom of a page and starts the text on the next page. Here, you will probably want to insert a required page break ahead of the title (to move it to the next page), then repaginate to combine the text with the title.

To insert a required page break, move the cursor to where you want the break, then press + (Insert Character) on the numeric keypad and Alt-B to make the insertion. Advantage displays a new page that contains the text that follows the required page break. Since this page is partially full, repaginate to adjust the rest of the document.

Special Print Formats

Besides underlining and bold print, Advantage can also produce subscripts, superscripts, and strikeouts. As with bold print, you get these formats by pressing a control key (Alt or Ctrl here) and another key before and after you enter the text.

Subscripts

If your report includes chemical formulas such as H_2O or mathematical notation such as A_i, you will need subscripts that appear below the line. To produce a subscript, press Alt-W before the text and Alt-Q after it.

Alt-W makes Advantage print text one-half line lower than usual (thereby producing subscripting); Alt-Q makes it print one-half line higher (thereby restoring the original line position). Advantage doesn't actually show subscripting on the screen. It displays a down-arrow symbol ($\downarrow$) for Alt-W and an up-arrow ($\uparrow$) for Alt-Q. The arrows indicate what the printer will do: move down, print the subscript, then move back up to the original position.

For example, to produce H_2O, enter **H,** press Alt-W, type **2,** press Alt-Q, and type **O.**

Superscripts

If your report includes footnotes, references, or mathematical formulas such as $E = mc^2$ or $c^3 = a^6 + b^9$, you will need superscripts that appear above the line. To produce a superscript, enter Alt-Q before the text and Alt-W after it—the reverse of what you do for a subscript. For example, to produce $E = mc^2$, enter **E = mc,** press Alt-Q, type **2,** and press Alt-W.

Strikeouts

When lawyers or legislators change a legal document, they often indicate what has been deleted by striking through it with slashes or hyphens. Advantage provides a "strikeout" command that lets you do this.

To apply the strikeout to new text, type Alt-O (Advantage shows +), enter the text, then type Alt-O again. To strike out existing text, insert Alt-O ahead of the text and after it. For example, suppose your will includes the sentence

```
The estate is to be equally distributed among John,
Mary, Elizabeth, and Jason Cane.
```

Later, in an act of heartless vengeance, you decide to disinherit Elizabeth. To do this, move the cursor to the *E* and press + (Insert Character) on the numeric keypad, then Alt-O. To turn strikeout off, move the cursor to the space that precedes *and* then press + and Alt-O again. When you print the will, the sentence appears as

```
The estate is to be equally distributed among John,
Mary, Elizabeth/ and Jason Cane.
```

Note that you have disinherited the extra comma as well.

Advantage will strike out characters with a slash (/) unless you tell it to use something else. To change the strikeout character, obtain the "Modify System Defaults" form (select "Other Utilities" from the Main Menu, then "Edit System Defaults") and enter the character you want in the "Strikeout Character" field.

Double Underscore

Besides underlining material, Advantage can also put a double underscore beneath it. To produce this, type Ctrl-underscore (Advantage shows a ⏷ symbol), enter the text, then type Ctrl-underscore again. To double-underscore existing text, insert Ctrl-underscore ahead of the text and after it.

Mixing Print Formats

You can apply more than one special print format to a given piece of text. For example, you can embolden an underlined title or embolden a subscript or superscript. To do this, simply apply the first format, then the second. At the end of the text, use these same commands to turn the formats off. For example, to embolden and underline a title, press Alt-Z and Alt-underscore, then enter the title and press Alt-Z and Alt-underscore again.

Footnotes

Advantage lets you add footnotes to any page. Once you have created a footnote, Advantage automatically numbers it and "attaches" it to the text that refers to it. That is, if repagination moves the reference to a different page, Advantage moves the footnote along with it. Similarly, if you delete a footnote reference, Advantage deletes its footnote as well.

Footnotes do not appear on the screen during regular editing, but Advantage prints them at the bottom of the page where their references appear. It also prints a dashed line above the footnotes to set them off from the main text.

Creating Footnotes

To create a footnote, enter the text that refers to it, then press Alt-V. Alt-V makes Advantage display a box or *window* at the bottom of the screen with a ♫ symbol at the beginning of it. Enter the text for your footnote (up to eight lines), then press Alt-V again to return to the regular text. Advantage places the ♫ symbol at the place where you pressed Alt-V; this marks where the footnote reference number will be printed.

For example, suppose you are writing a term paper on *Alaskan Explorers* that includes the sentence

```
Their journey took them through the Shelikov Strait.
```

and you want *Shelikov Strait* to refer to the footnote

```
A strait 30 miles wide between the Alaskan Peninsula
and the Kodiak and Afognak Islands.
```

To insert this footnote in your term paper, enter the reference sentence then press Alt-V. When Advantage displays the footnote window, enter the footnote text and press Alt-V again.

When you print the term paper, the reference sentence appears in the text in this form:

```
Their journey took them through the Shelikov Strait.¹
```

and the footnote will appear at the bottom of the page in this form:

```
-----------------
¹A strait 30 miles wide between the Alaskan Peninsula
and the Kodiak and Afognak Islands.
```

The superscript "1" here assumes that this is the first footnote in the term paper. If other footnotes precede it, the reference number will be higher.

If your printer cannot produce superscripts, Advantage will print footnote reference numbers enclosed in brackets (e.g., [1], [2], etc.).

Editing Footnotes

To edit a footnote, put the cursor on its ♫ symbol in the text and press Alt-V. When the footnote window appears, edit the footnote text just as you would regular text.

Deleting Footnotes

To delete a footnote, put the cursor on its ♫ symbol in the text, then press the − (Delete Character) key on the numeric keypad. Deleting the footnote marker also deletes the footnote it refers to.

Decimal Tabs

Advantage lets you use tabs to mark the position of the decimal point in a column of numbers. In that case, we call them *decimal tabs*.

To produce a decimal tab, press Shift-F4 (rather than Tab) to move the cursor to it. Advantage shows a small box (▮)—the decimal tab marker—just ahead of the tab location.

Suppose your organization is raising money for a charity and you want to list how much each member has collected, like this:

Member	Collections
Brown, John	$1,504.36
Carlson, Ray	965.77
Decker, Patricia	1,668.43
Eaves, Carter	769.03
Evans, Sue	779.56
Frisch, Paul	1,056.90
Gerard, Roy	1,567.00
Morton, Mary	800.50
Stevens, George	863.96

You must set the decimal tab directly below the *t* in *Collections*. Then you simply press Shift-F4 after entering each name and type the amount. Advantage automatically aligns it around the tab position.

For example, as you enter **$1,504** on the first line, Advantage puts each character just ahead of the tab position and shifts all preceding characters left. Then, when you type the decimal point, Advantage stops shifting and puts the next two digits (36) to the right of the decimal point.

Adding Rows and Columns of Numbers

Advantage can add rows and columns of numbers that you have entered using decimal tabs.

Adding Rows

To make Advantage add a row of numbers, you must first set a tab for each item (including one for the answer). Once you have done that, enter the numbers, pressing Shift-F4 to move between them. Finally, when you reach the place where the answer goes, press the left-arrow key to move the cursor to the decimal tab marker, then press Ctrl-F3 to produce the answer.

Suppose you are writing a report on a business trip taken by a group of employees, and you want to tabulate each person's expenses. The beginning of the summary table may look like this:

```
Employee         Travel    Lodging    Food    Misc.    Total

Denninger, P.L.  1272.36    765.34   654.60   45.33
```

Begin as usual: enter the heading and the longest line of data, and insert spaces until the columns are aligned the way you want them. To get the proper spacing, you may want to enter the data without using tabs and add this one line by hand.

When you have obtained the final spacing, insert a copy of the format line using Shift-F9, set a tab at the decimal point position for each column, and press F9 to get back to editing. (For our example, set tabs at columns 22, 31, 41, 49, and 61.) Enter the rest of the table using Shift-F4 to move between columns and Ctrl-F3 to get the *Total*.

Adding Columns

You can make Advantage add a column of numbers the same way you make it add a row, except you press Ctrl-F4 (rather than Ctrl-F3) to produce the total.

For example, if you are preparing the travel report mentioned in the preceding section, you will end up with a row of expenses for each traveler, and a row total at the right. When you finish, you can produce the column totals as follows:

1. Press Shift-F4 to reach the column.
2. Press the left-arrow key to put the cursor on the decimal tab marker.
3. Press Ctrl-F4 to produce the column total. Advantage leaves the cursor on the decimal tab marker.
4. Use the right-arrow key to move the cursor past the total.

When you finish producing column totals, the final table might look like this:

```
Employee          Travel    Lodging  Food      Misc.     Total

Denninger, P.L.  1272.36   765.34   654.60    45.33    2737.63
Edwards, F.C.    1284.88   856.00   532.07    87.45    2760.40
Maxwell, C.E.    1201.77   803.08   543.77    58.00    2606.62
Normand, M.G.     768.43    56.88    24.76     4.65     854.72
Sloan, L.J.      1432.61   951.00   698.60    94.56    3176.77

      Totals     5960.05  3432.30  2453.80   289.99   12136.14
```

Using Ctrl-F3 produces the entries in the *Total* column and Ctrl-F4 produces the entries in the *Totals* row.

Negative Numbers

To enter a negative number in a table, either precede it with a hyphen (the lowercase symbol on the underscore key) or enclose it in parentheses. For example, *-$123.45* and *($123.45)* mean the same thing. If adding a row or column produces a negative total, Advantage displays the answer in whichever form you used to enter the data—with a minus sign or in parentheses.

Changing Tables That Have Additions

If you change data in a table after performing an addition, you must make Advantage recalculate every total the change affects. To do this, make your changes, then move the cursor to the data tab marker for the total and press Ctrl-F3 to add a row or Ctrl-F4 to add a column. Advantage replaces the original total with the corrected one.

For example, if you change the *Lodging* amount for one of the employees in our sample travel report, you must recalculate the row total at the right, the column total at the bottom, and the grand total in the lower right-hand corner.

Indenting Lists

When people type a list of items, they often indent them and set them off with numbers, dashes, or "bullets." Suppose you want to indent three numbered sentences in a letter, as in

```
In response to our recent request, we need the following
information to complete a credit application:

    1)  Name and address of your bank, along with your account
        number.
    2)  Three credit references.
    3)  A signed corporate resolution indicating responsibility
        for payment.
```

To indent material, simply set a tab where you want the indented left-hand margin. Then, whenever you want to indent something, press F4 (rather than Tab) to start indenting. Advantage marks the indentation with a small right-arrow (→).

Advantage will indent everything you type until you press Return. In other words, it indents a paragraph worth of text.

You can also indent a paragraph you entered earlier. To do this, put the cursor on the first character, then press + on the numeric keypad (to insert a character) and F4. Of course, if there is a tab at the beginning of the paragraph, you can simply type F4 where the tab marker appears. Either way, Advantage will indent only the current paragraph.

Section Numbering

Many documents must be organized into numbered sections. This is especially common for term papers, research reports, legal contracts, and technical specifications and manuals. If the document has a lot of sections and subsections, the numbering can get quite complicated.

Normally, the writer must keep track of section numbers—an annoying job at best. It becomes even more tedious if he or she adds or deletes a subsection, because that changes the numbering on all subsequent subsections. Fortunately, Advantage can eliminate these problems.

If you give it a section title and tell it what level that title represents, Advantage inserts the proper section number when you print the document. It can also adjust the numbering if you insert a new section or delete an old one earlier in the document.

Numbering Styles

Advantage can number sections in two styles, Roman or numeric (that is, Arabic), with up to six different levels. Table 5-1 shows the first number at each level.

Table 5-1. Section-numbering styles.

Level	Roman Style	Numeric Style
1	I.	1.
2	I.A	1.1
3	I.A.1	1.1.1
4	I.A.1.a	1.1.1.1
5	I.A.1.a.(1)	1.1.1.1.1
6	I.A.1.a.(1).(a)	1.1.1.1.1.1

The section-numbering style is determined by the "Section Numbering Style" parameter on the "Modify Document Defaults" form that appears when you create a document. Advantage assumes you want the Roman style, and sets this parameter to R; to get the numeric style, change it to N.

Entering Section Titles

To make Advantage number sections, you must specify the level and enter the title. To specify the level, put the cursor where the section number is to appear and press Alt and U once for each level of numbering you want. Advantage displays a ∘ symbol wherever you type Alt-U. After specifying the numbering level, enter the title.

For example, suppose you are preparing a term paper on the life of Harry S Truman. The first section describes the years before he became President, and has subsections describing his childhood, early occupations, military career, and so forth. You might start as follows:

1. Enter your name and the centered title **The Life of Harry S Truman** at the top of the first page.
2. Move the cursor to where the title of the first section belongs and press Alt-U. Advantage displays the section-numbering symbol.
3. Press the space bar twice, type **The Early Years**, then press Return.
4. Enter your introduction, if any.
5. Move the cursor to where the title of the first subsection belongs and press Alt-U twice. Advantage displays two section-numbering symbols.
6. Press the space bar twice, type **Childhood**, and then press Return.
7. Enter the material for the subsection.

When you print the term paper, Advantage will produce

```
I.   The Early Years
```

for the section title (assuming you are using the Roman numbering style) and

```
I.A   Childhood
```

for the subsection title. It will number the next subsection *I.B*, the next section *II*, and so on.

Assigning Section Numbers

When you finish entering your document, you must make Advantage insert the section numbers. To do this, put the cursor anywhere in the document and press Ctrl-F2.

Recall from Chapter 3 that Ctrl-F2 is the Repaginate command. It displays a "Repagination" form that provides three options: "Repaginate Document", "Generate a Table of Contents", and "Reassign Section Numbers:". To make Advantage put section numbers in your document, set "Reassign Section Numbers:" to *Y* and press F10.

Advantage starts at the beginning of the document and inserts section numbers between the numbering symbol(s) and the title. (Note that although the numbering symbols remain on the screen, they will not appear on the printed copy.) If "Repaginate Document" is also set to *Y*, it repaginates as well, starting at the page the cursor is on. When this operation finishes, save the document on disk and print it.

Changing Section Levels

If you decide that a third-level section should really be second-level, or vice versa, you can easily make Advantage change the level. To do this, simply insert or delete one or more section numbering symbols (∘) on the title line, then do a "Reassign Section Numbers" operation. Each numbering symbol you insert lowers the section title one level, while each one you delete raises the title one level. Just remember that changing levels on one title may affect the numbering on titles that follow it.

Tables of Contents

An added benefit of using Advantage's automatic section numbering is that it lets you generate a table of contents document.

Creating a Table of Contents

To create a table of contents for a document:

1. Put the cursor anywhere in the document and press Ctrl-F2. Advantage displays its "Repagination" form at the bottom of the screen.
2. For "Lines per Page:", enter the page length you want for your table of contents document. (Use *055* for standard 8 1/2-inch paper.)

3. For "Generate a Table of Contents:", enter **y**.
4. If you have not yet inserted the section numbers, enter **y** for "Reassign Section Numbers:".
5. Press F10 to begin the operation.

When Advantage finishes, your data disk contains a new file that has the same name as the document file, but with the extension *.TOC*. For example, if your original document is in the file TERMPAPR.DOC, its table of contents is in TERMPAPR.TOC.

Editing a Table of Contents

To see what the table of contents looks like before you print it, select "Edit an Old Document" from the Main Menu, and when the "Edit an Old Document" form appears, press the F7 key. This makes Advantage switch to a similar form called "Edit a Table of Contents Document," in which only the available table of contents documents are listed. Enter the name of the one you want, press Return to proceed to the "Document Summary Screen" and then press F10 to obtain the text.

As with a regular document, Advantage uses the system format line to format the table of contents text. The text itself is arranged in standard table of contents form, but each line is preceded by the section numbering symbols you entered in your main document. (As with a regular document, these symbols appear only on the screen, not on the printed copy.) The beginning of a typical table of contents looks like this:

```
o      I. The Early Years . . . . . . . . . . . . . . . . . . . . . . . . . . . 1
o   o     I.A Childhood  . . . . . . . . . . . . . . . . . . . . . . . . 1
o   o     I.B Early Occupations . . . . . . . . . . . . . . . . . . . . . 3
o   o     I.C Military Service  . . . . . . . . . . . . . . . . . . . . 6
```

You may edit this text just like you would edit a regular document. Note, for example, that all section numbers are flush with the left-hand margin. You may want to insert tabs to indent the second-level entries. (Of course, you must also delete some of the dots, so the page numbers remain at the right-hand margin.)

Printing a Table of Contents

To print a table of contents document, start as usual but when the "Print a Document" form appears press the F7 key. Advantage switches to a "Print a Table of Contents Document" form. Enter the name of the table of contents you want and press Return to obtain the "Print Parameters for Document" form. Make any required changes and then press F10 to start printing.

Drawing Lines and Boxes

Advantage lets you draw lines and boxes in documents. This is particularly useful for creating bar charts. To draw a line or box, move the cursor to where you want it to begin, then press Alt-E. The bottom of the screen shows a list of patterns you can use. Type the number of the pattern you want, then move the cursor to form the shape. When you finish, press Alt-E again to get back to editing.

To use this feature, your printer must be able to produce the IBM Extended Character Set. Very few printers can do this; Appendix D of the *Advantage Reference Manual* lists them.

Multicolumn Material

Newspaper and magazine articles, newsletters, audiovisual scripts, and some legal documents are printed with several columns on a page. Advantage lets you produce two different column styles: "bound" columns and "snake" columns.

Bound columns keep different information together on a page, side by side. This is useful for entering tables, scripts, resumes, and inventory lists. In *snake columns*, Advantage continues the text from one column to the next in winding, newspaper-like fashion. You may want to use this style for a club newsletter.

Advantage can handle up to eight columns on a page, and show them all on the screen. Bound columns can have different widths; snake columns must have the same width. Further, to produce snake columns, the "Automatic Page Breaks" option on the "Modify Document Defaults" form must be on; that is, it must be set to *Y*. Bound columns can work with either setting, but they are much easier to use with page breaks on.

Creating Bound Columns

To create bound columns, you must first set up a format for them as follows:

1. Press F9 to reach the format line.
2. To make the first column begin anywhere other than column 1, move the cursor there and type [.
3. Move the cursor to where you want the column to end and type].
4. Press the space bar to reach the place where the next column should begin.
5. Repeat steps 2, 3, and 4 to define the remaining columns, but press Return (rather than]) to end the last column.
6. Press F9 to leave the format line.

Advantage now arranges everything you enter in column form. When you reach the end of a column, it moves to the next one automatically—provided "Automatic Page Breaks" is set to *Y*.

To end a column and start working on the next one, press Shift-F3 to put Advantage into Column mode. When *COLUMN MODE* appears at the top right-hand corner of the screen, press Return. (Advantage leaves Column mode when you press any key.)

To end a group of columns and start a new group, press Ctrl-Return.

Advantage continues arranging text in columns until you set up a format line that has no bracket markers ([and]). The easiest way to do this is to insert a copy of the system format line, by pressing Ctrl-F9.

Creating Snake Columns

To create snake columns, do the following:

1. Press F9 to reach the format line.

2. To make the first column begin anywhere other than column 1, move the cursor there and type [.
3. Move the cursor to where you want the column to end and type].
4. Type a number between 2 and 8 to indicate how many columns you want.

   Now you must tell Advantage how much space to put between the columns; this gap is called a "gutter." The gutter width is determined by the sum of
   a. The space between the left-hand margin and the [symbol.
   b. The number of spaces between the] symbol and the end of the line.
5. Press the space bar once for each additional space you want and then press Return. For example, if the first snake column begins at column 5, and you want seven spaces between columns, press the space bar three times and press Return.
6. Press F9 to leave the format line.

Advantage now arranges everything you enter in column form. When you reach the end of a column, it moves to the next one automatically.

To end a column and start working on the next one, simply move the cursor to the beginning of the new column and enter text as usual. To end a group of columns and start a new group, press Ctrl-Return.

Advantage continues arranging text in columns until you set up a format line that has no bracket markers ([and]). The easiest way to do this is to insert a copy of the system format line, by pressing Ctrl-F9.

Moving within Columns

When editing regular text, people rely mainly on the arrow keys to move the cursor around the screen. You can use the arrow keys to move through columnar material, too, but that's *awfully* slow. For example, consider how you would use the arrow keys to move to the middle of the previous column. You have to move all the way up the current column and then, when Advantage switches columns, continue moving up *that* column. Fortunately, there's an easier way.

Just as the regular editing mode has key commands that move the cursor directly from one place on the screen to the other (Home,

End, Ctrl-Home, and so on), the Column mode has its own collection of cursor-moving commands. To use any of them, press Shift-F3 to put Advantage in Column mode. When *COLUMN MODE* appears, you can move the cursor by using one of the commands listed in Table 5-2. To leave Column mode, press Esc.

Table 5-2. Cursor-moving keys for Column mode.

Press . . .	To move the cursor to . . .
Home	beginning of the column.
End	end of the column.
Up-arrow	last line of the preceding column group.
Down-arrow	first line of the next column group.
Left-arrow	preceding column.
Right-arrow	next column.
Alt-F3	beginning of same line in the first column.
Alt-F4	end of same line in the last column.

Handling Long Reports

Hard disks can hold millions of characters (i.e., thousands of pages), so hard disk users rarely run out of space for their documents. Floppy disk users, however, can run out of storage space by filling the data disk. Hence, if you are using floppy disks, you should have an idea about the amount of storage available.

With Advantage, a floppy disk can hold about 60 single-spaced pages or 144 double-spaced pages. Therefore, a long report may not fit entirely on one disk.

When you create a new document or edit an old one, Advantage tells you how much disk space is left (in characters and double-spaced pages). If you try to save a document on a full disk, Advantage simply stops and displays

```
-DISK FULL ERROR: UNABLE TO SAVE PAGE.
```

at the bottom of the screen.

When that happens, you must return to the Main Menu, at which point you will lose changes to the current page. Before leaving for the Main Menu, get a copy of the screen by switching your printer on and pressing Shift-PrtSc. PrtSc is the dark key between right Shift and 1 on the numeric keypad. When printing has finished, switch the printer off and press Esc to exit.

One way to make room on a disk is to remove documents you no longer need. For details on how to do this, see "Deleting Documents" in Chapter 2.

Organizing Long Reports

The most efficient way to organize long reports is to create a separate document for each section or chapter. This not only gives you logical stopping points if you need to switch to a new disk, but lets you make changes to one section without affecting others.

Copying Documents

Advantage keeps only one copy of a document on your data disk. Therefore, if you lose that disk, spill something on it, or destroy it in some other way, all of your work disappears. For safety's sake, make *backup* copies of important documents and keep the backup disks in a safe place, out of harm's way.

You may also want to copy to create a different version of a document. For example, you might have a standard contract form and variations for common situations. You might also have wholesale, retail, and promotional price lists.

Advantage lets you copy a document onto any disk, as long as it's formatted. The copying procedure is:

1. Select "Document Handling Utilities" from the Main Menu, then "Copy a Document" from the "Document Handling Utilities" menu. Advantage asks for the names of the drive and document you are copying from and to, and suggests *B* for both drive parameters.
2. For the *FROM* document, enter the name of the document you want to copy, then press Tab.
3. For the *TO* drive field, you have two choices:
   a) *To copy a document to the same disk,* press Tab.
   b) *To copy a document to a different disk,* type **a** and Tab.
4. For the *TO* document field, enter the name you want the copy to have and press F10. (If you are copying to a different disk, the name can be

the same as before. If you are copying to the same disk, you must give
the copy a different name.)

5. When Advantage shows

```
INSERT DISKETTE(S), PRESS ANY KEY WHEN READY
```

replace the System disk with the target disk (if appropriate), then
press the space bar.

6. When the operation is finished, replace the target disk with the System disk (if appropriate), then press Esc twice to return to the Main
Menu.

Moving Documents

If you are running out of space on a disk or just want to combine
related documents, you can move a document to a new disk. This
involves the same kind of procedure as copying a document, except
you select "Move a Document" from the "Document Handling Utilities" menu.

Producing Backup Files

Earlier we described how to copy a document to create a backup.
Advantage can save you the bother of copying documents manually—it makes backups automatically if you tell it to. When doing
this, Advantage gives the backup the same name, but with the extension *DBK*. For example, if you edit and save a document named
roster, Advantage saves the new version as *ROSTER.DOC* and the
original as *ROSTER.DBK.*

The procedure for making Advantage produce backups depends
on whether you want to back up every document or just selected
ones:

• To make it back up every document, select "Other Utilities" from the
Main Menu, then "Edit System Defaults". When the "Modify System
Defaults" form appears, move the cursor to *Backup before edit docu-*
ment? and type **y** for yes. Finally, press F10 twice to return to the
Main Menu.

- To make it back up an individual document, start creating the document as usual, but when the "Modify Document Defaults" form appears, move the cursor to *Backup before edit document?* and type **y** for yes. Then press F10 to begin preparing the document.

Using Backup Files

If you somehow foul up a document beyond repair, you may want to go back to the original. To begin, select "Document Handling Utilities" from the Main Menu, then "Restore a Backed-up Document" from the "Document Handling Utilities" Menu. Advantage shows its *RESTORE* form and lists the backed-up documents. Enter the name of the one you want and press F10.

Because restoring means that Advantage will have to delete the current version, it gives you a chance to change your mind by showing

```
<ESCAPE> to abort, any other key to continue.
```

To leave the documents as they are and return to the Document Handling Utilities Menu, press Esc. Otherwise, to reinstate the backup, press the space bar. When *OPERATION COMPLETE* appears, press Esc twice to return to the Main Menu. The backup has replaced the previous version of your document, and Advantage has deleted the backup (DBK) file.

Questions and Answers

Question: Advantage seems to have gone haywire. Everything I told it to embolden, it's printing in regular type—and vice versa. What's wrong?

Answer: You turned emboldening on and forgot to turn it off. To embolden something, press Alt-Z ahead of it *and* after it; you omitted the second Alt-Z. Find out where it's missing and insert it.

Question: How can I make Advantage print something emboldened and underlined?

Answer: Press Alt-Z and Alt-underscore, type the text, then press Alt-underscore and Alt-Z.

Question: My report consists of four different documents. The first page of each one includes the footer - # - to number the pages. When I print them, Advantage always numbers the first page *1*. How can I make it give the entire report consecutive page numbers?

Answer: When Advantage displays its "Print Parameters for Document" form, enter the starting page number for the document in the "Header/Footer First Page Number" field. For example, if each document is 20 pages long, enter **001** for the first one, **021** for the second, **041** for the third, and **061** for the fourth.

Question: I made some changes to pages 20 and 21 of my report. How can I print just those two pages?

Answer: Start the printing procedure as usual, but when Advantage displays its "Print Parameters for Document" form, enter **020** for "Start print at page number" and **021** for "Stop print after page number", then press F10. Since page 20 is deep in the heart of the document, it may take a while for Advantage to reach it.

Question: I want to print copies of five different letters from my disk. Do I have to wait until each letter has been printed before I can tell Advantage which one to print next?

Answer: No, you can simply give Advantage a series of print commands, one for each letter. That is, start the first print operation. When the Main Menu reappears, select "Print Document Utility" again and tell Advantage which document you want to print next. Repeat this procedure for the other three letters. Advantage will remember each operation, and perform them in the order you entered them.

Question: I put a table on a page of its own, but when I repaginated, Advantage combined it with the text. How can I keep the table separate?

Answer: Press Alt-B (rather than F2) to start or end a page that contains a table. Alt-B makes Advantage insert a required page break—a "start-a-new-page" command that is unaffected by repaginating.

Question: How can I indent a paragraph on both sides?

Answer: Before you type the paragraph, insert a copy of the page format line by pressing Alt-F9. On it, set a tab where you want the left indentation, then move the cursor to where you want the right indentation and press Return. Press F9 to return to editing and F4 to indent, then type the paragraph. Finally, press Alt-F9 to insert another copy of the page format line, then F9 to return to editing.

Question: I entered two consecutive tables showing sales figures for my company's Northeast and Southeast regions. At the end of each table, I entered a "Total" column and pressed Ctrl-F4 to get the total.

The total for the first table is correct, but the one for the second table is wrong. Why?

Answer: Advantage included numbers from the first table into the second total. To make it keep the tables separate, insert a format line between them using Shift-F9, then recalculate the second total. It should now be correct.

Question: I wrote a report that uses numbered sections, so I entered numbering symbols with Alt-U ahead of each title. However, when I printed the report, Advantage omitted the section numbers. What went wrong?

Answer: You forgot to make Advantage insert the section numbers. To do this, put the cursor anywhere in the document and press Ctrl-F2. When the "Repagination" form appears, set "Reassign Section Numbers:" to *Y* and press F10. When Advantage finishes inserting section numbers, save the report and print it again.

Hints and Warnings

1. To enter a centered table, type its headings and a line of data before determining the tab positions.
2. Remember that Advantage always displays text single-spaced. The only way to tell how it will be printed is by examining the line spacing value at the beginning of the format line.
3. Note the difference between using the "current page number" markers &PAGE& and # in a header or footer. &PAGE& always produces the actual page number (i.e., it is *1* on the first page, *2* on the second page, and so forth), and cannot be changed. # produces a page number relative to the value of the "Print Parameters for Document" form's "Header/Footer First Page Number" field.
4. When using a special print format (bold print, subscript, superscript, strikeout, or double underscore), be sure to turn the format off at the end of the affected material.
5. Underlining appears on the screen, but bold print, subscripts, superscripts, and double underscores will not. Emboldened material is enclosed with a solid rectangle, subscripted and superscripted material is enclosed with vertical arrows, and double-underscored material is enclosed with ↕ symbols.
6. Do not enter material with a tab if you must enter anything to the left of the tab position. Advantage will not let you do it.

7. When adding a row or column of numbers, remember to press the left-arrow key to put the cursor on the decimal tab marker (▮). If you simply press Ctrl-F3 or Ctrl-F4, Advantage displays

```
ERROR...CURSOR MUST BE ON A DECIMAL TAB.
```

8. If you use automatic section numbering, remember to make Advantage insert the numbers before you print the document; otherwise, the titles won't be numbered.

9. When inserting section numbers or building a table of contents, Advantage always starts at the beginning of the document. When repaginating, however, it starts on the same page as the cursor. To make it repaginate the entire document as it numbers sections or builds a table of contents, start with the cursor on the first page.

10. As with any new document, Advantage uses the system format line to create a table of contents. If your section titles are indented or you want the lines in the table of contents to be longer or shorter than in a regular document, modify the system format line before creating the table of contents. To obtain the system format line, select "Other Utilities" from the Main Menu, then select "Edit System Format Line."

11. Advantage tells you roughly how much space is left on a disk (in double-spaced pages) when you create a new document or begin editing an old one. If a disk is too full to store editing changes, Advantage displays a *DISK FULL* message and you lose the changes. To be safe, check the "Page(s)" status when you start creating or editing a document.

    If there are less than seven pages left, press Esc to return to the Main Menu. Then start your document on a new disk or get more space by either deleting documents you no longer need or moving documents to another disk.

12. If you plan to include multicolumn material (either bound or snake) in a document, set *Automatic Page Breaks?* to *Y* on the "Modify Document Defaults" form when you create the document. Snake columns require automatic page breaks; bound columns do not, but they are much simpler to enter with automatic breaks.

13. If you lose a disk or some other misfortune befalls it, you're out of luck unless you have a backup. Create backup copies of all your important documents by periodically copying them to another disk.

Key Point Summary

Table 5-3 summarizes the keys and functions we introduced in this chapter.

Table 5-3. Keys and functions introduced in Chapter 5.

Key(s)	Function
Alt-B	Required page break
Alt-E	Draw a line or box
Alt-F	Footer
Alt-H	Header
Alt-O	Strikeout
Alt-U	Section number
Alt-Q	Start superscript or end subscript
Alt-V	Footnote
Alt-W	Start subscript or end superscript
Alt-Z	Bold print
Ctrl-Break	Stop print operation
Ctrl-underscore	Double underscore
Ctrl-F3	Add row
Shift-F3	Column mode
F4	Indent
Ctrl-F4	Add column
Shift-F4	Decimal tab
Alt-F9	Insert page format line
Ctrl-F9	Insert system format line
Shift-F9	Insert current format line

1. To embolden text, press Alt-Z before and after the text.
2. To print text double-spaced, change the format line's line spacing value to 2.
3. To create a header for a document, put the cursor at the top of the first page where you want one and press Alt-H and Return. Enter the header text, press Alt-H, and press Return again.
4. To create a footer, put the cursor on the line at the bottom of the page where you want the footer to appear and press Alt-F and Return. Enter the footer text and press Alt-F and Return again.
5. To include a page number in a header or footer, enter # where you want it to appear. You may also enter &PAGE& or &LPAGE& for the number of the current or last page. &PAGE& and &LPAGE& may be used in regular text as well as in headers and footers.

6. To change the format within a page, insert a new format line by pressing Shift-F9 (current format), Alt-F9 (page format), or Ctrl-F9 (system format). Advantage will reformat the text between this format line and the next one.

7. Options on the "Print Parameters for Document" form allow you to produce multiple copies, print selected pages, and specify the starting page number for a header or footer that includes the page number symbol #.

8. Once printing has begun, you can create a new document or edit an existing one—simply select the new task from the Main Menu.

9. To stop a print operation, press Ctrl-Break. When the "Printer Queue Control" form appears, press **1** until all the document names disappear. Then press F10 to return to the Main Menu.

10. To force Advantage to start a new page , press Alt-B to enter a required page break.

11. To produce a subscript, precede it with Alt-Q and follow it with Alt-W (Advantage shows an up-arrow and down-arrow, respectively). To produce a superscript, do just the opposite: precede it with Alt-W and follow it with Alt-Q.

12. To strike out material, enter Alt-O before and after it.

13. To double-underscore material, enter Ctrl-underscore before and after it.

14. To create a footnote, enter the reference text and press Alt-V. When the footnote window appears, enter the footnote text and press Alt-V again to get back to editing.

15. To edit a footnote, obtain the footnote window by putting the cursor on the footnote reference marker (♫) and pressing Alt-V. To delete a footnote, delete the footnote reference marker.

16. Decimal tabs allow you to align numbers around a decimal point. Create them like normal tabs, but press Shift-F4 to reach them.

17. Advantage can add rows and columns of numbers you entered using decimal tabs. To make it do this, press Shift-F4 to move the cursor to the tab for the total and press the left-arrow key to put it on the decimal tab marker (▌). Then press Ctrl-F3 (add a row) or Ctrl-F4 (add a column).

18. You can change a paragraph's left-hand margin by indenting it. To do this, set a tab at the margin position and press F4 to reach it. Advantage will indent the next paragraph you enter.

19. Advantage can automatically number sections in a document and produce a separate table of contents document based on those numbers. It can produce up to six levels of section numbering in either Roman or numeric style.

20. To specify a section number level, type Alt-U once for each level just ahead of the title. To make Advantage insert the section numbers, put the cursor anywhere in the document, press Ctrl-F2 to obtain the "Repagination" form, then set "Reassign Section Numbers:" to Y and press F10.

21. To produce a table of contents document, put the cursor anywhere in the document, press Ctrl-F2 to obtain the "Repagination" form, then enter the page length you want in "Lines per Page:", set "Reassign Section Numbers:" to Y, and press F10.

22. To edit or print a table of contents document, start as usual but when the "Edit an Old Document" or "Print a Document" form appears, press the F7 key.

23. To draw a line or box in a document, press Alt-E. To use this feature, your printer must be able to produce the IBM Extended Character Set.

24. Advantage can arrange text in up to eight columns. These can be either *bound columns* that are side-by-side or *snake columns* in which text "winds" from one column to the next.

25. The Main Menu's "Document Handling Utilities" option lets you move or copy documents. Moving can open up space on a disk. Copying provides a backup capability and a starting point for new documents.

26. Advantage can produce backup copies of documents automatically. To make it do this, set "Backup before edit document?" to Y on either the "Modify System Defaults" form (to backup every document) or the "Modify Document Defaults" form (to backup only this document).

6

Revising

In the preceding chapters you learned how to change and correct characters, words, lines, sentences, and paragraphs. However, formal correspondence, reports, and large projects often require more extensive revisions.

For example, you may want to move material to improve continuity, combine related ideas or separate distinct ones, change emphasis, or balance the length of sections. Or you may need the same legal or technical terminology, table or figure heading, address, equation, or set of instructions in several places. You may also want to find occurrences of certain words, phrases, or sequences in a document, and perhaps change them to correct spelling, improve grammar, standardize terminology, or change dates, names, places, numbers, or titles.

Move and Copy Operations

In Chapter 3 you learned how to put text such as a name into a library and then insert it into a document. Advantage also lets you move or copy text directly. This is useful for single moves, whereas the library is better suited to repetitive situations.

Moving Text

You move text in Advantage much as you would in a rough draft of a typed document: you cut it from one place and paste it in another. With Advantage, however, you cut and paste blocks of text electronically.

The procedure for moving a block is:

1. Put the cursor where the block begins and press F7 to put Advantage in the move mode (it shows *MOVE WHAT?* at the top right-hand corner of the screen).
2. Move the cursor to where the block ends (Advantage highlights the entire block) and press F7 again. The prompt *TO WHERE?* appears in the top right-hand corner.
3. If the destination is on another page, use F1 to move there.
4. Move the cursor to where you want the block to go and press F7 once more.

Advantage automatically closes the gap on the page that held the block, but it will not repaginate. That's your job.

Copying Text

If you want to leave the original block in place, you can simply copy it. To copy a block, use the procedure we just described but press F8 (instead of F7) each time.

Suppose you type the following text:

```
Our firm specializes in tax-advantaged investments such as oil
and gas exploration and development, equipment leasing, and real
estate.
    Our background in oil and gas exploration and development
includes over 50 projects during the last ten years.
```

When you start the new paragraph, you notice the repetition of *oil and gas exploration and development*. Rather than typing it again, move the cursor up to the *o* in *oil* and press F8, then move it to the *t* in *development* and press F8 again. Now put the cursor back where it was (two spaces past *in*) and press F8 once again. The original phrase is still in place and a copy appears in the text.

Note that this copies something just once. If you are likely to need the same block repeatedly, put it in a library.

Preserving the Format

When you move or copy text using the preceding procedures, the text takes on the format line settings (line spacing, tabs, and line length) that are active at the new location. For example, if you move single-spaced material to a double-spaced page, Advantage makes it double-spaced.

To move or copy the format along with the text, press F9 when Advantage asks *MOVE WHAT?* or *COPY WHAT?*. Then, when you "paste" the block in its new location, Advantage precedes it with a copy of the original format line.

Of course, moving the format makes it the active format at the new location. This means that if you have inserted a block of single-spaced text on a double-spaced page, everything that follows the block suddenly becomes single-spaced. To restore the original format at the end of the block, press Alt-F9 to insert a copy of the page format line, change the line if necessary, then press F9 to return to editing.

Copying between Documents

Advantage can also copy a block of text from one document to another, even if they are on different disks. To begin, move the cursor to where you want the copy inserted and proceed as follows:

1. Press Shift and F8. Advantage displays *EXTERNAL COPY* at the top and this prompt at the bottom:

```
Drive: B DOC Name: _____    Shft F1 for directory, F7 switches to TOC
```

   and puts the cursor in the "Doc Name:" field.
2. If the document you want to copy from is on a different disk, press Return (to reach the *Drive* field) and type **a**. Then replace the System disk with the disk that contains the document.
3. Enter the name of the document you want to copy from and press F10. Advantage puts it on the screen and shows *START COPY WHERE?* in the top right-hand corner.

4. Move the cursor to the beginning of the text you want to copy and press Shift-F8. Advantage shows *COPY WHAT?* in the top right-hand corner.
5. If you want the copy to have the same format as the original, press F9.
6. Move the cursor to the end of the text to be copied (Advantage highlights it) and press Shift-F8 again.
7. If you changed disks in step 2, put the System disk back in drive A.

Advantage restores the original document, with the copied text now inserted.

Copying a Table of Contents

Chapter 5 described the procedure for creating a table of contents for documents that use Advantage's automatic section-numbering feature. Advantage puts the table of contents in a special kind of document, one that has the extension *.TOC*.

Generally, you will want to combine the table of contents with the main text to produce the final document. To do this, copy the table of contents using the procedure we just described, but when *EXTERNAL COPY* appears at the top of the screen, press the F7 key. Advantage changes the prompt at the bottom to

```
Drive: B TOC Name: _____    Shft F1 for directory, F7 switches to DOC
```

Enter the name of the table of contents document you want to copy and press F10. The rest of the procedure is the same as the one you use to copy a regular document.

Column Operations

Advantage can insert, delete, move, or copy columns of text or numbers. These operations can save a lot of time when you want to manipulate a table.

Inserting Columns

To insert a column into a table:

1. Change the tabs in the table's format line to reflect an additional column. To do this, set a tab for the new column and move the remaining tabs right to provide space for the insertion.
2. Put the cursor on the top line of the table, then move it to where you want to insert space for the new column.
3. Press Shift-F3 to put Advantage in the column mode (it shows *COLUMN MODE* at the top right-hand corner).
4. Press Ins to insert a column. Advantage shows *COLUMN INSERT* at the top right-hand corner and the following prompt at the bottom of the screen:

```
INSERT   # of Columns 00   # of Lines 00   Press F10 to Continue
```

where *# of Columns* means the number of characters you want to insert for the new column.
5. For *# of Columns*, enter the width of the new column and press Return. For example, to insert a ten-character column, type **10** and press Return.
6. For *# of Lines*, enter the line length of your table and press F10.

Advantage makes space for the new column by shifting the remaining columns to the right.

Column Insert Example

Suppose you have prepared a list of your company's major customers, as shown in Figure 6-1. As usual, you used tabs at the beginning of each column to enter the data. Here, they are at columns 16 and 33.

```
Account          Buyer            Sales Rep.

Wilburg Sons     Paul Wilkinson   R. Roberts
Jenco            Carrie Black     C. Chamber
Symtech          Wayne Beck       P. Grogan
Chicago Gear     Morris Daley     J. Wilkes
Hart Foods       Sandy Karras     P. Wallach
Pacifico         Bill Anderson    D. Kim
Storr Bros.      Lee Walters      B. Lloyd
```

Figure 6-1. Customer list before column insertion.

After finishing the list, you decide to insert a column for the buyer's telephone number between *Buyer* and *Sales Rep.* Since each number will be 12 characters long, and you want three spaces between it and the next column, the new column must be 15 characters wide. To insert it:

1. Put the cursor on the heading line and press F9 to reach the format line.
2. Set a new tab at column 47 (this is where the *Sales Rep.* column will move after the insertion) and press F9.
3. Put the cursor on the *S* in *Sales* and press Shift-F3 to put Advantage in the column mode.
4. Press Ins to insert a column.
5. For *# of Columns*, enter **15** and press Return.
6. For *# of Lines*, enter **09** (the list is nine lines long) and press F10. Advantage opens a gap for the new column, with a tab marker preceding each data position.

Now you can enter the heading and data for the telephone number column. The final list will look similar to Figure 6-2.

```
Account         Buyer           Phone #         Sales Rep.

Wilburg Sons    Paul Wilkinson  212-555-3589    R. Roberts
Jenco           Carrie Black    904-388-6743    C. Chamber
Symtech         Wayne Beck      404-783-8832    P. Grogan
Chicago Gear    Morris Daley    312-395-1904    J. Wilkes
Hart Foods      Sandy Karras    406-184-5683    P. Wallach
Pacifico        Bill Anderson   503-438-9532    D. Kim
Storr Bros.     Lee Walters     213-679-4260    B. Lloyd
```

Figure 6-2. Customer list with inserted column.

Deleting Columns

To delete a column, move the cursor to it:

1. Press Shift-F3 to put Advantage in the column mode.
2. Press Del. Advantage shows *COLUMN DELETE* in the top right-hand corner and this prompt at the bottom:

```
<↔> and <↔> to Define Width THEN <↓> to Define Length.
```

3. Press the right-arrow key until the cursor reaches the space that precedes the next column. (If you go too far, use the left-arrow key to
   backtrack.) As the cursor moves, Advantage displays characters in reverse video.
4. Press the down-arrow key until the cursor reaches the bottom line of
   the table. (Use the up-arrow key to backtrack, if necessary.) Advantage turns off the inverse video, but highlights column entries as the
   cursor moves down.
5. Press Del to delete the column. Advantage moves other columns left
   to close the gap.

Moving Columns

To move a column, put the cursor on it and do the following:

1. Press Shift-F3 to put Advantage in the column mode.
2. Press F7. Advantage shows *COLUMN MOVE* at the top right-hand
   corner and this prompt on the bottom:

```
<↔> and <↔> to Define Width THEN <↓> to Define Length.
```

3. Press the right-arrow key until the cursor reaches the space that precedes the next column, then press the down-arrow key until it reaches
   the bottom line of the table. As with the column delete procedure,
   Advantage displays characters in reverse video as the cursor moves
   right, then highlights entries as it moves down the column.
4. Press F7. Advantage asks *TO WHERE?* at the top right-hand corner.
5. Move the cursor to where you want the column and press F7 once
   more.

Copying Columns

To copy a column, use the procedure we just gave to move one,
but press F8 (rather than F7) each time.

Search and Replace Operations

Advantage has a search feature that searches a document for a specific *string* (any sequence of characters) and a replace feature that both searches for a string and replaces it. You can use these features to:

- Locate a customer's name in a mailing list.
- Correct a common misspelling throughout a document.
- Update a document to account for changes in names, titles, dates, or locations.
- Change prices, rates, or terms in an invoice or contract.
- Change a part number or order number in a technical manual.
- Replace an overused or inappropriate phrase throughout a report.
- Check for occurrences of obsolete or revised names, titles, dates, or terms.

Searching

The procedure to search for a string is:

1. Move the cursor to where you want the search to begin and press F6. Advantage displays *SEARCH MODE* at the top of the screen and *SEARCH FOR* at the bottom.
2. If you want to find only an exact match for the string, press Alt-G (Advantage shows *CASE* at the bottom right-hand corner). For example, press Alt-G to find only *First Quarter 1985*. Otherwise, to find all variations, such as *FIRST QUARTER 1985* and *First quarter 1985*, omit Alt-G.
3. Enter the string and press F6.
4. Advantage shows you each page while it searches. If it finds an instance of the string, it puts a flashing rectangle on the first character. Your options at this point are:
   a) To search for the next occurrence of the string, press F6.
   b) To change the string, type in the corrections directly. (This takes Advantage out of the search mode, however; press F6 *twice* to restart it.)
   c) To stop searching entirely, press Esc. When Advantage displays

   ```
   Do you want to escape without saving this page? (Y/N)
   ```

   type **n**.

For example, let's go back to our most recent sample text. To search for the phrase *oil and gas*, put the cursor ahead of where you want to start searching and press F6. When Advantage shows *SEARCH FOR*, press Alt-G, type **oil and gas** and press F6.

Changing the Search String

Once you have done a search, Advantage assumes that you want to look for the same string the next time. This is convenient if you want to resume a search after making changes or corrections. But if you actually want to search for a different string, you must enter it directly over the old one. If the new string is shorter than the previous string, you must erase any leftover characters. To do this, press Del (*not* −) once for each character you want to delete.

Advantage also retains the CASE setting between searches. To reverse it, press Alt-G.

Selecting Search Strings

If the string you are looking for is long or distinctive, such as "International Products Division" or "NASA", you probably won't have any trouble with unexpected matches. However, if it is not distinctive, Advantage may stop at places you never intended. For example, if you tell Advantage to search through a report on cigarette smoking for each mention of "tar", it will stop at "target", "start", and "retarding". And if you omit CASE, it will also stop at "Tarrytown" and "Tarleton".

One solution to this problem is to put a space in front of the string. For example, you can tell Advantage to search for " tar". If you put a space *after* "tar", Advantage will not find occurrences followed by a period, a comma, or other punctuation. Even a space in front can cause problems with occurrences such as "(tar)".

Replacing

If you have a specific replacement in mind, use Advantage's replace feature. Replace will even make all the changes automatically if you are sure there are no exceptions. You can make Advantage search and replace as follows:

1. Move the cursor to where you want the search to start and press Shift-F6. Advantage displays *REPLACE MODE* at the top right-hand corner and

```
TYPE OF REPLACE:       1) GLOBAL  2) DISCRETIONARY  3) ABORT
```

at the bottom.
2. Type one of three numbers:

- 1 (for GLOBAL) makes Advantage automatically replace all occurrences of the search string.
- 2 (for DISCRETIONARY) makes Advantage stop each time it finds the string and ask if you want to replace it.
- 3 (for ABORT) cancels the replace command.

If you type 1 or 2, Advantage shows *REPLACE WHAT?* on the bottom line.
3. To replace only exact matches of the string, press Alt-G. Advantage shows *CASE* in the bottom right-hand corner.
4. Enter the string you want to search for, then press F6. Advantage shows *REPLACE WITH?* on the bottom line.
5. Enter the replacement string and press F6.

Advantage begins searching when you press F6. If you selected *DISCRETIONARY* in step 2, it stops at each instance of the search string and shows the prompt

```
REPLACE?    Y/N/ANY OTHER KEY TO ABORT
```

Here, type **y** to replace the string, **n** to proceed to the next occurrence, or press the space bar to cancel the replace operation.

Replace Example

Figure 6-3 shows a document that illustrates the use of the replace options. We want to update this notice for the 1986 annual meeting to be held at the same place on Friday, June 6, 1986. To do this, we perform the following operations:

NOTICE OF STOCKHOLDERS' MEETING

The 1985 Annual Stockholders' Meeting for International
Consolidated Industries will be held at company headquarters,
19850 Pine Street, Des Moines, Iowa on Friday, June 7, 1985.
The following matters will be considered:

1)   Election of the Board of Directors for the 1985-86
      fiscal year.
2)   Designation of Smith, Brown, and Little as the
      company's independent auditors for the 1985-86 fiscal
      year.
3)   Amendments to the Employees' Qualified Stock Ownership
      Plan (ESOP) in accordance with new regulations.
4)   Other amendments and matters as they may be brought to
      the attention of the Secretary of the Corporation.

Anyone wishing to have matters considered at that meeting
must notify the Secretary by registered mail on or before May
15, 1985. In accordance with regulations adopted at the annual
meeting of June 11, 1982, such notifications must be presented
on forms provided by the Secretary and must contain notarized
signatures representing no fewer than 1% of the common stock of
the Corporation of record May 15th, 1985. In accordance with
guidelines adopted at a special Board of Directors meeting on
February 1, 1985, the board has the final authority on whether
to accept notifications that are presented after May 15th, 1985
or that contain an insufficient number of signatures.

Figure 6-3. Original search document.

1. Replace automatically each occurrence of *1985-86* with *1986-87*.
2. Replace automatically each occurrence of *June 7* with *June 6*.
3. Find all occurrences of *1985* and replace them with *1986*. We must be
   careful here to avoid changing historical dates accidentally.

To replace *1985-86* automatically with *1986-87*, do the following:

1. Put the cursor at the beginning of the first line of the text and press
   Shift-F6.
2. In response to *TYPE OF REPLACE*, press **1** for GLOBAL.
3. For *REPLACE WHAT?*, type **1985-86** and press F6.
4. For *REPLACE WITH*, type **1986-87** and press F6 again.

Advantage immediately makes the replacements and moves the cursor to the end of the document. Press Ctrl-Home to put it back at
the beginning.

To replace *June 7* with *June 6*, start by pressing Shift-F6 and 1 to select GLOBAL. For *REPLACE WHAT?*, enter **June 7,** press Del to delete the extra *6*, and then press F6. Enter the *June 6* replacement string similarly. Now the meeting notice looks like Figure 6-4.

```
                 NOTICE OF STOCKHOLDERS' MEETING

    The 1985 Annual Stockholders' Meeting for International
Consolidated Industries will be held at company headquarters,
19850 Pine Street, Des Moines, Iowa on Friday, June 6, 1985.
The following matters will be considered:

    1)   Election of the Board of Directors for the 1986-87
         fiscal year.
    2)   Designation of Smith, Brown, and Little as the
         company's independent auditors for the 1986-87 fiscal
         year.
    3)   Amendments to the Employees' Qualified Stock Ownership
         Plan (ESOP) in accordance with new regulations.
    4)   Other amendments and matters as they may be brought to
         the attention of the Secretary of the Corporation.

    Anyone wishing to have matters considered at that meeting
must notify the Secretary by registered mail on or before May
15, 1985.  In accordance with regulations adopted at the annual
meeting of June 11, 1982, such notifications must be presented
on forms provided by the Secretary and must contain notarized
signatures representing no fewer than 1% of the common stock of
the Corporation of record May 15th, 1985.  In accordance with
guidelines adopted at a special Board of Directors meeting on
February 1, 1985, the board has the final authority on whether
to accept notifications that are presented after May 15th, 1985
or that contain an insufficient number of signatures.
```

Figure 6-4. Revised document after automatic replacements.

To replace *1985* with *1986* selectively:

1. Press Ctrl-Home to reach the top of the page.
2. Press Shift-F6 to start a new replace operation.
3. In response to *TYPE OF REPLACE*, press **2** for DISCRETIONARY.
4. For *REPLACE WHAT?*, type **1985**, press Del twice, and then press F6.
5. For *REPLACE WITH*, type **1986**, press Del twice, and then press F6 again.

Advantage will immediately find a match in the second word. You must press **y** to make the replacement.

The next match is unexpected: Advantage finds *1985* at the beginning of the company's address. Here you must press **n** to make Advantage continue forward without replacing. You must do this again later when Advantage finds *1985* as part of *a special Board of Directors meeting on February 1, 1985*. That is a historical date, and you must not change it.

When Advantage finishes, the document looks like Figure 6-5.

NOTICE OF STOCKHOLDERS' MEETING

The 1986 Annual Stockholders' Meeting for International
Consolidated Industries will be held at company headquarters,
19850 Pine Street, Des Moines, Iowa on Friday, June 6, 1986.
The following matters will be considered:

1)   Election of the Board of Directors for the 1986⇒87
      fiscal year.
2)   Designation of Smith, Brown, and Little as the
      company's independent auditors for the 1986⇒87 fiscal
      year.
3)   Amendments to the Employees' Qualified Stock Ownership
      Plan (ESOP) in accordance with new regulations.
4)   Other amendments and matters as they may be brought to
      the attention of the Secretary of the Corporation.

Anyone wishing to have matters considered at that meeting
must notify the Secretary by registered mail on or before May
15, 1986. In accordance with regulations adopted at the annual
meeting of June 11, 1982, such notifications must be presented
on forms provided by the Secretary and must contain notarized
signatures representing no fewer than 1% of the common stock of
the Corporation of record May 15th, 1986. In accordance with
guidelines adopted at a special Board of Directors meeting on
February 1, 1985, the board has the final authority on whether
to accept notifications that are presented after May 15th, 1986
or that contain an insufficient number of signatures.

Figure 6-5. Final form of document.

Replacing Abbreviations

The replace feature also allows you to use abbreviations when typing a document. This is like the common practice in note-taking of jotting down UN for "United Nations" or DoD for "United States Department of Defense."

If, for example, you are writing a report on European sales, you may simply type UK for "United Kingdom," WG (West Germany) for "Federal Republic of Germany," and EEC for "European Economic Community." Then, when you have finished, do replace operations to expand the abbreviations. Make sure that your abbreviations are distinct (note, for instance, that you find US in USSR) and do not conflict (such as using UN for "United Nations" and "University of Nebraska").

In Chapter 3 we described how to use a *library* to expand abbreviations. Replace has the advantage that it lets you type without stopping to expand abbreviations. On the other hand, you must do a replace operation every time you want to expand an abbreviation. There is no dedicated function key or storage (in memory or on the disk), as there is with a library.

Reformatting Documents

Sometimes you must reformat an entire document. Suppose you have double-spaced a report (so you could edit it easily) but want to print the final version single-spaced. The easiest way to reformat a document, or a portion of one, is to make Advantage replace each page format line with one that has the format you want, then repaginate. This involves using the regular replace feature, but when Advantage asks for a replace string, specify the format line.

To reformat an entire document:

1. Put the cursor on the first page and press Shift-F6 to put Advantage in the replace mode.
2. When Advantage presents its *TYPE OF REPLACE* menu, enter **1** for *GLOBAL*.
3. When Advantage shows the prompt *REPLACE WHAT?*, press Alt-F9 to specify the page format line. A message of the following form appears at the bottom of the screen:

```
Search and replace format lines.  Format lines will be replaced with
the format line below.  Edit format line then enter F10 to continue or
ESC to abort.
              (Advantage shows the format line here)
              Single line spacing              right margin 65
```

4. Change the line spacing value, tabs, and right-hand margin to what you want, then press F10 to start the replace operation.

Advantage replaces every format line in the document. When it finishes, press F1 and Home to reach the first page and press Ctrl-F2 to repaginate.

Of course, many documents have format lines that change the spacing or tabs for a few paragraphs or a table or figure; you won't want to change *them*. To leave selected format lines intact, use the procedure we just gave but enter **2** in step 2, to select *DISCRETIONARY* instead of *GLOBAL*.

To reformat a portion of a document, use the same procedure as for an entire document, but start it on the page where you want reformatting to begin. Of course, since Advantage does not let you specify a range of pages for the replace operation, you must also select *DISCRETIONARY*. Then, when Advantage has changed all the format lines you want it to, press the space bar to return to editing.

Questions and Answers

Question: I searched for a phrase that I know is in my report, but Advantage couldn't find it. Why not?

Answer: The most likely reason is that you had the cursor past where the phrase occurred. Try searching from the beginning of the report. Also check the spelling and the CASE option. If you misspelled something, Advantage surely won't find the phrase. If you have CASE on and the phrase is in lowercase, Advantage won't find it if it's at the beginning of a sentence.

Question: I just finished my monthly sales report when the Northwest sales office called with some corrections. How can I find all the places where I might have mentioned their figures?

Answer: Move the cursor to the beginning of the report and start a search operation. If the *SEARCH FOR* line shows CASE, press Alt-G to turn it off. Then enter **Northwest** and press F6 to begin the search. Advantage will stop the first time it finds *Northwest*. To find the next occurrence, press F6. Otherwise, if something needs changing, move the cursor to it and make the changes, and then press F6 twice to resume the search.

Question: I misspelled *recommend* as *recomend* throughout a term paper. How can I correct it?

Answer: Move the cursor to the beginning of the document, then do a replace operation. Enter **recomend** for *REPLACE WHAT?* and **recommend** for *REPLACE WITH*. Be sure you don't put a space after either entry, so Advantage will correct such variations as *recomended* and *recomendation*.

Question: Our company's statement of qualifications always refers to us as *Smith, Brown, Jones, and Associates, Inc.* Unfortunately, after a minor argument and small lawsuit, Brown left and is now our chief competitor. How do I change the name to *Smith, Jones, and Associates, Inc.* and make sure Brown isn't mentioned anywhere?

Answer: You can remove Brown from the company name by doing a replace. Use *Smith, Brown* as the search string and *Smith* (no comma) as the replacement. Then search the entire statement for *Brown* and change the text as required. I would even do a final search for *Brown* just to make sure I hadn't missed any mentions. Better to be safe than to worry about a few keystrokes and some computer time.

Hints and Warnings

1. Watch the distinction between moving and copying text. Pressing F7 starts a move operation, which deletes text from its old position; pressing F8 starts a copy operation, which leaves the original as it was.

2. When performing a move (F7), copy (F8), or external copy (Shift-F8) operation, remember that Advantage does not preserve the original format automatically. To move or copy the format along with the text, you must start the operation and then press the F9 key.

3. To enter a search or replacement string that is shorter than the one you entered previously, be sure to press Del to erase each leftover character. If you try to use the space bar or the − key to erase characters, Advantage will simply add spaces or − characters to the string.

4. Be careful when using the automatic (global) replacement option. Advantage does not indicate what it replaced or how many replacements it made. If you aren't absolutely sure that you want to make the replacement each time, use the selective (discretionary) option instead. This may take some time, but it can avoid errors that are almost impossible to find.

5. Move, copy, and replacement operations may make pages too long. If they do, you must repaginate the document; Advantage doesn't do this automatically.

6. You can cancel an insert, delete, move, or copy operation at any time by pressing Esc. Pressing Esc can even undo the effects of a column

insert or delete operation *after* you have done it—provided you
haven't changed pages or otherwise saved it on disk.

Key Point Summary

Table 6-1 summarizes the editing keys and functions we introduced in this chapter.

Table 6-1. Keys and functions introduced in Chapter 6.

Key(s)	*Function*
Alt-G	*In search or replace mode:* Reverse CASE setting
Del	*In column mode:* Delete column
	In search or replace mode: Delete string character
Ins	*In column mode:* Insert column
Shift-F3	Column mode
F6	Search for string
Shift-F6	Replace string
F7	*In edit mode:* Move text
	In column mode: Move column
	During external copy: Switch from regular documents to table of contents documents, or vice versa
F8	*In edit mode:* Copy text
	In column mode: Copy column
Shift-F8	External Copy
F9	*In move, copy, or external copy mode:* Move or copy the format as well as the text

1. To move a block of text, put the cursor at the start of it and press
   F7. Then, if you want to preserve the original format at the new
   location, press F9. Next, put the cursor at the end of the block and
   press F7 again. Finally, move the cursor to the new location and
   press F7 once again.
2. To copy a block of text, use the same procedure as moving but press
   F8 each time.
3. Advantage can also copy text between documents. To begin, put the
   cursor where you want the copy inserted and press Shift-F8. If the
   other document is on a different disk, put that disk in drive A and
   enter its drive name and document name.

   When the second document appears, move the cursor to where
   you want to start copying and press Shift-F8, then move it to the end

of the copy block and press Shift-F8 again. Finally, put the System disk back in drive A if necessary.

4. To copy from a table of contents, follow the procedure described in key point 3, but when Advantage displays *EXTERNAL COPY* press F7 to switch to table of contents documents.

5. Besides ordinary text, Advantage can insert, delete, move, or copy columns of text or numbers.

6. To insert a column, set a tab for it and move the remaining tabs right. Then put the cursor where you want the insertion and press Shift-F3 then Ins. Give Advantage the width of the column ("# of Columns") and its length ("# of Lines"), then press F10 to make the insertion.

7. To delete a column, move the cursor to it and press Shift-F3 then Del. Specify the width of the column using the right-arrow key and its length using the down-arrow key, then press Del to delete it.

8. To move or copy a column, put the cursor on it and press Shift-F3, then F7 (move) or F8 (copy). Specify the boundaries as in keypoint 6, then press F7 or F8 again. Finally, move the cursor to the destination and press F7 or F8 once more.

9. Advantage can search a document for a specified *string* (a sequence of characters). To start a search, press F6. When Advantage displays its *SEARCH FOR* prompt, press Alt-G to make it find only exact matches for the string. Then enter the search string and press F6.

10. Advantage's search feature can search a document for a string and replace it with another of your choice. To start a replace, press Shift-F6.

11. Before starting a replace operation, Advantage displays three options. *GLOBAL* makes it replace every occurrence of the search string automatically; *DISCRETIONARY* makes it stop each time and ask whether you want to replace the occurrence; *ABORT* cancels the replace operation.

12. The replace operation displays two more prompts. Enter the search string in response to *REPLACE WHAT?* and the replacement string in response to *REPLACE WITH,* and press F6 after each one.

13. Replace allows you to use abbreviations while typing. It provides automatic replacements, but does not remember the abbreviations as a library does. Still, replace makes Advantage (*not* you) expand the abbreviations.

14. To reformat a document, do a replace operation in which you specify the format line for the *REPLACE WHAT* text.

7

Key Procedures

In Chapter 3, we described using libraries to store text you need frequently in your documents. Advantage also provides a similar, but more versatile, way of storing information: you can store it in a special disk file called a *key procedure*.

A key procedure is simply a sequence of keystrokes that Advantage plays back when you tell it to. In that respect, a key procedure is similar to a library entry. However, a library entry may contain only text, while a key procedure may include commands as well. Besides the standard Advantage commands (e.g., F6 for search), key procedures may include *pause* commands that let you enter information from the keyboard and *prompt* commands that make Advantage repeat the procedure.

The pause command is convenient for producing key procedures that include "personalized" items such as names or addresses. Typical users include the following:

- Attorneys who want to produce stock or *boilerplate* paragraphs that refer to a specific person or company.
- Businesspeople who want to use a form letter to reply to someone who has requested the address of a local dealer or the price of a specific item.
- Engineers who want to prepare status reports that include variable items (e.g., dates, manpower estimates, and costs) within set tables or blocks of text.
- Anyone who wants to produce periodic meeting notices or bulletins that differ only in time, place, or purpose.

Here we describe the general process for creating key procedures that include pause commands. Later in this chapter, we will suggest some uses for key procedures that have no pause commands.

Using Key Procedures

To use a key procedure, you must first create or *build* it, then tell Advantage where to play it back or *execute* it.

Building a Key Procedure

To build a key procedure:

1. Create the document in which you first want to use the key procedure.
2. When the blank first page appears, make any required changes to the format line, then press Ctrl-F5 to start a key procedure. Advantage shows this prompt on the bottom line:

```
KEY PROCEDURE FILE NAME:     (F10 TO CONTINUE, ESCAPE TO ABORT)
```

3. Enter a name for the key procedure (up to eight characters), and press F10. Advantage shows a *B* in reverse video at the bottom right-hand corner, to indicate that you are "building" a key procedure.
4. Enter the material you want Advantage to play back. Besides text, this can include tabs, special print formats (e.g., boldface, subscripts, and superscripts), formatting keys (e.g., F3 for centering), or anything else you can use in a regular document.
5. Wherever you want Advantage to pause for a keyboard insertion, press Ctrl-F6. Advantage shows *PAUSE* in the bottom left-hand corner, but does not indicate the pause point in the text.
6. When you finish entering the key procedure, press Ctrl-F5 again. Advantage saves the procedure on your data disk and removes the *B* from the bottom.
7. Delete the entire key procedure.

Executing a Key Procedure

When you reach the place in a document where you want to execute a key procedure, do the following:

1. Press Ctrl-F8. Advantage displays this prompt at the bottom of the screen:

   ```
   KEY PROCEDURE FILE NAME: name (F10 TO CONTINUE, ESCAPE TO ABORT)
   ```

   Here, *name* is the key procedure you defined most recently.
2. To replay the key procedure suggested by Advantage, press F10. To select a different one, type its name and press F10.
   Advantage displays *E* (for execute) at the bottom right-hand corner and begins playing the key procedure. When it encounters your first pause (Ctrl-F6) command, it stops and displays

   ```
   PRESS (C) TO CONTINUE. PLEASE ENTER DATA, THEN CTRL-F6 TO RESUME.
   ```

3. Press the *C* key, then enter your insertion text and press Ctrl-F6. Advantage resumes playing the key procedure and stops when it reaches the next pause command (if any). This time it shows

   ```
   PLEASE ENTER DATA, THEN CTRL-F6 TO RESUME.
   ```

4. For this pause, and any subsequent ones, enter the insertion text immediately (do *not* precede it with C), then press Ctrl-F6.
5. When Advantage finishes executing the key procedure, it removes the *E* from the bottom right-hand corner. Now you may enter any remaining text, then save the document and print it.

Example

Suppose you want to notify a customer that your company is discontinuing credit due to unpaid bills. Figure 7-1 shows the general form of a letter you could use. The underlined material in square brackets indicates the places where Advantage should allow you to insert personalized items.

```
                              211 Washington Street
                              San Diego, CA 92121
                              [Current date]

[Customer's name and address]

Dear [Name]:

As of the close of business on [Date], your company has
outstanding invoices over 30 days old totaling [Amount].  We
must request immediate payment of these invoices or we will be
forced to add a 1 1/2% monthly service charge.

Until we receive payment, we cannot extend credit to your
company or process further orders.  Please remit this payment to
my attention as soon as possible.

                              Sincerely yours,



                              Marie F. Gerard
                              Assistant Credit Manager
```

Figure 7-1. Generalized letter showing insertion points.

To define this letter as a key procedure:

1. Create a new document. If you want to first send this letter to someone named Rogers, name it *rogersnc* (where "nc" stands for "no
   credit").
2. When the blank first page appears, delete the automatic tabs and set
   a new tab at the center (column 32).
3. Press Ctrl-F5 to start building a key procedure.
4. When Advantage shows the prompt

```
KEY PROCEDURE FILE NAME:      (F10 TO CONTINUE, ESCAPE TO ABORT)
```

   enter *nocredit* and press F10.
5. Enter the return address as shown in Figure 7-1. On the line below
   it, press Tab to reach the center and Ctrl-F6 to insert a pause command for the date. Then press Return twice to reach the line where
   the customer's address belongs.
6. Press Ctrl-F6 again, to insert a pause command for the customer's
   address, and then press Return twice to reach the salutation line.
7. Enter the start of the salutation (*Dear*) and press Ctrl-F6 to insert a
   pause command for the name.

8. Complete the letter, inserting two more pause commands in the first sentence—one after *close of business on* and the other at the end of the sentence.
9. Press Ctrl-F5 to save the key procedure on disk.
10. Delete the entire text of the key procedure.

Let's use this procedure to produce a credit cancellation letter to Harold "Bug" Rogers of Pest-B-Gone, Inc. As of October 11, 1985, Mr. Rogers' company has accumulated $1287.67 in unpaid invoices. With the now-blank page of the *rogersnc* letter still on the screen, proceed as follows:

1. Press Ctrl-F8 to start a key procedure. Advantage shows this prompt at the bottom of the screen:

```
KEY PROCEDURE FILE NAME: nocredit  (F10 TO CONTINUE, ESCAPE TO ABORT)
```

2. Since *nocredit* is the key procedure we want, press F10. Advantage produces the return address, pauses, and shows

```
PRESS (C) TO CONTINUE. PLEASE ENTER DATA, THEN CTRL-F6 TO RESUME
```

3. Press **c**, then type **October 16, 1986** and press Ctrl-F6. Advantage skips to the line where Mr. Rogers' address belongs, then displays

```
PLEASE ENTER DATA, THEN CTRL-F6 TO RESUME
```

(Note that this time you do *not* press C before entering the data.)
4. Enter

```
Mr. Harold "Bug" Rogers
Pest-B-Gone, Inc.
2786 Mayflower St.
San Diego, CA 92121
```

and press Ctrl-F6.
5. When Advantage pauses after *Dear* in the salutation, type **Mr. Rogers** and press Ctrl-F6 again.
6. When Advantage pauses after *close of business on*, type **October 11, 1986** and press Ctrl-F6 again.
7. When Advantage pauses after *totaling*, type **$1286.67** and press Ctrl-F6 again.

At the end of the letter, Advantage removes *E* from the bottom right-hand corner. Save the completed letter and print it.

Replaying a Key Procedure

Once you execute a key procedure, you can replay it by pressing Alt-R. This saves you from entering the procedure's name each time you want to use it.

Prompt Commands

In addition to pause (Ctrl-F6) commands, key procedures may also include *prompt* commands. A prompt command lets you tell Advantage whether to continue the procedure or cancel it. To insert a prompt command, press Ctrl-F7.

When Advantage encounters the prompt command within a procedure, it pauses and shows

```
DO YOU WISH TO CONTINUE OR STOP? (C/S)
```

To continue executing the key procedure, press **c;** to leave it, press **s.**

If you put a prompt command at the end of a procedure, pressing **c** makes Advantage *repeat* the entire procedure. This lets you play a procedure continually until you tell Advantage to stop.

Key Procedures That Reformat Documents

Chapter 6 described how to reformat documents by making Advantage replace each format line with one that has a different line spacing value. A possible drawback to this technique is that Advantage automatically changes the *tabs* as well as the line spacing each time. To preserve the tab settings, we can use a key procedure, rather than a replace operation, to change the format.

For example, a key procedure that converts a document to single-spacing should do three things:

- Find the next format line.
- Change the line spacing value on the format line to *1*.
- Ask whether to repeat the procedure or stop.

To create this procedure:

1. Select for editing the first document you want to single-space.
2. When the first page appears, press Ctrl-F5 to build a key procedure.
3. When Advantage asks for the procedure's name, type **single** and press F10.
4. Do the following:
   a. Press the F6 key. Advantage shows *SEARCH FOR* on the bottom line and *SEARCH MODE* at the top.
   b. Press F9. Advantage finds the next format line and puts the cursor below it.
   c. Press F9 again to move the cursor to the format line.
   d. Press the left-arrow key on the numeric keypad to reach the line spacing value.
   e. Press **1** on the top row of the keyboard to change to single-spacing.
   f. Press F9 to leave the format line.
   g. Press Ctrl-F7 to enter a prompt command.
   h. Press Ctrl-F5 to save the key procedure on disk.

Note that Advantage actually performs the commands as you enter them in the key procedure. At this point, the cursor should be below the second format line in your document (which means it is probably at the top of page 2).

Now that the *single* key procedure is on the data disk, press Ctrl-F8 to execute it. Each time Advantage changes a format line, it asks whether you want to repeat the procedure. If you are on the last page, type **s** to stop; otherwise, type **c** to continue.

When you finish, move the cursor to the first page (press F1 and Home) and change the page format line to single-spacing (press F9, left-arrow, **1,** and F9 again). Finally, repaginate the document and print it in its new, single-spaced form.

A key procedure that converts a document to double-spacing (call it *double*) requires the same sequence of instructions, except you must enter **2** (instead of **1**) in step 4e.

Editing Key Procedures

Sometimes you may want to change or *edit* a procedure after you have saved it—perhaps to add a new feature or correct an error. Editing a key procedure involves using the Advanced Utilities disk. To begin, select "Return to DOS" from the Main Menu. The computer displays its A> prompt (or C>, if you have a hard disk). What you do next depends on which kind of computer you have.

If you have floppy disks, move the System disk to the right-hand drive (B) and insert your Utilities disk in the left-hand drive (A). Then type **util** and press Return. When this prompt appears:

```
CAN'T FIND MULTIMATE SYSTEM FILE
WPHELP.TXT
ENTER A NEW DRIVE AND PATH, F1D; OR ESCAPE TO ABORT
```

enter **b:** and press F10.

If you have a hard disk, type **util** and press Return.

Advantage's Advanced Utilities Menu appears (see Figure 7-2) and shows the "Printer Tables Editor" line covered with a band of reverse video. This band or *light bar* shows which option is currently selected.

```
MultiMate Advanced Utilities Version 3.40


          Printer Tables Editor

          Key Procedure Files Utility

          File Conversion

          Modify Display Defaults

          Document Recovery



Use Spacebar to Select Option, F1D to Continue
          ESCAPE to exit to DOS
```

Figure 7-2. Advanced Utilities menu.

To edit a key procedure, we want the "Key Procedure Files Utility", so press the space bar once to put the light bar on it, then press F10. Advantage displays a "Key Procedure File Utility" menu (see Figure 7-3).

```
Advantage Key Procedure File Utility


              Edit an Old File
              Create a New File
              Delete a File
```

Figure 7-3. Key Procedure File Utility menu.

Note that "Edit an Old File" is selected. If you have floppy disk drives, replace the System disk in drive B with the data disk that contains the key procedure you want to edit. Then, for either type of drive, press F10.

Advantage lists the available key procedures and assumes you want the first one. To edit a different key procedure, press the space bar to select it. Finally, press F10.

Pressing F10 makes Advantage display its Key Procedure Editing form. As Figure 7-4 shows, the top of this form contains a menu that lets you choose from three modes (CURSOR, INSERT, or DELETE) or EXIT. Below the dashed line is a list of the keystrokes in your key procedure, with spaces and key commands enclosed in angular brackets < and >.

For example, if you were to edit the *single* key procedure we described earlier, the bottom of the form would show

```
<F6><F9><F9><<-->1<F9><Ctrl F7>
```

The choices at the right of the form let you tell Advantage what you want to do, as follows:

- *Cursor Mode,* Advantage's initial selection, lets you move the cursor to the place where you want to insert or delete something.
- *Insert Mode* makes Advantage insert whatever you enter at the cursor location.
- *Delete Mode* makes Advantage delete a character or command whenever you press Del.
- *Exit* saves your changes, then returns to the previous menu.

```
         MULTIMATE KEY PROCEDURE FILE EDIT UTILITY

                                            CURSOR MODE
Use SPACEBAR to Select Mode                 INSERT MODE
Press <F10> to Continue, ESCAPE to Abort    DELETE MODE
                                            EXIT
```

Figure 7-4. Key Procedure Editing form.
Courtesy of Multimate International Corp.

To edit a key procedure, press F10 to reach its text. Advantage shows the prompt

```
Use Cursor Keys to Move Cursor
Press Ctrl-M to Change Mode
```

Use the arrow keys to move the cursor where you want to insert or delete material. To insert, press Ctrl-M to reach the menu at the top, press the space bar to select *INSERT MODE*, then press F10 to get back to editing. Now Advantage will insert whatever you type. Deleting is similar, except you select *DELETE MODE* and press Del to erase characters.

When you finish editing, press Ctrl-M to reach the menu, select *EXIT*, then press F10 to save the revised key procedure. Finally, press Esc twice to get back to the A> prompt. When it appears, replace the Utilities disk in drive A with the System disk.

Operating on Key Procedure Files

So far, we have described how to build, execute, and change key procedures. All these tasks involve operating on the contents of a key procedure. If you want to delete, copy, or rename a key procedure *file* on the disk, you must use the resources of the computer's disk operating system, or *DOS*.

As we mentioned in Chapter 2, to get ready to use DOS, select "Return to DOS" from Advantage's Main Menu. The computer clears the screen and shows *A>* at the top left-hand corner; it is waiting for you to enter a DOS command.

We will now describe how to delete, copy, and rename key procedure files, and how to obtain a list of the key procedure files on a disk. In each case, we assume that the file you want is in drive B.

Deleting Files

To delete a key procedure file, enter a command of the form

erase b:*keyproc.***key**

and press Return. For example, to delete a key procedure named *address*, enter

erase b:address.key

and press Return.

Copying Files

You may copy a key procedure file onto any formatted disk. To do this, put the new disk in drive A (replacing the System disk), and enter a command of the form

copy b:*keyproc.***key a:**

and press Return. When the A> prompt reappears, return the System disk to drive A.

Renaming Files

If a key procedure name is inappropriate or hard to remember, you can rename it. To do this, enter a command of the form

rename b:_oldname._**key** _newname._**key**

Listing the Available Key Procedures

To delete, copy, or rename a key procedure file, you must (of course) know its name. You must also know a procedure's name before you can use it; Advantage does not list the choices, as it does for documents and libraries. If you forget which key procedure files are on a data disk, enter the DOS command

dir b:*.key

DOS displays a list of key procedure files in the form

```
ADDRESS  KEY      368   2-06-86   9:45p
```

This shows the name (ADDRESS), the key procedure "extension" (KEY), the file's size in characters (368), and the date (2-06-86) and time (9:45p) it was most recently saved.

Questions and Answers

Question: I set up a key procedure that includes pauses for me to enter a name, address, and date. However, when I execute it, Advantage always ignores the first letter I type for the name. What's going on?

Answer: You forgot to press **c** before entering the name. Advantage requires the **c** for the first pause, but not for the rest.

Question: I just realized that I made a mistake in entering a previous data item in a key procedure. How can I correct it?

Answer: Finish the procedure, then move the cursor to where the error is and make your changes. Once a key procedure has been executed, Advantage treats the resulting document like ordinary text.

Hints and Warnings

1. You must type **c** before entering the data for the first pause command in a key procedure. For subsequent pause commands, enter the data directly; do not precede it with **c.**
2. When building a key procedure, remember to press Ctrl-F5 at the end of it as well as at the beginning. If you don't press Ctrl-F5 the second time, Advantage will simply continue building the procedure indefinitely.

Key Point Summary

Table 7-1 summarizes the keys and functions we introduced in this chapter.

Table 7-1. Keys and functions introduced in Chapter 7.

Keys	*Function*
Alt-R	Replay a key procedure
Ctrl-M	Change modes while editing a key procedure
Ctrl-F5	Build (create) a key procedure
Ctrl-F6	Pause command
Ctrl-F7	Prompt command
Ctrl-F8	Execute a key procedure

1. A key procedure is a sequence of keystrokes that Advantage plays back when you tell it to. To create or *build* a key procedure, put Advantage in a document (either old or new) and press Ctrl-F5. Enter a name for the key procedure (up to eight characters) and press F10. Then type whatever you want Advantage to play back or *execute.* When you finish, press Ctrl-F5 to save the procedure on disk.
2. To make Advantage execute a key procedure, put the cursor where you want the insertion and press Ctrl-F8. When requested, enter the key procedure's name and press F10.
3. Key procedures may include pause and prompt commands.
4. A pause command makes Advantage stop while you insert text from the keyboard. To insert one in a key procedure, press Ctrl-F6.
5. Once you execute a key procedure you can replay it by pressing Alt-R.
6. A prompt command tells Advantage to stop and ask whether you want to continue the procedure (type **c**) or leave it (enter **s**). To insert one in a key procedure, press Ctrl-F7.
7. Advantage lets you edit key procedures. To begin, put your Utilities disk in drive A and your System disk in drive B, then enter **util** and press Return. Advantage eventually leads you to the Key Procedure Editing form, which provides four choices:

   - *Cursor Mode,* lets you move the cursor to the place where you want to insert or delete something.
   - *Insert Mode* makes Advantage insert whatever you enter at the cursor location.
   - *Delete Mode* makes Advantage delete a character or command whenever you press Del.
   - *Exit* saves your changes and returns to the previous menu.

Use Cursor Mode to reach the place you want to change, then press Ctrl-M to switch to the Insert or Delete Mode. When you finish editing the key procedure, select Exit to save it on disk.

8. To operate on a key procedure file, leave Advantage and enter DOS by selecting "Return to DOS" from the Main Menu. DOS provides commands that let you delete (erase), copy, or rename a file, as well as one that produces a listing or *directory* of files on a disk.

8

Form Letters

Sometimes you must send the same letter, such as a request for payment, notice of credit terms, order acknowledgment, or report on account status, to an entire list of recipients. Direct mail solicitors often use personalized letters that have the recipient's name and address in various places. The following is typical of the kind of letters that fill our mailboxes and wastebaskets:

```
Dear Mr. Brown:

Would you like the name James C. Brown to be associated with success?
Yes, Mr. Brown, you can be a dynamic, successful person if you attend
our seminar.
```

With Advantage, creating this kind of personalized form letter takes three steps:

1. Prepare a model of the letter in which you name places or fields that will vary (e.g., the recipient's name, address, account number, and outstanding balance.)
2. Prepare a data file containing the items Advantage must insert into the multiple copies.
3. Use the Main Menu's "Merge Print Utility" to combine the form with the data and print the letters.

The Advantage manuals refer to the generalized letter as the *Primary Document* (or the *Merge Document*) and to the printed copies as *Result Documents*. Hence, the Merge Print Utility's job is to combine a Primary Document with data items in a Data File to produce a group of Result Documents.

First we discuss the simple situation in which Advantage replaces fields in the Primary Document with items from the Data File on a one-for-one basis. We then describe Advantage's features for creating more elaborate form letters. These include conditional insertion of text, customizing individual letters from the keyboard, and using several data entries in a single document.

Simple Form Letters

As an example of a simple form letter, let us produce an invitation to a company's anniversary party. All we will do here is insert an individual address, a salutation, and a single reference to the recipient's affiliation.

Contents of Data Files

A *Data File* is a document containing a description of the entries and the entries themselves. The description (the Advantage manuals call it a Template) comes first.

A *Template* is simply a blank form that Advantage displays for each entry in the Data File. It contains the name or *label* of each data item, followed by one or more blank lines. The blank line or lines are underscores representing the item's *data field*—the place where the user fills in the data (say, the name or street address). Note the following rules:

- A label may be up to 79 characters long and must end with a colon (:).
- The first 12 characters of a label must be different from any other label in the Template. (Advantage pays attention to case, however, so it treats Name and NAME as different labels.)
- If a label consists of several words (e.g., First Name:), you must separate them with "hard" space. To enter a hard space, press Alt-S. Advantage marks it with a ∅ symbol.
- The length of the data field determines the maximum number of characters that can be entered for a given item. Data fields can be up to 255 characters long.

The rest of the Data File consists of the entries or *records* for the recipients. Each must be on a separate page. Whenever you change pages to start a new record, Advantage displays the Template form.

Creating a Data File

Creating a Data File involves constructing a Template, then filling in records—one for each addressee. To create a Data File for the invitation, begin as usual by selecting "Create a New Document" from the Main Menu. Name the document *address*. When the Document Summary Screen appears, press Shift-F10. Advantage displays the still-blank Template page.

Figure 8-1 shows the Template for the invitation data. It includes a centered title, the labels and data field lines for each of the five fields in the generalized letter or Primary Document, and some instructions to the operator.

```
                    Address Entry for Invitation


Name:    _____
Company: _____
Street:  _____
City:    _____
First⌀Name:  _____


    To enter another address, press F2.  To leave, press F10.
```

Figure 8-1. Template for a simple form letter.

Enter the material shown in Figure 8-1, and note the following:

- The *Name:* and *Company:* fields are 30 characters long (press Alt-underscore 30 times to enter their data field lines); the *Street:* and *City:* fields are 20 characters long; and the *First Name:* field is 10 characters long.
- The ⌀ symbol in the *First Name:* label is a hard space mark; to produce it, press Alt-S.

When you finish, press F2 to leave the Template and start entering data.

Since Advantage will apply the Template to every record in the Data File, it wants to make sure that you are satisfied with what you have entered so far. It displays

```
ARE YOU SURE YOU WANT TO LEAVE THE TEMPLATE PAGE? (Y/N)
```

Press **y** to proceed to the page for the first record.

On this page (and those that follow), Advantage displays a copy of the Template. Because the page represents a record in a Data File, the status line at the top shows *REC#:, TOT#:,* and *SELECTED* instead of the usual *PAGE:, LINE:,* and *COL:.* The *REC#:* value is the record number; the *TOT#:* value gives a running total of the number of records in this Data File. *SELECTED* means that Advantage will use this record to produce a form letter unless you tell it otherwise (we will say more on this later).

Figure 8-2 shows two records we can use to produce the invitation. Put them on separate pages (i.e., press F2 after entering the Grange data), then press F10 to save the Data File on disk.

```
                   Address Entry for Invitation

Name: Mr. Phillip T. Grange_____
Company: Newton Plastics Corporation___
Street: 1865 Industrial Way___
City: Newton, FL 32786___
First◊Name: Phil_____


     To enter another address, press F2.  To leave, press F10.
```

(A) Grange data

```
                   Address Entry for Invitation

Name: Mrs. Viola Wilson_____
Company: Wilson and Associates, Inc.___
Street: 4399 Beach Street___
City: Ocala, FL 32787___
First◊Name: Vi_____


     To enter another address, press F2.  To leave, press F10.
```

(B) Wilson data

Figure 8-2. Data records for a simple form letter.

Creating a Primary Document

To begin, create a new document called *invite* and enter the generalized letter shown in Figure 8-3. As usual, set a tab at the center (column 32) for the return address, the closing, and the writer's name and title.

```
                              Gutenberg Printing, Inc.
                              1243 Flamingo Lane
                              Newton, FL 32786
                              September 24, 1986


⊢Name⊣
⊢Company⊣
⊢Street⊣
⊢City⊣


Dear ⊢First∅Name⊣:

This year is Gutenberg Printing's fifth anniversary in
business.  To mark the occasion, we are hosting a cocktail party
on Wednesday, October 1, from 4:30 to 7:00 PM at the Newton
Inn.  As one of our most valued customers and friends at
⊢Company⊣, we would be honored by your presence.  I hope to see
you there!


                              Best wishes,



                              James A. Anderson
                              President
```

Figure 8-3. Simple form letter before merging.

The material enclosed with ⊢ symbols are fields in which Advantage is to insert data when it prints the letters. This ⊢ symbol, called a *merge code*, does not appear on the keyboard; you must press Alt-M to produce it. Note also that as in the Data File, there is a hard space (Alt-S) within *First Name:*.

When you finish entering the letter, press F10 to save it on the disk. Now you may create the Data File.

Printing Form Letters

To print our personalized invitations (that is, our Result Documents), proceed as follows:

1. Select "Merge Print Utility" from the Main Menu. Advantage displays its "Merge Print a Document" form (Figure 8-4).

```
┌─────────────────────────────────────────────────────────────────┐
│                    MERGE PRINT A DOCUMENT                         │
│                                                                   │
│        MERGE DOCUMENT                    MERGE DATA FILE           │
│          Drive: __                         Drive: __              │
│          Name:_____                   Name:_____   │
│    Approximately 00000000 characters [00000 Page(s)] available on __│
│                                                                   │
│        (Documents on the selected drive are listed here.)         │
│                                                                   │
│      Press F10 to continue, Esc to abort, PgDn to switch drives   │
│   Press Ctrl Home to select default directory, Ctrl End to select next directory│
│                                                         S:l N:l   │
└─────────────────────────────────────────────────────────────────┘
```

Figure 8-4. Merge Print a Document form.
Courtesy of Multimate International Corp.

2. For *MERGE DOCUMENT Name:*, type **invite** and press Tab.
3. For *MERGE DATA FILE Name:*, type **address** and press F10. Advantage shows

```
Record(s) [00001] to [99999]
```

It assumes you want to print a letter for every individual in your Data File.

4. To print just selected letters, change these values, and then press F10.
5. When the "Print Parameters for Document" form appears, make any required changes (e.g., request justification or multiple copies), then press F10 again.

Advantage clears the screen and shows

```
PLEASE WAIT ... PRINTING A DOCUMENT
```

while it prints the invitations. When it finishes, the Main Menu reappears.

Figure 8-5 shows the completed letter to Phillip Grange. Note that Advantage has replaced all the names with specific entries from the Data File.

```
                                    Gutenberg Printing, Inc.
                                    1243 Flamingo Lane
                                    Newton, FL 32786
                                    September 24, 1986

Mr. Phillip T. Grange
Newton Plastics Corporation
1865 Industrial Way
Newton, FL 32786

Dear Phil:

This year is Gutenberg Printing's fifth anniversary in
business.  To mark the occasion, we are hosting a cocktail party
on Wednesday, October 1, from 4:30 to 7:00 PM at the Newton
Inn.  As one of our most valued customers and friends at Newton
Plastics Corporation, we would be honored by your presence.  I
hope to see you there!

                                    Best wishes,



                                    James A. Anderson
                                    President
```

Figure 8-5. Printed form letter after merging.

Variable Form Letters

Advantage lets you tailor letters to groups of recipients. For example, you can:

- Include a company name in letters to business customers.
- Print "Enclosures" on letters to people who are to receive additional material.
- Insert "The charges below include a $50.00 late-payment penalty." on invoices to delinquent customers.
- Print special messages such as "Remember to add 6% California sales tax." for in-state customers or "Please remit in U.S. currency with checks drawn on a U.S. bank." for international customers.

The instruction *OB* (for "omit if blank") lets you exclude a specified entry from selected letters. The general form is:

```
⊢field⊣ ⊢OB⊣
```

This tells Advantage to omit the *field* text for every letter whose Data File record has no *field* entry.

Suppose you are mailing a retail catalog and want to offer preferred customers a 15 percent discount. To do this, put the following entry on each preferred customer's Data File page:

```
Preferred: And as a preferred customer, you are entitled to
           deduct an additional 15 percent!
```

(We enter two spaces after the exclamation point to separate this sentence from the next one.) You can then use the following paragraph in the cover letter:

```
    As you can see, our prices are among the lowest in the
business. ⊢Preferred⊣ ⊢OB⊣Don't delay; order TODAY!
```

Advantage will print all three sentences for preferred customers and the abridged version for everyone else.

Of course, this approach requires you to reproduce the "Preferred" text on every Data File record to which it applies. (To save retyping this material each time, enter it where it first occurs and then copy it onto subsequent rcords.) An alternative is to create a separate letter and Data File for preferred customers, and include the sentence directly in their letter.

Operating on Records

Advantage lets you easily operate on records in a Data File. You can add or delete individual records, select specific records for merging, or sort the entire file.

Adding and Deleting Records

To add a record, put the cursor in the record that is to precede it (or in the Template, if you want a new first record) and press the F2 key. Advantage shows the Template for the new record, at which point you can fill in data as usual.

To delete a record, put the cursor in it and press Shift-F2. When Advantage shows

```
ARE YOU SURE YOU WANT TO DELETE THIS RECORD? (Y/N)
```

type **y**. The record disappears and Advantage displays the next one.

Selecting Records for Printing

When you create a Data File, Advantage assumes you want to merge every record to produce the copies. It marks each new record *SELECTED* for printing. As we have already mentioned, you can merge a specific range of records (say, Records 4 through 18) by changing the starting and ending values in the *Record(s) [00001] to [99999] prompt*. However, this only works for consecutive records in a File. As an alternative, you can unselect the records you don't want and leave the prompt as it is. Advantage will then print only the records that remain *SELECTED*.

To unselect a specific record, put the cursor anywhere in it and press Alt-F1. Advantage removes *SELECTED* from the status line. (Pressing Alt-F1 also does the opposite; it changes an unselected record to *SELECTED*.)

You can also select or unselect the remaining records in a Data File. To do this, put the cursor in the first one you want to change and press Alt-Y. Advantage displays

```
ALL REMAINING RECORDS WILL BE: 1) SELECTED 2) UNSELECTED 3) ABORT
```

If you accidentally put the cursor in the wrong record, type **3** to remove the prompt; otherwise, type **1** or **2**.

Sorting Records

Advantage can sort records in ascending or descending order, based on any field you specify. To begin, put the cursor in the desired data field of any record in the file and press the F5 key. When Advantage shows

```
SORT ORDER: 1) ASCENDING  2) DESCENDING  3) ABORT
```

type your choice. When sorting finishes, the cursor is in the sorted data field of the first record.

Modifying Templates

Advantage also lets you change a Data File's Template. You can rename labels, shorten or lengthen data fields, or add, delete, or move labels and their data fields. To begin any of these operations, load the Data File document using "Edit an Old Document." Advantage puts the cursor in the Template.

Changing Data Field Sizes

You can make a data field longer or shorter by inserting or deleting underscore characters. If you shorten a data field, Advantage displays this warning when you leave the Template:

```
SHORTENED FIELD LENGTH MAY CUT OFF DATA, DO YOU WISH TO CONTINUE? (Y/N)
```

Press **y** once for each shortened field.

Renaming Labels

You can change a label as you would ordinary text. Of course, changing a label gives it a different name than the corresponding label in the records. To warn you of this difference, Advantage displays `field` MISSING, HAS IT BEEN RENAMED? (Y/N)

(where *field* is the name of the label you have changed). Since you have indeed renamed a label, type **y**. At this point, Advantage forgets the original name and asks

WHAT IS THE NEW LABEL NAME?   PRESS F10 TO CONTINUE

Enter the revised name and press F10.

Inserting, Deleting, and Moving Items

To insert, delete, or move a label and its data field, perform a standard Ins, Del, or F7 procedure.

Printing Envelopes

You can also use Advantage to address envelopes. Here, your Primary Document contains only your return address (unless you have preprinted envelopes) and fields for the recipient's name, title, company, street address, and city. Figure 8-6 shows a typical Primary Document for use on standard 4 1/8-inch by 9 1/2-inch business-size envelopes.

```
Susan Briggs
Universal Bridge Co.
12366 West 10th Street
Bridge City, PA 16589
```

```
                                        |Name|
                                        |Title| |OB|
                                        |Company| |OB|
                                        |Street|
                                        |City|
```

Figure 8-6. Primary Document for printing envelopes.

We have started the recipient's fields at line 12 and column 45, so they print two inches from the top and 4 1/2 inches from the left

edge. (You may want different values.) Furthermore, printing envelopes also requires two changes to the "Print Parameters for Document" form: you must set "Pause between pages?" to *Y* and
"Document page length" to, say, *25*.

Using Multiple Entries in a Letter

So far, we have shown examples in which Advantage uses only one
Data File entry per letter. Sometimes, however, you may want to use
more than one. The *NEXT* instruction lets you do this—it simply
tells Advantage to advance to the next record (that is, the next page)
in the Data File.

Suppose you are sending the letter shown in Figure 8-7 to prospective new members of an investment club. Here, each copy contains two names and addresses: the prospective member's and the
sponsor's. Of course, you must arrange records in the Data File in
the order the letter expects to find them: first a member, then a
sponsor, and so on.

Note that only new members get the letter in Figure 8-7. Once
you use NEXT, Advantage never returns to the previous entry.
However, we can use the same Data File to send reminders and
schedules to both members and sponsors. Letters and Data Files are
independent documents. Advantage does not associate one with the
other unless you merge them using the "Merge Print Utility."

```
                              12568 Easy Street
                              Moolah, MI 67432
                              October 1, 1986


|Title| |First∅Name| |Last∅Name|

|Street|

|City|


Dear |First∅Name|:

    We are pleased to inform you that you have been selected for
membership in the Make-a-Million Investment Club.  This honor is
reserved for a selected few in the investment community.  You
will be inducted into the club at our annual general meeting on
October 15, 1986, at 8:00 P.M. at the Bay City Inn.  Your
sponsoring member is:

|NEXT|
      |Title| |First∅Name| |Last∅Name|

      |Street|

      |City|


We extend our congratulations to you on this achievement.


Sincerely yours,



D. Bigbucks
Secretary
```

Figure 8-7. New members' letter using the NEXT instruction.

Summarizing Data Files

   To summarize the entries in a Data File, precede NEXT with another instruction, *REPEAT*. The general form is:

```
|REPEAT:nn|
|NEXT|
(Enter items to be repeated here.)
|END REPEAT|
```

This makes Advantage print the material between NEXT and END REPEAT for *nn* consecutive entries.

For example, the form in Figure 8-8 produces a list of a company's 40 salespeople, giving the person's name, region, home address, and home telephone number. The blank line after the final item (<u>Home∅Phone</u>) provides spacing between entries.

```
           SALES ROSTER - 1986

           Chic Shoes, Inc.

|REPEAT:40|«
|NEXT|«
|Name|«
|Region|«
|Home∅Address|«
|Home∅Phone|«
«
|END REPEAT|«
```

Figure 8-8. Sales roster using the REPEAT instruction.

Producing Forms and Form Letters from the Keyboard

So far, we have discussed how to produce form letters by merging a Data File with a Primary Document. However, you don't have to have a Data File; you can instead enter data directly from the keyboard when Advantage asks for it.

This feature is especially convenient for filling out order-entry forms. It is also useful for preparing standard reply letters. For example, an employee of a Customer Service Department could use it to answer someone's request for the name of his or her local dealer; a Personnel employee could use it to acknowledge receipt of a resume.

To create a form or form letter from the keyboard:

1. Create the Primary Document then select the Merge Print Utility as usual.

2. When Advantage asks for the "Merge Document Name," enter the name of your Primary Document and press F10 (that is, leave the Merge Data File Name field blank).
3. When the *Record(s)* prompt appears, press F10 again. This makes the "Print Parameters for Document" form appear.
4. Enter your print parameters and press F10. When Advantage encounters a merge item name, it displays a prompt of the form

```
REPLACE:     (merge item name)
WITH:
```

5. Type the information for that name, then press Return.
6. Repeat steps 4 and 5 for each merge item in the document.

Questions and Answers

Question: Advantage won't insert anything into my form letters. It just prints entry names as if they were regular text. What's wrong?

Answer: Either you selected the "Print Document Utility" instead of "Merge Print Utility" or you entered the merge code symbol incorrectly. To enter ⊦, press Alt-M.

Question: Advantage omitted a data item from one of my form letters. Why?

Answer: You omitted the data from the addressee's page in your Data File.

Question: I have a Data File with the names and addresses of my company's 120-person sales staff, and want to send a memorandum to the six regional managers. What's the easiest way to do this?

Answer: Unselect all the records in the file, then select the managers' records and print the memoranda. To unselect the entire file, put the cursor in the first record and press Alt-Y. When the prompt appears, type **2**. After that, move the cursor to each manager's record and press Alt-F1 to mark it *SELECTED*. When you finish, save the Data File and do a "Merge Print."

Hints and Warnings

1. Like a regular document print operation, a merge print operation uses the "Print Parameters for Document" options to determine how

many copies and which pages to print. Remember that the default
values are one copy and the entire document printed.

2. When using field names consisting of two or more words, be sure to
insert a hard space (press Alt-S) between the words in both your Primary Document and the Template for your Data File. If you omit the
hard space in either place, Advantage will print a blank where that
item belongs.

3. When using the NEXT instruction, note that the advancement in the
Data File is permanent. Advantage does not provide a way to go back
to the previous entry (i.e., there is no PREV instruction). Nor will
Advantage ever use the current entry again. That is, when it proceeds
to the next letter, it also advances to the next page in the Data File.

Key Point Summary

Table 8-1 summarizes the keys and functions introduced in this
chapter.

Table 8-1. Keys and functions introduced in Chapter 8.

Keys	Function
Alt-M	Merge code (⊢)
Alt-S	Hard space (∅)
Alt-Y	*From within a Data File:* Select or unselect the remaining records.
Alt-F1	*From within a Data File:* Select or unselect a record.
F2	*From within a Data File:* Start a new record.
Shift-F2	*From within a Data File:* Delete a record.
F5	*From within a Data File:* Sort the records based on the field where the cursor is.
Shift-F10	*From the Document Summary Screen:* Create a Data File

1. Advantage can produce form letters by combining a generalized letter (the *Primary Document*) with entries or *records* from a Data File.

2. Create a Data File just as you would an ordinary document, but
when the "Document Summary Screen" appears, press Shift-F10.

3. A Data File contains a Template followed by a page for each record.
The Template is a blank form that includes a *label* for each data
item, followed by one or more *data field* lines. If a label consists of
several words, separate them with "hard space" symbols (∅) by

pressing Alt-S. To leave the Template and start entering data, press the F2 key.

4. Whenever you start a new record in a Data File, Advantage displays the Template as a fill-in form. Further, it automatically marks records as SELECTED for printing. Enter text in each data field, then press F2 to start a new record or F10 to save the Data File on disk.

5. The Primary Document is a regular document that includes a field name wherever Advantage is to insert a data item. Each field name must be enclosed with *merge code* symbols (⊦); to enter a merge code, press Alt-M.

6. To print form letters, select "Merge Print Utility" from the Main Menu.

7. Form letter documents may include the following instructions:

   - *OB* excludes a specified item from letters whose Data File record has no corresponding data.
   - *NEXT* lets you use more than one data record in a single copy. It makes Advantage advance to the next record. This is useful for letters containing more than one address.
   - *REPEAT* lets you summarize records in a Data File by repeating NEXTs a specified number of times. This is useful for compiling lists.

Table 8-2 summarizes these instructions.

Table 8-2. Form letter instructions.

⊦field⊦ ⊦OB⊦

Omits *field* for Data File records that have no corresponding data.

⊦NEXT⊦

Makes Advantage advance to next record entry in the Data File.

⊦REPEAT:*nn*⊦
(Material to be repeated)
⊦END REPEAT⊦

Makes Advantage repeat *nn* times the material between REPEAT and END REPEAT. Generally, a NEXT instruction follows the REPEAT, to make Advantage summarize entries in a Data File.

8. Advantage lets you add or delete individual records, select specific records for merging, or sort an entire Data File.

9. To add a record, put the cursor in the record that precedes it (or in the Template) and press F2. To delete a record, put the cursor in it and press Shift-F2.

10. To select or unselect a record, press Alt-F1.

11. To select or unselect the remaining records in a file, press Alt-Y.

12. To sort the records in a Data File, put the cursor on the data field on which you want to sort, then press F5.

13. Advantage lets you enter data items from the keyboard instead of from a Data File, which is handy for filling out forms and responding to individual letters. To select keyboard entry, start the "Merge Document Utility" as usual, but press F10 after entering the "Merge Document Name."

9

Customizing Advantage

When you begin working on a document, Advantage gives you built-in or "default" values for its various system parameters. For example, if you use Advantage in its original form, it sets the right-hand margin at column 75 and puts tabs at columns 5, 10, and 15. It also assumes that you want to print 55 single-spaced lines on 11-inch paper, starting on the first line of every page and the left-hand edge.

These are Advantage's guesses at what you need for most work. If they are not right for you, you can select more convenient ones. For example,

- If you want shorter lines or double-space most material, you can alter the *system format line* to produce these features automatically.
- If you print on legal-size paper, you can change the *system defaults* to produce the required number of lines.
- If you print on letterhead paper or generally justify your text, you can change the *printer defaults* to produce the top margin or justification automatically.

In this book we have shown you how to change Advantage so that it starts with the right-hand margin at column 65 and prints with specified margins at the top and left-hand sides. We have also described how to tell it which printer you have. You may want to make other changes.

To customize Advantage, you must change the default parameters on the System disk. In general, you should prepare and label a separate System disk for each format you use often. For example, you might create separate System disks for formal correspondence, memoranda, and reports. To do this, prepare a backup copy for each format (see "How to Set Up Your Advantage System" in the *Advantage User's Guide*), then tailor the copies.

Hard disk users may want to create a separate subdirectory for each unique format. LETTERS, MEMOS, and REPORTS would be suitable names for these subdirectories.

Changing the System Format Line

To change the system format line, select "Other Utilities" from the Main Menu, then select "Edit System Format Line". Advantage displays its "System Format Line Modification" form and puts the cursor at column 3. The changes you can make are:

1. *Different spacing.* The default value of 1 makes Advantage print single-spaced. To get double- or triple-spacing, change it to 2 or 3. To get space-and-a-half, change it to +.
2. *Different tabs.* Advantage's default tabs are at columns 5, 10, and 15. To add a tab, press the Tab key; to delete one, press the space bar.
3. *Different line length.* The Return symbol ($\leqslant$) at the end of the line marks the right-hand margin setting, so it determines the line length. To get shorter lines, move the cursor to where you want the right-hand margin and press Return. To get longer lines, keep moving the cursor until it is where you want it; the right-margin marker moves with the cursor.

When you finish changing the system format line, press F10 to restore the Other Utilities Menu. To return to the Main Menu, press F10 again.

Changing the System Defaults

To change the system defaults, select "Other Utilities" from the Main Menu, then select "Edit System Defaults". Advantage displays its "Modify System Defaults" form. Figures 9-1 shows Advantage's original settings. When you finish changing this form, press F10 to restore the Other Utilities Menu, then press F10 again to restore the Main Menu.

```
                    MODIFY SYSTEM DEFAULTS

Insert Mode [(D)rop Down / (P)ush]?    D    Acceptable Decimal Tab [ . or , ]?         .
Allow Widows And Orphans?              Y    Number Of Lines Per Page?                 55
Automatic Page Breaks?                 N    Display Spaces As Dots [.]?                N
Destructive Backspace?                 N    Keep Document Closed For Safety?           Y
Backup Before Editing Document?        N    Strikeout Character?                       /
Display Directory?                     Y
(T)ext Or (P)age Associated Headers And Footers?                                       T

System Date Standard [(U)SA,(E)urope,(J)apan, Or (D)OS]?                               D
Print Date Standard [(U)SA,(E)urope,(J)apan, Or (D)OS]?                                D

Section Numbering Style [(R)oman Or (N)umeric]?                                        R

Acceleration Rate [0 - 9]?             5    Acceleration Responsiveness [0 - 9]?       5
Main Dictionary?                 WEBSTER    Custom Dictionary?                    CLAMFL

            Press F10 to Continue, Press ESC to Abort                       S:1 N:1
```

Figure 9-1. Modify System Defaults form.
Courtesy of Multimate International Corp.

Insert Mode

This parameter tells Advantage what to do to the text on the screen when you press the Ins key. The original value, *D* (for Drop-Down), makes it remove all text from where you pressed Ins to the end of the screen. The alternate choice, *P* (for Push), makes it insert characters directly into the screen text, by pushing existing characters to the right as you type new ones.

Allow Widows and Orphans

This parameter tells Advantage how to treat paragraphs when it repaginates. The original value, *Y*, makes it fill each page to capacity, as specified by "Number of lines per page." *N* makes it keep the first and last two lines of paragraphs together on a page. With *N*, Advantage will not end a page with the first line of a paragraph, nor will it begin a page with the last line of a paragraph.

Automatic Page Breaks

Advantage's default, *N*, requires you to start each new page manually, by pressing F2 (new page) or Alt-B (required page break). When you have filled a page, the computer beeps and flashes the *LINE* number at the top of the screen. The opposite choice, *Y*, makes Advantage start a new page automatically when you pass the line number specified by "Number of lines per page."

Destructive Backspace

The original value, *N,* makes the Backspace key act just like the left-arrow key: it simply moves the cursor to the left. *Y* makes Backspace erase characters as it moves the cursor.

Backup before Editing Document

Advantage normally keeps only one copy of each document on disk. Therefore, if you change a document and save it, the original version disappears. However, if you set "Backup Before Editing Document?" to *Y*, Advantage automatically saves a backup copy of the original whenever you select the document for editing.

Acceptable Decimal Tab

Advantage comes set up to use a period for aligning numbers you enter using a Decimal Tab (Shift-F4) command. This parameter lets you tell it to align numbers around a comma instead, which is the European standard.

Number of Lines per Page

This parameter determines how many lines of text Advantage accepts before it considers a page "full." The original value, *55,* is designed for standard 11-inch paper. You must change this parameter if you are printing on longer or shorter paper. For example, to print on 14-inch legal-size paper, change it to *72.*

Strikeout Character

This parameter lets you tell Advantage which character to use for overprinting with the Strikeout (Alt-O) command. The default is a slash (/), but you may want it to use a hyphen.

Section Numbering Style

This lets you tell Advantage whether to use the Roman style or the numeric style to number sections. The original value is *R* (Roman).

Acceleration Rate

This parameter determines the speed at which keys repeat when you hold them down; *0* is slowest, *9* is fastest. The original value is *5.*

Changing the Printer Defaults

To change the printer defaults, select "Printer Control Utilities" from the Main Menu, then select "Edit Printer Defaults". Advantage displays its "Modify Printer Defaults" form. Figure 9-2 shows Advantage's original settings.

The Advantage manual fully describes these parameters, so we will discuss only the ones you are most likely to want to change. When you finish, press F10 to restore the Printer Control Utilities Menu, then press F10 again to restore the Main Menu.

```
                        MODIFY PRINTER DEFAULTS


Start Print At Page Number        001    Lines Per Inch [6 or 8]                6
Stop Print After Page Number      999    Justification: [N or Y or M(icro)]     N
Left Margin                       000    Proportional Spacing: [N or Y]         N
Top Margin                        000    Char Translate / Width Table     ____
Pause Between Pages: [N or Y]        N    Header / Footer First Page Number    001
Draft print: [N or Y]               N    Starting Footnote Number [1-871]     001
Default pitch [4 = 10 CPI]          4    Number of Original Copies            001
                                         Document Page Length                 066
Printer Action Table          TTYCRLF    Sheet Feeder Action Table        ____
Sheet Feeder Bin Numbers [0 - 3]:        First page: 0  Middle: 0  Last page:   0
P(arallel) / S(erial) / L(ist) / A(uxiliary) / F(ile)                          P
                                         Device Number                        001


Print Doc. Summary Screen:  [N or Y]  N  Print Printer Parameters: [N or Y]     N
Background / Foreground:  [B or F]    B  Remove Queue Entry When Done: [Y or N] Y



Press F1 for Printers, F2 for Sheet Feeders - only the first 16 are displayed

                  (Printer types are listed here.)

        Press F10 to Continue, Press ESC to Abort            S:1 N:1
```

Figure 9-2. Modify Printer Defaults form.
Courtesy of Multimate International Corp.

Left Margin

This parameter tells Advantage how far to indent before it starts
printing. If you have positioned the paper to allow for a left margin,
keep the original value, *000*. Otherwise, enter the number of spaces
you want. For example, to produce a one-inch left margin, enter **010**
if your printer uses standard 10-pitch (pica) type or **012** if it uses
12-pitch (elite) type. The "Default pitch" parameter on this form
specifies the print type.

Top Margin

This tells Advantage how many lines to skip before it starts to
print. The original value, *000*, makes it start printing immediately. If
you have positioned the paper to allow for a top margin, keep *000*;
otherwise, enter the number of lines you want. For example, to pro-

duce a one-inch top margin, enter **006** (Advantage's "Lines per inch" parameter is set to 6).

Pause between Pages

The original parameter value, *N*, assumes you are printing on continuous form paper. To print on single-sheet paper, change it to *Y*.

Default Pitch

Advantage assumes your printer uses 10-pitch (pica) type, so it makes the "Default pitch" *4*. To use a different type size, enter a number between 1 and 9. For example, *5* selects 12-pitch (elite) type and *8* selects 16.5 characters per inch. Of course, your printer must be able to produce the pitch you specify.

Lines per Inch

Advantage assumes you want 6 lines per inch, but you may change it to *8*. You might do this to print with a small type size—say, 16.5 characters per inch.

Justification

The original value, *N*, makes Advantage print documents with a ragged right-hand margin. If you generally justify text, enter *Y*. Advantage will then produce even right-hand margins by inserting spaces between words. The third choice, *M* (for Micro), makes Advantage insert a small amount of space within words as well as between them.

Proportional Spacing

If you set this parameter to *Y*, the printer gives each character the amount of space equal to its width. Of course, your printer must be able to produce proportional spacing.

Number of Original Copies

Advantage assumes you want to print just one copy. However, if you need multiple copies for filing purposes, you can change this parameter to *002* or *003* or whatever amount you need.

Document Page Length

This parameter tells Advantage how long your paper is, in sixths of an inch. The original value, *066*, is for standard 11-inch paper. To print on 14-inch legal-size paper, enter **082**.

Hints

For most writing on standard paper with no letterhead, we recommend the following defaults:

- On the *system format line,* change the line spacing value to **2** for double-spaced text and set the right-hand margin to column **65** for a 6 1/2-inch line and one-inch side margins.
- For the *system defaults,* change "Allow Widows and Orphans?" to *N,* "Destructive Backspace?" to *Y,* and "Acceleration Rate [0-9]?" to a small number such as *0, 1,* or *2.*
- For the *printer defaults,* enter **010** for "Left margin" and **006** for "Top margin" to produce one-inch left and top margins. Further, change "Pause between pages?" to *Y* if you are using single-sheet paper and change "Justification?" to *Y* or *M* if you want text justified or micro-justified.

Key Point Summary

The *system format line, system defaults,* and *printer defaults* determine what values Advantage uses when you turn the power on. You can change these default settings by selecting "Other Utilities" or "Printer Control Utilities" from the Main Menu.

The original system format line values are:

- Line spacing: 1 (single-spacing)
- Text tabs: three, at columns 5, 10, and 15
- Right-hand margin: column 75

The original system default settings are:

- Insert Mode?: Drop down (pressing Ins clears the rest of the screen)
- Allow Widows and Orphans?: Yes
- Automatic Page Breaks?: No (the computer beeps when you have filled a page)
- Destructive Backspace?: No (the Backspace key acts like left-arrow key; it moves the cursor, but does not delete characters.)
- Backup before Editing Document?: No
- Acceptable Decimal Tab [. or ,]?: Period
- Number of Lines per Page?: 55 (for 11-inch paper)
- Strikeout Character?: /
- Section Numbering Style [(R)oman or (N)umeric]?: Roman (i.e., I, I.A)
- Acceleration Rate [0-9]?: 5

The original printer default settings are:

- Left Margin: 0 (no indentation)
- Top Margin: 0 (start printing on current line)
- Pause between Pages: No (for continuous paper)
- Default Pitch: 4 (produces 10 characters per inch, or pica)
- Printer Action Table: TTYCRLF (general-purpose printer)
- Lines per Inch: 6
- Justification: No
- Proportional Spacing: No
- Printer type: Parallel
- Number of Original Copies: 1
- Document Page Length: 66 (measured in sixths of an inch; 66 assumes 11-inch paper)
- Print Doc. Summary Screen: No

You can look up the parameters we have not mentioned in the *Advantage Reference Manual*.

10

Using Other Programs with Advantage

Throughout this book we have been treating Advantage documents as complete and final products. In practice, you may want to combine a document with a financial report generated by a spreadsheet or a list obtained from a database.

If every computer program produced results in the same form, you could simply copy material between them. For example, you could use Advantage's External Copy (Shift-F8) command to copy a *Lotus 1-2-3* spreadsheet directly into a report you are writing. Alas, things aren't that easy.

Spreadsheet programs generally produce results in a different form than word-processing programs. Likewise, database programs produce results in a different form than spreadsheets or word processors. In general, most programs are incompatible.

Fortunately, Advantage includes a program that can convert the results of various kinds of programs into Advantage documents. Conversely, it can also convert Advantage documents into a form that can be used by another program. This chapter describes the conversion procedure. It also includes examples of using the results of spreadsheets and databases with Advantage.

File Conversion

Advantage contains a special program called *UTIL* (for Utilities) that can, among other things, convert material from one format to another. The formats UTIL can convert are:

- *ASCII*, short for "American Standard Code for Information Interchange," is the format in which most computers transfer information internally. It is, if you will, the generic computer format. Nearly every program can both read ASCII information and produce ASCII results. You use ASCII to communicate with programs that cannot produce any of the other formats. For example, ASCII is useful for converting documents produced by other word processors to the form that Advantage uses.
- *COMM* is the format used by modems (devices that transfer data over telephone lines).
- *DIF* (Data Interchange Format) is used by many spreadsheets, such as Lotus 1-2-3, to represent numerical data.
- *JW* is the format used by Just Write, Multimate International's entry-level word processor.
- *MM* is the format used by MultiMate and Advantage.

Upon request, Multimate International will also provide conversion programs for other formats. Consult the *Advanced User's Guide* or Multimate International for details.

Conversion Procedure

In the process of using UTIL for the first time, you must put two files it needs onto the Advanced Utilities disk. You copy one from the System disk and tell UTIL to create the other.

To begin, leave Advantage by selecting "Return to DOS" from the Main Menu. When the A> prompt appears, move the System disk to drive B and insert the Advanced Utilities disk in drive A. Then type

copy b:wpsysd.sys

When A> reappears, remove the System disk from drive B and replace it with the data disk that contains the file you want to convert. To start UTIL, type **util** and press Return. Pressing Return here calls up Advantage's *Advanced Utilities* list, which provides these six choices:

Printer Tables Editor
Key Procedure Files Utility
File Conversion
Modify Console Defaults
Document Recovery
Custom Dictionary Utility

You want "File Conversion," so press the space bar twice to highlight it, then press the F10 key. When this message appears:

```
CANNOT FIND UTILITY SYSTEM FILE
        CONSYSD.SYS

Create a New File or Try Again  Create  Try Again

    F10 to Select  ESCAPE to Abort
```

press F10 to create the CONSYSD.SYS file.

Pressing F10 here calls up Advantage's *File Conversion* list, which provides just two choices: Convert Document(s) and Edit Conversion Defaults. The one we want now, Convert Document(s), is already highlighted, so press F10 to obtain the *Convert a Document* form.

This form lets you give UTIL information about the file you want to convert (the "Source") and the converted form of this file (the "Destination"). For each, you must specify the file's name and extension, its *Type* (ASCII, DIF, MM, etc.), and a *Path*. For the Source, Path tells UTIL where to find the file; for the Destination, Path tells it where to store the converted result. In both cases, Path is normally **b**: for floppy disks and **c**: for a hard disk. To perform the conversion, fill in these fields (use the arrow keys to move between them), then press F10 to start the conversion operation.

UTIL always assumes you want to perform another conversion. Now you can do any of four things:

- To convert another file, enter its Source and Destination parameters and press F10.
- To make another choice from the Advanced Utilities list, press Esc to obtain it.
- To start Advantage, press Esc until the A> prompt appears. Then replace the Advanced Utilities disk with the System disk and enter **wp**.
- To stop working altogether, simply switch the computer off.

Electronic Spreadsheets

Without a doubt, the most popular business program is the electronic spreadsheet. If your reports involve tables of numbers requiring arithmetic manipulation, an electronic spreadsheet can save you a lot of hand calculations.

To explain what an electronic spreadsheet does, let us consider a practical application. Suppose you own a clothing store and want to find out how your business is doing. You could take a large piece of paper and rule it off into rows and columns. Each row would correspond to a different department: men's suits, children's wear, sportswear, women's fashions, and so on.

The first 12 columns would be monthly sales totals, followed by yearly totals, comparisons with previous months or previous years, commissions, sales taxes, and so forth. You could add down the monthly columns (giving monthly totals) and add across the rows (giving annual totals for a given department). You could also figure annual receipts, net profits (receipts minus costs), and other results.

How would you do this by hand? You would enter the numbers from your account books and use a calculator to add each row and column, one after the other. Surely, this would be a long, tedious, error-prone task. The electronic spreadsheet can do all the calculations simultaneously. It lets you label rows and columns and tell the computer how they are related.

For example, you could label the monthly columns with the names of the months. You could then specify that the *Yearly Total* column is the sum of the monthly columns. Similarly, you could say that the *Monthly Cost* row is the sum of all departmental costs for a particular month. After you tell the computer what the rows and columns mean, you then enter your data.

The computer quickly and automatically performs all the calculations at once. It's like having many calculators, each doing its specific task and passing its results on if other calculators need them. You can also change any number on the spreadsheet, and the program will instantly recalculate everything the number affects.

You can copy the results of a spreadsheet such as Lotus' 1-2-3 or Microsoft's *Multiplan* into an Advantage document. For example, you might be preparing a loan proposal to a bank for a possible expansion of your clothing store. To begin, you develop a spreadsheet that lists income, costs, and profits for the last five years and uses them to make five-year projections under reasonable assumptions about inflation rates, profit margins, operating costs, and so forth.

You save this spreadsheet as a file on your data disk, then use the UTIL program to convert it to an Advantage document. When you reach the point where the spreadsheet is to appear, copy it into the loan proposal document with an External Copy (Shift-F8) command. After that, you can reformat, expand, or otherwise change the spreadsheet just as you would standard Advantage text.

An electronic spreadsheet is a great timesaver for an accountant, banker, insurance agent, purchasing manager, sales manager, broker, or anyone else who works with figures. Furthermore, it ensures greater accuracy and allows the user to calculate more results and try out variables such as inflation, interest rates, market penetration, or foreign exchange rates.

Lotus 1-2-3 Procedure

Lotus 1-2-3 produces spreadsheets in its own unique format called *WKS* (for "worksheet," which is what Lotus Development Corp. calls a spreadsheet). Advantage cannot convert the WKS format directly, but the Lotus 1-2-3 program contains a procedure to convert a WKS file to a DIF file—and DIF is a format Advantage can handle. Hence, we must make two separate conversions: WKS to DIF (using Lotus 1-2-3), then DIF to Advantage (using Advantage). The procedure is:

1. Start Lotus 1-2-3 as usual.
2. Create the worksheet or load it in from disk with a */File Retrieve* command.
3. Put your Advantage data disk in drive B.
4. Select */File Xtract*, then *Formulas*.

5. When Lotus 1-2-3 asks for the Xtract filename, enter **b**: and the name you want to give the file. (For example, **b:salespro** would be suitable for a table of sales projections.)

6. When Lotus 1-2-3 asks for the Xtract range, enter the beginning column and row, two periods, the ending column and row, and then press Return. For example, to extract rows 6 through 24 of columns A through G, enter **A6..G24**.

7. When the top right-hand corner of the screen shows *READY*, select */Quit* and Yes to leave Lotus 1-2-3.

8. When the Lotus Access System command menu appears, select *Translate*, then WKS to DIF.

9. For the source disk drive, specify B.

10. When the computer asks you to *Select file for processing*, use the down-arrow key to highlight the filename you entered in step 5, then press Return.

11. For the destination disk drive, specify B.

12. Select Yes to proceed with the translation.

13. When the screen shows *Press any key to clear display and continue*, press Return.

14. When the File Translation System Menu reappears, select Quit and Yes.

15. When the Lotus Access System command menu appears, select Exit and Yes to leave Lotus 1-2-3.

Your data disk now contains two versions of the worksheet, one in Lotus 1-2-3 worksheet format (e.g., SALESPRO.WKS) and another in DIF format (e.g., SALESPRO.DIF). To convert the DIF file to an Advantage document:

1. Put your Advantage Advanced Utilities disk in drive A, replacing the Lotus 1-2-3 disk, and enter **util**.

2. Select "File Conversion" from the Advanced Utilities menu, then select "Convert Document(s)" from the File Conversion menu.

3. When the Convert a Document menu appears:

    a. For Source File, enter the filename and **.dif** (e.g., enter **salespro.dif**).

    b. For Source Type, enter **dif.**

    c. For Destination File, enter the same filename, but give it the extension *.doc* (e.g., enter **salespro.doc**).

    d. For Destination Type, enter **mm**.

4. Press the F10 key to start the conversion.

5. When the conversion operation finishes, press Esc twice to return to the Main Menu.

Multiplan Procedure

To prepare a Multiplan spreadsheet for copying into an Advantage document:

1. Start Multiplan as usual.
2. Create the spreadsheet or load it in from disk with a Transfer Load command.
3. Put your Advantage data disk in drive B.
4. Select the Print Margins command. When its parameter list appears, change "left" and "top" to 0. Press Tab twice to reach "print length" and enter the number of spreadsheet rows you want to copy into your Advantage document. Enter the same value for "page length," then press Return.
5. Select Print Options. For "area," enter the row and column ranges for the portion of the spreadsheet you want and press Return. For example, to extract rows 6 through 24 of columns 1 through 7, enter **r6:24c1:7**.
6. To save the spreadsheet material on disk, use a Print File command. When Multiplan asks for the filename, enter **b:**, the name you want to give the file, and the extension **.txt**. (For example, **b:salespro.txt** would be suitable for a table of sales projections.) Press Return to start the save operation.
7. When the Command menu reappears, select Quit to leave Multiplan.

Your **.txt** file is in ASCII format. To convert it to an Advantage document:

1. Put your Advanced Utilities disk in drive A, replacing the Multiplan disk, and enter **util**.
2. Select "File Conversion" from the Advanced Utilities menu, then "Convert Document(s)" from the File Conversion menu.
3. When the Convert a Document menu appears:
    a. For Source File, enter the filename and **.txt** (e.g., enter **salespro.txt**).
    b. For Source Type, enter **ascii**.
    c. For Destination File, enter the same filename, but give it an extension of **doc** (e.g., enter **salespro.doc**).
    d. For Destination Type, enter **mm**.

4. Press the F10 key to start the conversion.

5. When the conversion operation finishes, press Esc twice to return to the Main Menu.

Copying Spreadsheets into Documents

Once you have converted a spreadsheet to an Advantage DOC file, you can copy it into another document using the standard External Copy (Shift-F8) operation we described earlier; see "Copying between Documents" in Chapter 6. If the spreadsheet has a different format than your text, be sure to press F9 before you respond to the *COPY WHAT?* prompt. Of course, if your document contains text following the spreadsheet, you must also insert a page format line (using Alt-F9) after the spreadsheet to restore the text format.

A problem with spreadsheets is that they are often wider than your paper. (For example, Multiplan provides 63 columns of up to 32 characters each—a width of over 2000 characters.) To use a wide spreadsheet, simply copy it as we just described, then distribute it over several pages with column move and copy operations; see "Column Operations" in Chapter 6.

Database Management Programs

Database management programs let you create, search, sort, combine, and perform arithmetic operations on lists of text and numbers. For example, you can enter purchase orders into a database, then have it produce a list of customers who bought more than, say, 100 units in the last year. Or you could make the database produce a file of customers in a given state, sorted by city.

Producing Form Letters from Database Files

In Chapter 8 we described how to produce form letters with Advantage. To do this, you must merge a generalized copy of the letter with a data file containing the items you want to insert (e.g., name, address, account status). Let us now describe how to use a data file produced by *dBASE II*, the popular database management program from Ashton-Tate. This approach allows you to use dBASE II to select entries and sort them (say, alphabetically or by zip code) before using Advantage to print the form letters.

Suppose you have a dBASE II file called CUSTMRS that holds current information about your company's customers. Each entry or *record* in the file has the following format:

```
company, street, city, state, zipcode, indtype, buyer,
salutation, telephone, salesyr, region
```

At the beginning of a new year you want to write a letter offering special terms to each customer who bought at least $100,000 worth of goods last year. So you must select these customers' records from the dBASE II file and list them in a form Advantage can use.

To begin, start dBASE II, then enter the following commands to select the qualifying customers (assuming your data files are on drive B):

```
USE B:CUSTMRS
COPY TO B:BIGSLS.TXT FOR SALESYR>=100000 SDF DELIMITED WITH "
QUIT
```

The dBASE II commands and qualifiers here have the following meanings:

- *USE B:CUSTMRS* specifies which database file dBASE II is to use.
- *COPY* copies from the database in USE to another file.
- *TO B:BIGSLS.TXT* assigns the name of the new file.
- *FOR SALESYR> = 100000* selects records with yearly sales greater than or equal to 100000 (> = means "greater than or equal to").
- *SDF* indicates that the file should be in a standard (ASCII) format that Advantage can use.
- *DELIMITED WITH* " not only encloses each data item in double quotation marks but also separates fields with commas. The quotation marks are necessary because company names and addresses could include commas, as in Pierce, Colby, and Smith, Inc. or 3800 Fifth Avenue, Suite 1205. If the commas are not within quotation marks, Advantage will think they are separate data items.

The entries in the BIGSLS.TXT file will look like the following:

```
"Bay Tea Co.","105 Federal Ave.","Boston","MA","01284","Food","Mr.
Thomas Wheaton","Tom","617-555-1776","123000","NE"
"XYZ Computers","34 Lake Rd.","Big Palm","FL","32650","Computer","Ms.
Carrie Raye","Carrie","904-987-2854","140000","SE"
```

This represents two records, one for Bay Tea Co. and another for XYZ Computers

Finally, you can prepare the Merge document—the letter you want to send to the BIGSLS customer list. This letter, shown in Figure 10-1, begins with a *DEFINE* block. The first line in this block specifies what kind of data file you are using. dBASE II produces "sequential" files; some other database programs produce "random" files (see the *Advanced User's Guide* for descriptions of these file types).

The rest of the lines in the DEFINE block list the items' field names in the order in which they occur in the data file. If you aren't sure of this order, you can enter DISPLAY STRUCTURE while in dBASE II to obtain it. When you finish the letter, select "Merge Print Utility" from the Main Menu to print the copies.

```
|DEFINE|
file type sequential
field name company
field name street
field name city
field name state
field name zipcode
field name indtype
field name buyer
field name salutation
field name telephone
field name salesyr
field name region
|END DEFINE|
```

                              February 6, 1986

|buyer|
|company|
|street|
|city|, |state| |zipcode|

Dear |salutation|:

    We are pleased to inform you that your company has qualified
for our 1986 Special Discount Program. As a valued customer,
you are entitled to the following privileges:

    1) 45-day terms on all purchases.

    2) An extra 2% discount in advance, as well as our usual 2%
       discount for payments made within 15 days.

    3) Free returns (you pay shipping costs only) on all goods
       unsold after 90 days.

We appreciate your patronage and plan to do all we can to
continue this important relationship.

                              Sincerely,

                              Ray Cornell
                              National Sales Manager.

**Figure 10-1. Form letter to be sent to customer list selected by
dBASE II.**

11

MultiMate On-File

What Is On-File?

The MultiMate On-File Information Manager is a program that computerizes the standard index card filing system you find in offices. With it, you can do anything you would with 3-by-5 cards, but you do it on the computer rather than with real cards. That is, On-File lets you create cards, edit them, and sort them into decks based on some criteria (i.e., all cards having a certain zip code). And because these tasks are performed electronically, you can do them quicker and easier than you could with cards.

In this chapter we introduce On-File and suggest a few simple, yet useful, jobs you can do with it. In Chapters 12 and 13, we discuss operations that use some of On-File's more advanced features.

Major Features

MultiMate On-File can perform the following tasks:

- Create card boxes, each having a specified name.
- Create new cards, and add them to those in a card box.
- Edit or delete cards.
- Search for cards having a specific subject, index word, color, or date. Cards that match the search criteria form a "deck."
- Display or print cards that have been selected by a search operation.
- Allow you to create templates for commonly-used card formats.
- Sort cards based on the information they contain.
- Print mailing labels.

- Merge cards with MultiMate documents to produce form letters, reports, or mailing labels.
- Convert the data on cards to files that can be used by spreadsheets, databases, and other programs.
- Convert files produced by other programs to cards.

Typical Uses

MultiMate On-File can keep track of any kind of information for which you would normally use 3-by-5 index cards. Typical uses include:

- Lists of names, addresses, and telephone numbers.
- Logs of business conversations.
- Lists of customers, contacts, and contributors.
- Mailing lists.
- Personnel records.
- Accounts payable and receivable.
- Lists of items in a book, stamp, or record collection.
- Club and class rosters.
- Medical, insurance, and real estate records.
- Indexes and bibliographies.
- Recipe files.
- Research notes.
- Inventories of credit cards and personal effects.
- Christmas card lists.
- Lists of birthdays, anniversaries, and special occasions.
- "Flash cards" to help students learn material.

Setting Up On-File

The "First Things First" chapter in the MultiMate On-File manual describes how to set up On-File for your daily work. For a computer with floppy disks, the manual tells you:

1. How to make working copies of the System and Utilities disks.
2. How to create a blank data disk (the manual calls it a "non-bootable diskette") to store card boxes you will create with On-File. This is the same procedure you use to create data disks for Advantage.

For a computer with a hard disk drive, the manual tells you how to install DOS on the hard disk, how to create a *path* to the DOS subdirectory, and how to create a CONFIG.SYS file. You already did these things when you set up Advantage, so you can skip them here. However, you must perform the manual's procedure for copying the On-File disks to a hard disk subdirectory.

The manual suggests that you copy the On-File disks to a new subdirectory called *of*. However, you can copy them to your Advantage subdirectory (*mm*), to keep everything together.

Installation

Once you have made working copies of the On-File disks (or have copied them onto a hard disk), you must customize On-File for your own computer. To do this, you run a special *install* program in which you:

1. Specify which kind of display you have, monochrome or color.
2. Record your name, address, and Advantage serial number.
3. Specify the *default drives* that you will use for card boxes and external files. (In each case, enter **B** for floppy disk drives or **C** for a hard disk drive).
4. Specify the *installed drives*—A and B for floppy disks, A and C for a floppy disk and a hard disk.
5. Tell On-File whether you want it to run with or without sound. (Unless you're a masochist, I suggest you turn the sound off.)

Starting On-File

Starting On-File is similar to starting Advantage, except when the DOS prompt (A> or C>) appears, you enter **mm** rather than **wp**. (Hard disk users: this assumes you have created the MM.BAT startup file we describe in Chapter 1.) This makes Advantage display the *Boot-up Menu* shown in Figure 11-1 instead of the usual Main Menu.

Note that the Boot-up Menu lets you get into Advantage (labeled "MultiMate Professional Word Processor" here) or the Advantage utilities ("MultiMate Advanced Utilities and Conversions"). But

```
        MultiMate Advantage*
    Professional Word Processor Version 3.60
          (C) Copyright 1986
      Multimate International Corporation


      1) MultiMate Professional Word Processor
      2) MultiMate On-File
      3) MultiMate Advanced Utilities and Conversions
      4) MultiMate On-File Utility

      8) Execute Other Programs
      9) Return to DOS

              DESIRED FUNCTION:
      Enter the number of the function; press RETURN

      THE PROXIMITY/MERRIAM-WEBSTER LINGUIBASE
        (C) Copyright 1983, Proximity Devices Corporation
        (C) Copyright 1983, Merriam-Webster, Inc.

          (C) COPYRIGHT 1986, SWFTE, Inc.**

      *Trademark of Multimate International Corporation
      **Trademark of SWFTE, INCORPORATED
```

Figure 11-1. Advantage Boot-up Menu.
Courtesy of Multimate International Corp.

what interests us here is that it lets you get into MultiMate On-File.
To start On-File from the Boot-up menu, type **2** and press Return.

When On-File's copyright information appears, press the space
bar. On-File shows a title screen and asks for a Box Name. We don't
have any card boxes yet (unless you have copied the DEMO box
that comes with On-File), so we must create one.

Creating a Card Box

On-File card boxes are like the real ones you keep on a desk,
except they are electronic. On-File boxes can also hold more cards

than real boxes; about 750 cards on a floppy disk or thousands of cards on a hard disk.

To create a card box, enter its name (up to 25 characters) on the title screen, then press Return. Let's create a card box to hold questions and answers for a trivia game. Enter trivia in the *Box Name*: field and press Return.

When On-File asks:

```
Start a new box? (y/n)
```

at the bottom of the screen, type **y**. On-File displays:

```
New box is being created
```

then:

```
Setup of your box was successful...
Press any key to continue
```

Press Return to obtain On-File's *Main Menu* (see Figure 11-2).

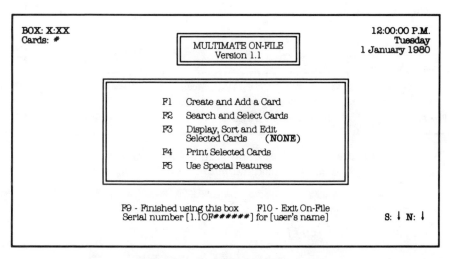

Figure 11-2. On-File's Main Menu.
Courtesy of Multimate International Corp.

Figure 11-2 shows a generalized version of the Main Menu. Your screen should show *B:TRIVIA* (or *C:TRIVIA*, for a hard disk) and *Cards: 0* at the top left-hand corner. The current date and time are at the top right-hand corner, and your name and serial number are at the bottom.

Creating Cards

To add a card to your new card box, press F1 to choose "Create and Add a Card" from the Main Menu. This makes On-File display a *Create and Add a Card* screen. Figure 11-3 shows this screen, and labels some key areas on it. Before continuing, let's discuss the areas.

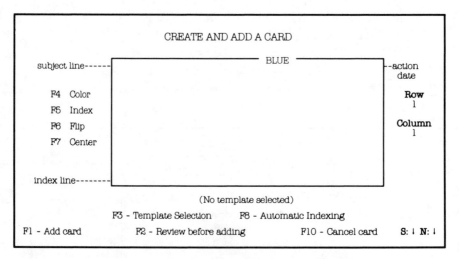

Figure 11-3. Create and Add a Card screen.
Courtesy of Multimate International Corp.

Areas on a Card

Each card has five areas: subject line, color, action date, text, and index line.

The *subject line* can hold words or phrases (up to 35 characters) that describe the contents of the card.

The *color* word indicates the card's color. This is for the benefit of people who have a monochrome display, which doesn't show colors. The card in Figure 11-3 is blue, but you can change it to brown, green, pink, purple, red, white, or yellow. To change the color, press the F4 (Color) key. Each time you press F4, On-File switches to the next color in the preceding list.

On-File automatically sets the *action date* to the date when you create a card. It shows the date in the form

```
dd MMM yyyy
```

where *dd* is the day, *MMM* is the first three letters of the month, and *yyyy* is the year. For example, it would show March 24, 1986 as 24 MAR 1986. The On-File manual describes five other date formats you can use.

There are two *text areas* where you can enter data, 10 lines on the front and 12 on the back. To see the back of a card, press the F6 (Flip) key. Pressing F6 again flips to the front. To center a line of text, press the F7 (Center) key. Note that this differs from Advantage, where you press F3 to center a line.

The *index line* holds key words that help you cross-reference the card with other cards. Typical index words are the abbreviation for a state (e.g., CA), the name of an industry group (e.g., Food), or the ranking of a company (e.g., A or B). Index words can be up to 18 characters long. You can put as many as you want on the index line as long as you don't exceed 50 characters.

On-File lets you use the color, subject, date, or index words to search the box and form a deck. We discuss this procedure later in the chapter.

Finally, at the right-hand side of the "Create and Add a Card" screen are Row and Column values that indicate the cursor position. These are On-File's equivalent of Advantage's LINE and COL indicators.

Our trivia game is to have questions and answers in four categories: geography, sports, entertainment, and history. On the front of each card, we will put the category on the subject line, the question in the text area, and one or more cross-reference words on the index line. We will put the answer on the back.

Filling in a Card

Figure 11-4 shows the front and back of the first card we want to put into our box. The subject (*Geography*) is on the top row, the question is on row 5, and the index words are on row 12, the index line. The answer is on row 1 of the back.

```
_____ BLUE _____
Geography



What is the capital of Pennsylvania?




US Capitals
_____


_____ BLUE _____
Harrisburg






_____ back of card _____
```

Figure 11-4. Sample card.

Enter the front of this card now. On-File has started the cursor at the beginning of the subject line, so you can enter **Geography** immediately. (Note that when you type the *G* in *Geography*, On-File displays the date at the top right-hand corner.) Press Return to move down the card; the Row value shows what line you are on. If you accidentally pass row 5, where the question belongs, press the up-arrow key to backtrack.

On-File also lets you correct mistakes, but does not provide all the handy features that Advantage does. For example, to insert characters, press Ins (not +); to delete them, press Del (not -). You may also press the Backspace key to delete the preceding character.

When you finish the front, press F6 to flip the card over, then type the answer on the back. Finally, press the F1 key to add this card to the box. On-File returns you to the Main Menu.

Creating Additional Cards

Now add nine more cards to the box, using the same procedure as before. The data is as follows:

1. *Subject:* Geography
   Text: What is the capital of Pennsylvania?
   Index words: US Capitals
   Text on back: Harrisburg
2. *Subject:* Sports
   Text: In which stadium do the Washington Redskins play their home games?
   Index words: Football Stadiums
   Text on back: Robert F. Kennedy (RFK) Stadium
3. *Subject:* Sports
   Text: Who is the head coach of the Pittsburgh Steelers?
   Index words: Football Coaches
   Text on back: Chuck Noll
4. *Subject:* Sports
   Text: What is Billie Jean King's maiden name?
   Index word: Tennis
   Text on back: Billie Jean Moffitt
5. *Subject:* History
   Text: The ancient Greeks called the god of wine Dionysus. What did the Romans call him?
   Index words: Greece Ancient Mythology
   Text on back: Bacchus
6. *Subject:* History
   Text: What does the "S" in Harry S Truman stand for?

Index words: US Presidents
Text on back: Nothing. Truman had no middle name, just an initial.
7. *Subject:* Entertainment
   Text: What was the theme song of the Duke Ellington Orchestra?
   Index words: Music Jazz
   Text on back: Things Ain't What They Used to Be
8. *Subject:* Entertainment
   Text: What is Frank Sinatra's middle name?
   Index words: Music Popular Singers
   Text on back: Albert
9. *Subject:* Entertainment
   Text: By what name was Claude Dunkenfield better known?
   Index words: Movies Comedians
   Text on back: W. C. Fields

Automated Indexing Techniques

To create the trivia cards, you typed in the index words manually. In some cases (e.g., "Music" and "Football"), this involved repeating index words that appear on previous cards. Well, I have good news: On-File can save you from typing index words. Specifically, it can copy to the index line any word that appears on the current card or any index word you used earlier. To copy a word on the current card to the index line, put the cursor on it and press the F5 key.

To use an existing index word, press the F8 key to get *automatic indexing*. On-File displays the first available index word (alphabetically) at the bottom of the screen. To copy that word to the index line, press the F5 key. Otherwise, to see the next word or preceding word in the list, press the right- or left-arrow key.

Because On-File displays only one word at a time, the automatic indexing feature is of questionable value. Its primary use is to check an existing index word, so you don't accidentally re-enter it with a different spelling.

Searching for Cards

Quite often you want to select similar cards from a box so you can review them or print them. Suppose you want to obtain a list of all your company's customers in a certain state.

On-File lets you search a card box for a specific subject, color, action date, or index word. When the search ends, you can display the cards it found. If they are indeed the ones you want, you can *select* them to form a "deck." You can then display, edit, or print the cards in the deck. In Chapters 12 and 13, we describe some other things you can do with selected decks, such as merge the data on them with an Advantage document.

Search Operations

To search a card box, obtain the Main Menu, then press the F2 key to choose "Search and Select Cards." This makes On-File display its *Search and Select Cards* menu (see Figure 11-5). Here, you may search the card box by subject (F1), index (F2), color (F3), or date (F4). You may also select all of the cards without searching; we discuss that option shortly.

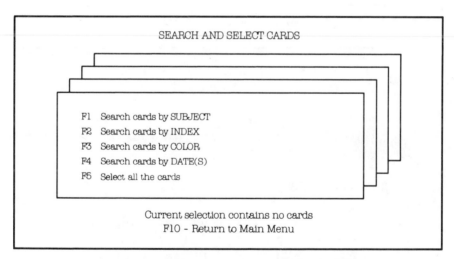

Figure 11-5. Search and Select Cards menu.
Courtesy of Multimate International Corp.

When you search by subject, index, or color, On-File lists the available choices on the screen. Use the arrow keys to highlight the item you want to search for, then press the F1 key to start searching.

Searching by date is a little different. When you press F4, On-File displays a *Search Cards by Date(s)* screen (Figure 11-6), and assumes you want to find cards that have a specific action date. If you do, enter the date in On-File's regular format (e.g., **11 SEP 1986**) and press F1. Otherwise, press the down-arrow key to choose one of the three other options.

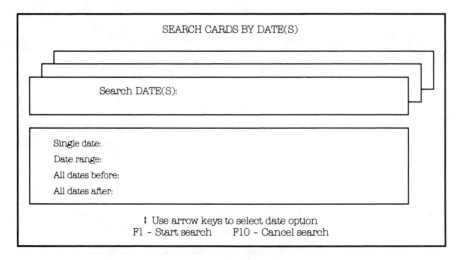

Figure 11-6. Search Cards by Date(s) screen.
Courtesy of Multimate International Corp.

For the "Date range:" option, you must enter a starting and ending date. For example, to search for cards having dates in September of 1986, you enter

1 SEP 1986 to **30 SEP 1986**

The "All dates before:" prompt is somewhat misleading in that it *includes* the specified date in the search. The prompt should actually read "All dates on or before:". Thus, to search for cards dated prior to September 5, 1986, enter

4 SEP 1986

Similarly, the "All dates after:" option searches for cards dated on or after the specified day.

When On-File has finished searching, it displays a *Create and Edit Card Selection* menu (Figure 11-7) and tells how many cards it found. The menu provides five choices, of which you often want the last one, "Display these new cards."

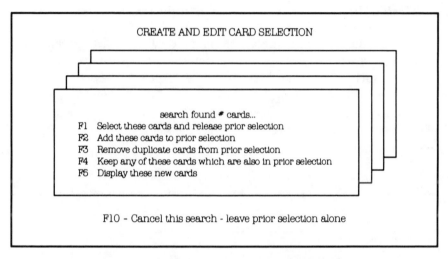

CREATE AND EDIT CARD SELECTION

search found # cards...
F1   Select these cards and release prior selection
F2   Add these cards to prior selection
F3   Remove duplicate cards from prior selection
F4   Keep any of these cards which are also in prior selection
F5   Display these new cards

F10 - Cancel this search - leave prior selection alone

Figure 11-7. Create and Edit Card Selection menu.
Courtesy of Multimate International Corp.

Displaying Cards Found by a Search

To display the cards a search has found, press the F5 key. On-File shows the first five cards (if it found that many) on a *Temporary Display of Cards Found By Search* screen. The cards are stacked so that only the top card is entirely visible. Now you can flip the card over (press F6) or display the next card (F1). When you finish, press F10 to return to the Create and Edit Card Selection menu.

Selecting the Search Cards

If On-File's search has found the cards you want, tell it so by pressing F1 to choose "Select these cards—release prior selection" from the Create and Edit Card Selection menu. On-File now assumes you want to search through the selected deck—to narrow in on even fewer cards—and displays the Search and Select Cards menu. To stop searching and return to the Main Menu, press F10; to do another search, press F1 through F4 or a new option, F6.

Searching for Words or Phrases

By pressing F6 from the Create and Edit Card Selection menu, you can search a deck for cards that contain a specific word or phrase such as a name. Here, On-File displays a *Match Selected Cards for Word or Phrase* screen (Figure 11-8) that looks like the screen you use to create a new card. On it, enter the word or phrase you want to find, then press F1 to start the search, or "scan," in On-File's terminology.

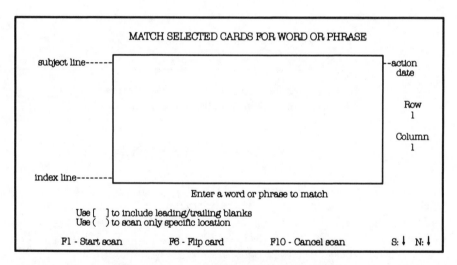

Figure 11-8. Match Selected Cards for Word or Phrase screen.
Courtesy of Multimate International Corp.

The way you enter the word or phrase tells On-File how much latitude to take when it searches the deck. Specifically,

- To search for a word or phase and any variations of it, just enter it. For example, entering **adjust** makes On-File locate not only *adjust*, but *adjustment, adjusted, readjust,* and so forth.

- To search for only the word you enter, precede it with a left bracket ([) and follow it with a right bracket (]). For example, to search for only *adjust*, enter **[adjust].**

Here, you can enter the word or phrase anywhere on the card. In turn, On-File will check everything on the cards (including the back) for a match.

On-File can also check for matches at a specific location on the cards. To make it do this, you must enter the word or phrase inside parentheses at that location. This option is mainly useful when you're using templates. We discuss templates in Chapter 12.

Building Decks through Multiple Searches

On-File also lets you build a deck from the results of several searches. Suppose you want to select the green, white, and brown cards. To build a deck in this way, perform the first search and select it using the "Select these cards—release prior selection" option on the Create and Edit Card Selection menu. Then obtain the Search and Select Cards menu, press F10 to return to the Main Menu, and perform the second search. This time, when the Create and Edit Card Selection menu appears, press F2 to "Add these cards to prior selection." Repeat this search-and-add procedure until your deck is complete.

Search Example

To see how a search works, let's find all the Sports cards in our TRIVIA box. Do this as follows:

1. Press F2 to choose "Search and Select Cards" from the Main Menu.
2. When the Search and Select Cards menu appears, press F1 to search by subject. On-File lists the available subjects—in fact, it repeats them to fill the screen!

3. Press the down-arrow key to highlight Sports, then press F1 to start searching. When On-File finishes searching, it shows the Create and Edit Card Selection menu and reports "search found 3 cards..." at the top.

4. To see the cards the search has found, press F5. This produces the three cards, with the Billie Jean King card in front. To see the next card, press F1.

   By the way, note that On-File has capitalized the index words and arranged them in alphabetical order. It does this whenever it adds a card to the box.

5. Press F10 to leave this display.

6. When the Create and Edit Card Selection menu appears, press F1 to *select* the search cards. On-File shows the Search and Select Cards menu, and reports "Current selection contains 3 cards" at the bottom.

7. Press F10 to return to the Main Menu.

Note that the F3 option now reads "Display, Sort and Edit Selected Cards (3)." The (3) reminds you that On-File has a deck of three cards that you can display, sort, or edit.

Selecting All Cards

You can also select all the cards in a box by pressing F5 when the Search and Select Cards menu appears. When you do this, On-File asks

```
Are you sure? (y/n)
```

Type **y**, then press Esc to return to the Main Menu.

Editing the Selected Cards

When displaying a deck, you may spot some errors on one or more cards. To correct them, press F3 to choose "Display, Sort and Edit Selected Cards" from the Main Menu. This makes On-File display the first five cards in the deck, in a format like the one shown in Figure 11-9.

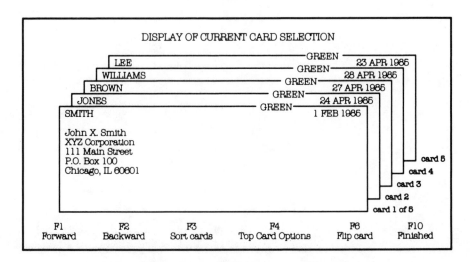

DISPLAY OF CURRENT CARD SELECTION

LEE — GREEN — 23 APR 1985
WILLIAMS — GREEN — 28 APR 1985
BROWN — GREEN — 27 APR 1985
JONES — GREEN — 24 APR 1985
SMITH — GREEN — 1 FEB 1985

John X. Smith
XYZ Corporation
111 Main Street
P.O. Box 100
Chicago, IL 60601

card 5
card 4
card 3
card 2
card 1 of 5

F1	F2	F3	F4	F6	F10
Forward	Backward	Sort cards	Top Card Options	Flip card	Finished

Figure 11-9. Typical display of selected cards.
Courtesy of Multimate International Corp.

You can only operate on the top (front) card. Therefore, to do something to a card that is deeper in the deck, press F1 until it is on top. (If you accidentally pass it, press F2 to backtrack.) When you reach the card you want, press F4 for "Top Card Options." On-File displays the options shown in Figure 11-10. To edit the front of the card, press F4; to edit the back, press F6, then F4. On-File shows the card on an *Edit Card* screen (see Figure 11-11).

Now you can move the cursor to the material you want to change and make the changes. When you finish, press F1 to save the card or, if you accidentally got the wrong card, press F10.

Deleting Cards

After selecting a deck, you can delete cards you no longer want. Further, if you have searched specifically to find unneeded cards, you can delete the entire deck!

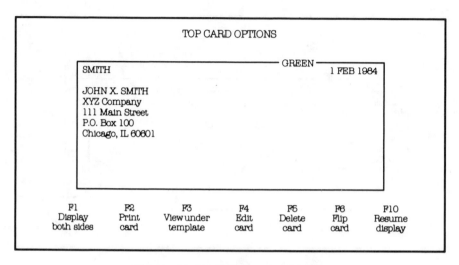

Figure 11-10. Top card options.
Courtesy of Multimate International Corp.

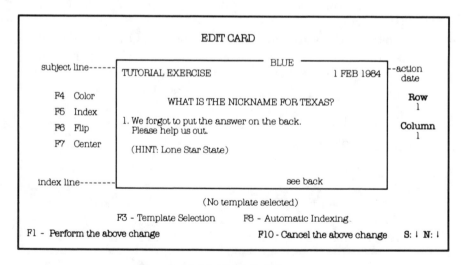

Figure 11-11. Edit Card screen.
Courtesy of Multimate International Corp.

Deleting Individual Cards

To delete a card, start as you would to edit one, but when the Top Card Options screen appears, press F5. Then, when the card appears, press F1.

Deleting a Deck

To delete all selected cards at once, obtain the Main Menu and choose "Use Special Features" by pressing F5. When On-File displays its *Use Special Features* menu (Figure 11-12), press F4 for "Delete selected cards."

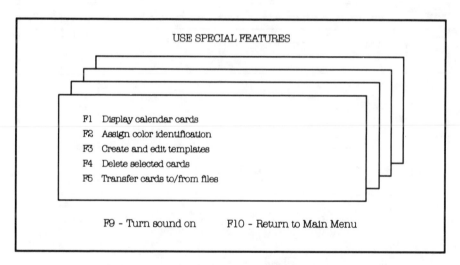

USE SPECIAL FEATURES

F1   Display calendar cards
F2   Assign color identification
F3   Create and edit templates
F4   Delete selected cards
F5   Transfer cards to/from files

F9 - Turn sound on   F10 - Return to Main Menu

Figure 11-12. Use Special Features menu.
Courtesy of Multimate International Corp.

Since deleting an entire deck is a drastic action, On-File lets you change your mind. It displays

```
# cards will be deleted
Confirm by entering (y/n)
```

Type **y** to delete the deck or **n** to cancel the delete operation. Either way, On-File next tells you to "Press any key" to continue. To get

back to the Use Special Features menu, press Return; to get back to
the Main Menu, press Esc.

Printing Cards

To print a card deck, press F4 from the Main Menu. When On-
File displays its *Print Selected Cards* menu (Figure 11-13), press F2
for "Print cards."

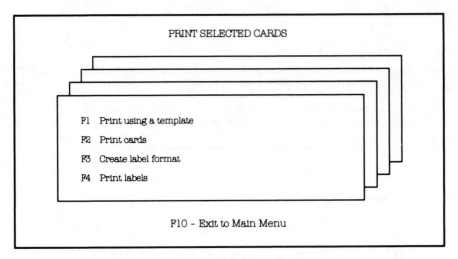

Figure 11-13. Print Selected Cards menu.
Courtesy of Multimate International Corp.

On-File shows how it will print cards by presenting a *Print On-
File Cards* screen (Figure 11-14). Here, it displays a box and the
message "Margin: 0"; this means On-File assumes you want to start
printing at the left-hand edge. To create a left margin, press the
right-arrow key (or the left-arrow key, if you move too far).

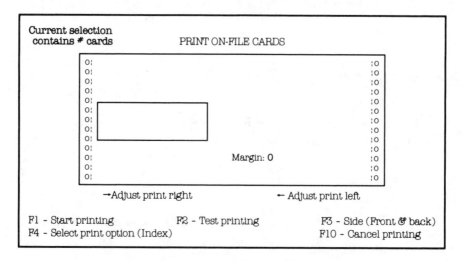

Figure 11-14. Print On-File Cards screen.
Courtesy of Multimate International Corp.

Before printing, you may choose from three options:

- *F2—Test printing* previews the print format, which helps ensure that the margin is where you want it. Specifically, it prints two rows of 50 Xs at your margin setting to show where the front and back sides will appear. You can then adjust the margin if necessary.
- *F3—Side* lets you print just the front, just the back, or both sides of the cards.
- *F4—Select print option* lets you print on 3-by-5 index cards or on continuous 11-inch paper. If you select 11-inch paper, On-File will print both sides of the cards. However, if a back side is blank, it simply prints "Back of card is blank" for the back.

To print the three-card *Sports* deck you have selected, switch your printer on and press F4 to specify 11-inch paper (assuming that's what you are using). Then press F1 for "Start printing." When On-File shows:

```
Ready printer
Press any key
```

press Return.

When printing finishes, press Return to get back to the Print Selected Cards menu, then F10 to obtain the Main Menu.

Leaving On-File

If you are done working with On-File, press F10 from the Main Menu. When the screen shows:

```
Are you sure? (y/n)
```

type **y**. This clears the screen and puts the DOS prompt (A> or C>) at the top. Now your choices are:

1. To work on an Advantage document, enter **wp** and (if you wish) a document name, then press Return.
2. To get back into On-File, type either **mm** and Return (to obtain Advantage's Boot-Up Menu) or **onfile** and Return (to go directly to On-File's Main Menu).
3. To format a disk, or do something else that requires the DOS facilities, enter a DOS command.
4. To quit altogether, switch the computer off.

Listing the Available Card Boxes

When On-File's title screen asks for the name of a card box, it doesn't tell you which ones are available. Thus, to use an existing box, you must know its name beforehand. To produce a list of card boxes on a disk, put the DOS prompt on the screen and enter the DOS Directory command

  dir b:*.crd

(or **dir *.crd**, if you have a hard disk).

Copying Card Boxes

Sometimes you need two similar card boxes. For example, you may want one box that contains telephone numbers for both your friends and business acquaintances, and another that contains just business numbers. To create the second card box, simply copy the first box, then change the copy (i.e., add or delete cards) as needed.

Copying a card box involves using the DOS COPY command. With the DOS prompt on the screen, enter a command of the form

copy *oldbox.** **b:***newbox.**

DOS copies three files: *oldbox*.idx (the card box), *oldbox*.crd (cards in the box), and *oldbox*.tem (templates).

Copying Cards between Boxes

Sometimes you want to copy a set of cards from one box to another. For example, if you have six separate card boxes that contain customer data for your company's six sales regions, you may want to combine them to form a box that has all the customers.

Copying cards between boxes involves two operations: writing the cards to be copied to a temporary holding file on disk, then reading the contents of the holding file into the box that is to receive the cards.

Writing Cards to a File

To begin, select the cards you want to copy and return to the Main Menu. To create the holding file:

1. Choose "Use Special Features" from the Main Menu and "Transfer cards to/from files" from the Use Special Features menu. On-File shows its *Transfer Cards to/from Files* menu (see Figure 11-15).

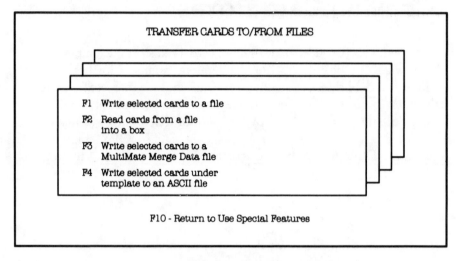

TRANSFER CARDS TO/FROM FILES

F1   Write selected cards to a file

F2   Read cards from a file
     into a box

F3   Write selected cards to a
     MultiMate Merge Data file

F4   Write selected cards under
     template to an ASCII file

F10 - Return to Use Special Features

Figure 11-15. Transfer Cards to/from Files menu.
Courtesy of Multimate International Corp.

2. Choose "Write selected cards to a file," then enter the name of the holding file and press Return. To keep things simple, enter the name of the first card box here.
3. When On-File finishes writing the cards, press Return to get back to the Transfer Cards to/from Files menu, then Esc to get back to the Main Menu.

Now you must select the second box and read the temporary file into it. Begin by pressing F9 from the Main Menu to tell On-File you are finished using the first box. When the title screen appears, enter the name of the second box and press Return to obtain the Main Menu.

Reading Cards from a File

To create cards using the temporary file, read the file as follows:

1. Choose "Transfer cards to/from Files" from the Use Special Features menu and "Read cards from a file into a box" from the Transfer Cards to/from Files menu.
2. Enter the name of your holding file and press Return.

3. When On-File finishes reading the cards, press Return to get back to the Transfer Cards to/from Files menu and Esc to get back to the Main Menu.

Deleting Temporary Files

When a copy operation finishes, you no longer need the temporary holding file. To delete it, return to DOS and enter a command of the form:

erase b:*tempfile.***mof**

If you don't remember the name of the file, get a list of all files that have the temporary file extension, *.mof*, by entering:

dir b:*.mof

where **.mof* tells DOS to list all files that have the extension *.mof*.
You can also delete all the temporary files on your disk, by entering:

erase b:*.mof

Questions and Answers

Question: I have cards that log this year's sales bookings, where the colors signify the quarter: blue for first quarter, green for second, red for third, and white for fourth. One of the index words is a state abbreviation. How can I find the cards for California bookings during the third quarter?

Answer: Choose "Search and Select Cards" from the Main Menu and "Search cards by COLOR" from the Search and Select Cards menu. When the Search Cards by Color menu appears, highlight *RED* and press F1. When On-File finishes searching, press F10 to return to the Search and Select Cards menu, then choose "Search Cards by INDEX." When the Search Cards by Index screen appears, use the arrow keys to highlight *CA* and press F1 to start searching again.

Question: I have a card box that holds telephone numbers for both my friends and business acquaintances. To distinguish them, I put the index word *PERSONAL* on friends' cards. How can I form a deck containing only business cards?

Answer: You must select the entire box and then deselect the non-business cards. To begin, choose "Search and Select Cards" from the Main Menu and "Select all the cards" from the Search and Select Cards menu. When the Main Menu reappears, do another search, but this time choose "Search cards by INDEX" from the Search and Select Cards menu, and tell On-File to search for *PERSONAL*. When the second search finishes, choose "Remove duplicate cards from prior selection" from the Create and Edit Card Selection menu.

Question: How can I form a deck of all cards dated either January or April of 1986?

Answer: This takes two search operations. To begin the first one, choose "Search and Select Cards" from the Main Menu, then "Search cards by DATE(S)." When the "Search Cards by Date(s)" screen appears, press the down-arrow key to choose the *Date range:* option and enter

1 JAN 1986 to **31 JAN 1986**

Finally, press F1 to start searching.

When On-File finishes searching, it displays the Create and Edit Card Selection menu. Choose "Select these cards—release prior selection," then press F10 to return to the Search and Select Cards menu. Now do another search by dates and enter:

1 APR 1986 to **30 APR 1986**

for *Date range:*. At the end of this search, choose "Add these cards to prior selection" and press Esc to return to the Main Menu.

Hints and Warnings

1. On-File accepts card box names of up to 25 characters, but you should limit them to eight characters, because that's all DOS displays if you ask for a listing or *directory* of box names.
2. You cannot use bold print, underlining, or any other special print format on cards.
3. When performing multiple searches, be aware of the difference between searching the selected deck (to reduce the number of selected cards) and searching the card box (to add new cards to the selected

deck). To search the selected deck, use the options on the Create and Edit Card Selection menu. To search the card box, choose "Search and Select Cards" from the Main Menu.

4. You can also *deselect* cards from a deck. To do this, search for the cards you want to deselect using the Main Menu's "Search and Select Cards" option. When the Create and Edit Card Selection menu appears, choose "Remove duplicate cards from prior selection."

5. Generally, pressing F1 tells On-File to complete an operation, while pressing F10 tells it to cancel the operation (i.e., return to the preceding screen). Pressing Esc also cancels an operation, and returns you to the Main Menu.

Key Point Summary

Table 11-1 summarizes the On-File keys and commands introduced in this chapter. There are more in Chapters 12 and 13, and a complete list in Appendix B.

Table 11-1. Commands introduced in Chapter 11.

Main Menu

F1—Create and Add a Card
F2—Search and Select Cards
F3—Display, Sort and Edit Selected Cards
F4—Print Selected Cards
F5—Use Special Features
F9—Finished using this box
F10—Exit On-File (return to DOS)

Create and Add a Card menu (F1 from Main Menu)

F1—Add card (to box)
F2—Review before adding
F4—Color (change color)
F5—Index (use current text word as index word)
F6—Flip
F7—Center (current text line)
F8—Automatic Indexing (choose from previous index words)
F10—Cancel card

Search and Select Cards menu (F2 from Main Menu)

F1—Search cards by SUBJECT
F2—Search cards by INDEX (word)
F3—Search cards by COLOR

Table 11-1. Commands introduced in Chapter 11. (continued)

> F4—Search cards by DATE(S)
> *Create and Edit Card Selection menu* (after F1, F2, F3, or F4)
> F1—Select these cards—release prior selection
> F2—Add these cards to prior selection
> F3—Remove duplicate cards from prior selection
> F4—Keep any of these cards which are also in prior selection
> F5—Display these new cards
> F10—Cancel this search—leave prior selection alone
> F5—Select all the cards (without searching)
> F6—Match selected cards for word or phrase (appears when cards
> have been selected)
> F1—Start scan
> F6—Flip card
> F10—Cancel scan
> F10—Return to Main Menu

Display of Current Card Selection menu (F3 from Main Menu)

> F1—Forward (next card)
> F2—Backward (preceding card)
> F4—Top Card Options
> F1—Display both sides
> F2—Print card
> F4—Edit card
> F1—Perform the above change
> F8—Automatic indexing
> F10—Cancel the above change
> F5—Delete card
> F6—Flip card
> F10—Resume display
> F6—Flip card
> F10—Finished (return to Main Menu)

Print Selected Cards menu (F4 from Main Menu)

> F2—Print cards
> F10—Exit to Main Menu

Use Special Features menu (F5 from Main Menu)

> F4—Delete selected cards
> F5—Transfer cards to/from files
> F1—Write selected cards to a file
> F2—Read cards from a file into a box
> F10—Return to Use Special Features
> F10—Return to Main Menu

1. MultiMate On-File is a computerized version of a standard 3-by-5 index card filing system. Like an office index card system, On-File stores cards in boxes.

2. To start On-File, either type **onfile** and Return or **mm** and Return at the DOS prompt. Typing *mm* makes Advantage display its Boot-up Menu. To start On-File from the Boot-up Menu, type *2* and press Return. Either way, On-File displays its title screen.

3. From the title screen, you can either "unlock" an existing card box or create a new one, by entering a box name. Once a box has been unlocked, On-File displays the Main Menu.

4. To create a card, choose "Create and Add a Card" from the Main Menu.

5. On-File cards have five areas: subject line, color, action date, text, and index line. The text area consists of 10 lines on the front and 12 lines on the back. The index line holds words that help you cross-reference cards.

6. The Create and Add a Card screen lets you change the color (press F4), choose an index word from the text (F5) or from previous index words (F8), flip the card over (F6), center text (F7), review the card (F2), or add the card to the current box (F1) or cancel it (F10).

7. To search the card box for similar cards, choose "Search and Select Cards" from the Main Menu.

8. On-File lets you search the card box by subject (press F1), index word (F2), color (F3), or date (F4).

9. At the end of a search operation, press the F5 key to display the first five cards it found. These are stacked with only the top card entirely visible. To flip the card over, press F6; to display the next card, press F1; to exit, press F10.

10. To make On-File copy the search cards into a *deck*, press F1 from the Create and Edit Card Selection menu. You can also select the entire card box by pressing F5 from the Search and Select Cards menu.

11. Once you have selected a deck, you may select a subset of it by searching again with a different criteria. A multiple search of this kind is handy to form a deck of, say, blue cards that contain the index word *OVERDUE*.

12. You can also build a deck using the results of several searches. To do this, perform the first search and select the resulting cards by choosing "Select these cards—release prior selection" (F1) from the Create and Edit Card Selection menu. Then return to the Main Menu and do another search. But this time, when it finishes, choose "Add these cards to prior selection" (F2) from the Create and Edit Card Selection menu.

13. To change any card in a selected deck, choose "Display, Sort and Edit Selected Cards" from the Main Menu. This makes the first five cards appear. You can only operate on the top card, so if the one you want is deeper in the deck, press F1 until it is on top. To edit the top card, press F4 for "Top Card Options."

14. On-File can also delete individual cards or an entire deck. To delete a card, start as you would to edit one, but when the Top Card Options screen appears, press F5. Then, when the card appears, press F1. To delete a deck, choose "Use Special Features" from the Main Menu and "Delete selected cards" from the Use Special Features menu.

15. To print a deck of cards, choose "Print Selected Cards" from the Main Menu. Before printing, you can produce a test printing (F2), specify whether front, back, or both sides are to be printed (F2) and whether you are using actual cards or 11-inch paper (F4). You can also move the left-hand margin by pressing the left- or right-arrow key.

16. To leave On-File and return to DOS, press F10 from the Main Menu.

17. To list the available card boxes, you must leave On-File. When the DOS prompt appears, type:

dir b:*.crd

and press Return.

18. To copy a card box, enter a DOS command of the form

copy *oldbox.* **b:***newbox.**

19. To copy selected cards between boxes, write the cards to a temporary holding file, then unlock the box that is to receive the cards and read the holding file into it.

20. To write selected cards to a holding file choose "Use Special Features" from the Main Menu, then "Transfer cards to/from files" and "Write selected cards to a file." Enter the file's name and press Return. When On-File finishes writing the cards, press Return to get back to the Transfer Cards to/from Files menu, then Esc to get back to the Main Menu.

21. To read cards from a holding file, follow the same procedure as to write them, but when the Transfer Cards to/from Files menu appears, choose "Read cards from a file into a box."
22. After copying cards, you can delete the temporary holding file by entering a DOS ERASE command of the form:

erase b:*tempfile***.mof**

12

Advanced On-File Operations

Chapter 11 described how to create card boxes and cards, how to operate on the cards, and how to search and select decks of similar cards. In most cases, you will want to *sort* the cards in some prescribed order. You may also want to use the cards to print data summaries or labels, or copy cards between boxes. Most of these jobs require using a template.

Templates

A template is a form that makes On-File prompt you for data items, one at a time, when you create a new card. That is, when you use a template, On-File displays the name of each field or *area* on the card, and shows a highlighted bar whose length indicates the number of characters you can enter.

Templates also let you specify the *sequence* in which On-File is to ask for data. This means you can, for example, enter a person's first name and then last name, even though the last name area precedes the first-name area on the card. Finally, using a template lets you *sort* cards based on data they contain.

In short, like the Advantage templates we encountered in Chapter 8, On-File templates can save you a lot of time and trouble. They make the computer, not you, do the work.

Creating Templates

Template operations are included in the Main Menu's "Use Special Features" option, so press the F5 key to obtain the Use Special Features menu. To create a template, press F3. When the *Create and Edit Templates* menu appears (Figure 12-1), press F1 to choose "Create a new template."

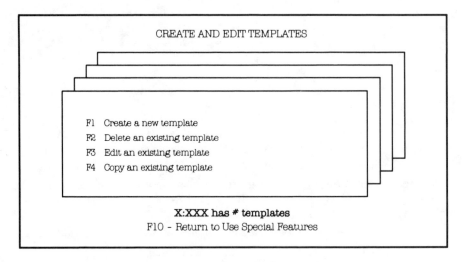

Figure 12-1. Create and Edit Templates menu.
Courtesy of Multimate International Corp.

Pressing F1 makes On-File display a *Create a New Template* screen that has a blank rectangle or "card" in which you construct the template. If you got here by mistake, press F10 to return to the Create and Edit Templates menu. Otherwise, enter a name for the template (up to 20 characters) and press Return. On-File posts the name above the blank card.

The cursor is now at the top left-hand corner of the card. The prompt at the bottom:

```
Press any alpha key to define desired
template area length
```

means that On-File is waiting for you to define a data area for the template.

Defining Template Areas

To define a template area, you must indicate where it starts and how long it is, then give it a name (label). To reach the starting point, move the cursor there using the Return and arrow keys. *Row* and *Column* values at the right of the card indicate the cursor position.

To specify an area's length, press any letter key (being right-handed, I generally use *L*) once for each character position you want. A *Length* counter at the right shows a running total of your keystrokes. If you go too far, backtrack with the left-arrow key.

Regardless of which letter key you press, On-File displays a letter of its own on the screen. The letters indicate the order in which you have set-up areas on the template. (That is, On-File displays As for the first area, Bs for the second, and so on.) They also indicate the order in which On-File will ask for data when you create new cards.

After defining a template area, you must give it a name. To do this, press the F1 key. When the screen shows:

```
Enter a title for the area designated X:
and press return
```

(where *X* is On-File's sequence letter), enter a name in the highlighted bar, and then press Return.

Define the rest of the areas in the template using the same three steps. That is, move the cursor, press a letter key, and label the area. When you finish, press F10 to exit, and then press Esc to return to the Main Menu.

Card Box Example Using a Template

To see how templates work, let's set up a new card box and use a template to create cards for it. Suppose you are national sales manager for Acme Corporation, and want to use On-File to keep track of your key accounts. To begin, set up a new card box called *keyaccts*.

Each card is to include the company's address, the buyer's name and telephone number, and the name of Acme's sales representative for that account. Further, the color of the card is to indicate the sales region, as follows:

Region	Card Color
Northeast (NE)	Blue
Southeast (SE)	Green
Midwest (MW)	Red
Mountain (MT)	White
Northwest (NW)	Yellow
Southwest (SW)	Pink

To keep the cards uniform, you design a general format, shown in Table 12-1, that specifies the name and length of each area, and where it starts. Here, the company name is the card's subject (because it is on row 1) and the last two fields—State and Rep's name—are index words (because they are on row 12, the index line). This format serves as the definition for a data-entry template.

Table 12-1. Template definition.

Area Description	Area Name	Row	Column	Area Length
Company	Company	1	1	30
Street	Street	3	1	30
City	City	4	1	20
State	ST	4	24	2
Zip	Zip	4	28	5
Buyer's last name	Buyer lastname	6	1	20
Buyer's first name	Buyer firstname	6	23	15
Area code	AC	7	1	3
Telephone number	Phone	7	5	8
Rep's name	Rep name	8	1	25
State	ST	12	1	2
Rep's last name	Rep lastname	12	4	20

To create the template:

1. Obtain On-File's Main Menu and press F5 for "Use Special Features."
2. When the Use Special Features menu appears, press F3 to choose "Create and Edit Templates."

3. When the Create and Edit Templates menu appears, press F1 to choose "Create a New Template."

4. For the template name, enter **acctdata** and press Return. On-File puts the cursor at row 1 and column 1 of the template form.

5. To define the Company area, press the L key (or the A or Z key, if you're left-handed) until the *Length* counter shows 30. On-File displays an A for each keystroke, to indicate that this is the first area on the template.

6. To label the Company area, press the F1 key. When the screen shows:

```
Enter a title for the area designated A:
and press return.
```

type **Company** and press Return.

7. Press the Return key twice to move the cursor to column 1 of row 3 (watch the *Column* and *Row* indicators) and set up the Street area using the same approach you used in steps 5 and 6.

8. Set up the rest of the areas listed in Table 12-1, then press the F10 key to return to the Create and Edit Templates menu.

9. Press Esc to return to the Main Menu.

Editing Templates

Once you have created a template, On-File lets you add new data areas or lengthen, shorten, or delete existing areas. You can also rename a template or any area within it. Finally (and perhaps most importantly), you can *resequence* the template. That is, you can make On-File ask for data in any order you want, not just in the order areas appear on the cards.

To edit a template, obtain the Use Special Features menu and press the F3 key to choose "Create and edit templates," then press F3 again. When On-File displays its *Edit an Existing Template* menu, press F9 until the template's name appears at the bottom of the screen. Now you have three choices:

1. To change the length of an area or add new areas, press F1.
2. To rename the template or an area within it, press F2.
3. To delete areas or resequence the template, press F3.

Adding and Editing Areas

Pressing F1 from the Edit an Existing Template menu makes On-File display the template on an *Add or Edit Template Areas* screen, with the cursor at the end of the subject area. To add a new area, perform the same procedure you used to create the template. That is, use the arrow keys to reach the place where the area belongs, then press the L key until the *Length* counter indicates the proper length. Finally, press F1, enter the area's name, and then press Return.

Note that when you enter length characters for a new area, On-File substitutes the next sequence letter in the alphabet. For example, if you create a card that has six areas, they get sequence letters A through F. Then, if you later add a new area, On-File gives it the letter G. This means that when you enter data for a card, On-File will ask for this area last. If that isn't what you want, you can change the entry sequence; we discuss resequencing later in this section.

To change an area's length, use the arrow keys to reach it, then press the numeric keypad's + or − key to lengthen or shorten it. These operations only work properly for the *last* area on a line, however. If you lengthen any other area, each character position you add replaces a space between areas. Similarly, if you shorten any other area, each position you delete widens the gap between this area and the next one. To lengthen or shorten any area but the last area, you must delete all remaining areas on the line (more about this later), then redefine them.

Renaming Templates and Areas

Pressing F2 from the Edit an Existing Template menu makes On-File display a *Rename Template or Area Names* screen, with the current template name at the bottom. To change the name, enter your replacement in the "Rename template to:" field and press Return; to keep the name, just press Return.

Either way, On-File assumes you now want to rename one or more areas. It displays the first area name at the bottom and supplies a "Rename area to:" field where you can enter a replacement. To change the name, enter your replacement and press Return; to keep the name and move to the next area, just press Return; to leave this screen, press the F10 key.

Deleting and Resequencing Template Areas

Pressing F3 from the Edit an Existing Template menu makes On-File display a *Delete or Resequence Template Areas* screen that shows the areas on the template and their names. To delete an area, press Return until you reach it, then press Del to delete it.

Deleting an area has no effect on other areas. Thus, if you delete, say, the second of three areas on a line, the first and third areas remain where they were, with a gap between them. To close the gap, delete the remaining areas on the line, then leave this screen by pressing F10. When the Edit an Existing Template menu reappears, press F1 to "Add or Edit Template Areas," then add the areas you just deleted at the positions where you want them.

You can also use this delete-and-restore technique to lengthen or shorten an area, but keep the same spacing between areas. To do this, delete the areas to the right of the one you want to change, then change the length and redefine the deleted areas.

When you create a template, On-File assumes you want to enter data in the order in which you have defined the areas. If you want some other order (say, to enter a person's first name before his or her surname) or you have added an area to a template, you may want to change the entry sequence.

To resequence a template, use Return to reach the area you want to enter first and press the Home key. On-File removes the area from the template, but shows its name at the right-hand side of the screen. Then move to the area you want to enter second and press Home again (its name appears below the first one). Continue doing this until you have worked through the entire template.

At this point, the right-hand side of the screen lists the sequence you have selected. If it's not what you had intended, resequence the template again; otherwise, press F10 to exit.

Using Templates

Once you have a template, you can use it to create cards. To begin, start On-File and tell it which card box to use. When the Main

Menu appears, choose "Create and Add a Card." Then, to select a template for your new cards, press F3.

When the *Template Selection* screen appears, press F3 to display the first template in this card box. On-File shows the template's data areas (but not their names) and the template name at the bottom. If you want a different template, press F3 to obtain the next one; otherwise, select the current template by pressing F9.

Creating Cards

Creating cards using a template is easier than creating them manually in that, with a template, you never move the cursor between areas. On-File displays the area names, one by one, at the bottom of the screen. You simply enter the data for each area and press Return. On-File records your data on the card and waits for you to enter data for the next area.

When you finish entering data for the card, the template is out of the picture, and you can do anything you would do with a card you have filled out manually. That is, you can press F2 to view the card without the highlighting, F4 to change the color, F6 to flip the card, and so forth. As usual, when you finish, press F1 to add this card to the box.

Adding Cards to the Example Card Box

To see how our *acctdata* template works, let's create five cards for our KEYACCTS box. The data is:

1. *Color:* Blue
   Company: Wilburg Sons
              47 Rockridge Road
              Main City, NY 10015
   Buyer: Wilkinson, Paul
   Buyer's phone number: 212 555-3589
   Sales rep: R. Roberts
   Index words: NY Roberts

2. *Color:* Green
   Company: Symtech
             6750 Peanut Blvd.
             Shells, GA 30319
   Buyer: Beck, Wayne
   Buyer's phone number: 404 783-8832
   Sales rep: P. Grogan
   Index words: GA Grogan

3. *Color:* Green
   Company: Jenco
             339 Oak Palms Rd.
             Palmville, FL 32605
   Buyer: Black, Carrie
   Buyer's phone number: 904 388-6743
   Sales rep: C. Chamber
   Index words: FL Chamber

4. *Color:* Red
   Company: Chicago Gear
             1854 Minnesota Ave.
             Chicago, IL 60611
   Buyer: Daley, Morris
   Buyer's phone number: 312 395-1904
   Sales rep: J. Wilkes
   Index words: IL Wilkes

5. *Color:* Yellow
   Company: Pacifico
             5757 E. Mountain Hwy.
             Valleyview, OR 99117
   Buyer: Anderson, Bill
   Buyer's phone number: 503 438-9532
   Sales rep: D. Kim
   Index words: OR Kim

To create the first card (the one for Wilburg Sons):

1. With the Main Menu on the screen, press F1. On-File shows the "Create and Add a Card" screen.
2. To select a template, press F3 until *acctdata* appears to the right of the F3 prompt.
3. To make On-File use this template, press F9.
4. When On-File asks you to *Enter Company:*, type **Wilburg Sons** and press Return.
5. Repeat step 4 for the remaining items in the data list.

6. Review the completed card by pressing F2. If you find a mistake, press F2 to rework the data (starting at step 4). Press Return until you reach the area that contains the error, and correct it. Correct any other errors and then press F3 to stop entering data.
7. Press F1 to add the card to the KEYACCTS box.

On-File puts the Main Menu back on the screen.

Now, repeat the procedure for the four remaining cards. Just remember to press F4 when you need to change colors.

Sorting Cards

On-File can sort a deck of selected cards on up to three areas. For each area, you can tell On-File to sort in ascending or descending order. Being able to sort on three areas is convenient for such things as:

- Sorting a mailing list by zip code, last name, and first name.
- Sorting an inventory of a record collection by artist's name (last and first) and album title.
- Sorting a book index by main entry (e.g., Florida), secondary entry (e.g., tourism in), and page number.

You can also tell On-File to use the card color as a sort area, but it will only sort the colors in alphabetical order.

Before sorting, you must select a deck of cards by doing a "Search and Select Cards" operation. With that done, proceed as follows:

1. From the Main Menu, press F3 for "Display, Sort and Edit Selected Cards."
2. When the Display of Current Card Selection menu appears, press F3. On-File displays its *Sort Cards* screen.
3. If the screen shows *(No template selected)*, press F3 until the template name you want appears.
4. To start specifying sort areas, press F1.
5. To select an area, press Return to reach it, then F3 or F5 to specify an ascending or descending sort. To select the color as a sort area, press F7.

6. If you want additional sort areas, select them by repeating step 5. If you select three areas, On-File starts sorting automatically. Otherwise, if you select only one or two areas, press F1 to start the sort operation.

When On-File finishes sorting, it displays the first five cards on its "Display of Current Card Selection" screen. To view specific cards, press the keys listed at the bottom of the screen. When you finish, press F1 to return to the Main Menu.

Copying Templates

Sometimes you want to create cards that are similar in format to those you already have, but contain a few more or a few less data areas. Instead of entering a new template from scratch, you can simply copy the existing template and change the copy to meet your needs. To copy a template:

1. From the Main Menu, press F5 to "Use Special Features."
2. Press F3 to "Create and edit templates," then press F4 to "Copy an existing template."
3. Press F4 until the name of the template you want is selected, then press F1 to copy the template.
4. When On-File displays

```
Confirm by entering (y/n)
```

type **y**.
5. When requested, enter a name for the template and press Return.
6. At the end of the copy operation, press Esc to return to the Main Menu.

Now that you have a new template, you can add areas to it, erase areas from it, or edit it in any other way you want. For the procedures, refer back to the "Editing Templates" section.

Printing Cards with a Template

Once you have selected a deck of cards, and perhaps sorted them, you can print a summary of their data. To do this, create a template that tells On-File which areas to print and what order to list them.

On-File's card summary is not very elegant; it simply prints straight across the page, and starts a new line if a data area extends beyond the column 80. Still, this listing is adequate to show what's on the cards.

To print with a template, create the template using the copy-and-edit procedure just described, then do the following:

1. From the Main Menu, press F4 to "Print Selected Cards."
2. When the Print Selected Cards menu appears, press F1 to "Print under template."
3. The *Print Using a Template* menu shows the current template (if one has been selected) and gives you four choices:

   - *F1—Print* cards makes On-File start printing.
   - *F4—Select template* lets you cycle through the names of the templates in your card box until you come to the one that is to be used for printing.
   - *F9—Select vertical spacing* lets you tell On-File how many blank lines to put between card summaries. The default value, *1*, puts one line between them, *2* puts two lines between them, and so forth. By repeatedly pressing F9, you can specify any spacing value up to 9.
   - *F10—Cancel printing* returns On-File to the Print Selected Cards menu.

4. When you press F1, On-File shows:

```
Ready printer
Press any key
```

   at the top left-hand corner. To start printing, switch your printer on and press Return.

   On-File prints the current date, time, and page number, then skips four lines and prints the template name and a header showing the area names. Finally, it prints the data for each card. On-File single-spaces the card summaries, but separates them by the number of blank lines you have specified using the F9 key.

5. When the screen shows

```
Printing complete...# cards had template information
Press any key to continue
```

press Esc to get back to the Main Menu.

Summarizing the Key Account Cards

Suppose you want to print an alphabetical list of your company's key accounts from the cards in the KEYACCTS box. Each entry should show the company's name, city, and state, and the name of the sales representative.

To begin, you must create a printing template that selects only those four areas. To do this, copy the *acctdata* template and name the copy *prtaccts.* Then edit the new template by deleting every area except *Company, City, ST,* and *Rep name.* (Coincidentally, the new template's sequence is just what we want. Some other combination of areas may require resequencing the template after deleting.)

Now, with the Main Menu on the screen, do the following:

1. Press F2 to "Search and Select Cards."
2. When the Search and Select Cards menu appears, press F5 to "Select all of the cards."
3. When On-File asks "Are you sure? (y/n)," type **y** and press F10 to return to the Main Menu.
4. Press F3 to "Display, Sort and Edit Selected Cards." On-File shows the Display of Current Card Selection menu.
5. To sort the cards, press F3. Then press F3 again until the *prtaccts* template is selected, and F1. The Define the Sort Criteria menu appears.
6. Press F3 to make On-File sort the *Company* area in ascending order, then press F1 to make it perform the sort.
7. When the Display of Current Card Selection menu reappears, press Esc to return to the Main Menu.
8. Press F4 for "Print Selected Cards," then F1 for "Print under template."
9. When the Print Using a Template menu appears, press F1 to print the cards.
10. Switch your printer on, when instructed, and press Return. The printed listing of the KEYACCTS cards should look like Figure 12-2.

When printing finishes, press Esc to return to the Main Menu.

```
May 29, 1986
2:42 p.m.
Page 1



                              prtaccts


Company                      City                ST Rep name


Chicago Gear                 Chicago             IL J. Wilkes

Jenco                        Palmville           FL C. Chamber

Pacifico                     Valleyview          OR D. Kim

Symtech                      Shells              GA P. Grogan

Wilburg Sons                 Main City           NY R. Roberts
```

Figure 12-2. Printed summary of cards.

Printing Labels and Envelopes

So far we have described how to print On-File cards on index cards or paper (see Chapter 11) and print summaries of specific areas for reference purposes (see the preceding "Printing Cards with a Template" section). On-File can also print labels and envelopes from cards. Here, you use a template to tell it which areas to print and a special *Label Format Container* to tell it where to put areas on the labels. On-File can print up to eight 70-character lines on each label or envelope.

You can specify either of two print formats: *Fixed* or *Float*. To make On-File print every data item (even empty ones) exactly where it appears on the "Label Format Container," choose the Fixed format. To make it omit blanks and "close up" the data, choose the Float format. Fixed format labels look like this:

```
George            Atkins
12365 River Street
Bell City          FL 32651
```

while Float format labels look like this:

```
George Atkins
12365 River Street
Bell City FL 32651
```

You will probably use the Float format for most printing jobs.

To begin, select the cards you want printed and create a template that selects data areas within those cards. Then tell On-File where to print the data by specifying the print format.

Specifying the Print Format

Specify the print format as follows:

1. Choose "Print Selected Cards" from the Main Menu and "Create label format" from the Print Selected Cards menu.
2. When On-File shows its "Create Label Format" screen, press F3 until the name of your label-printing template appears, then press F1 to "Create using this template." This makes the *Cut and Paste the Label Format* screen appear (see Figure 12-3).

   The upper box on the screen, called the *Label Format Container*, will hold the printing format. The lower box, called the *Template Container*, shows the template you have selected for printing. To construct the printing format, you must "cut" data areas from the Template Container and "paste" them where they belong on the Label Format Container.
3. To cut-and-paste a data area, use the Return and the arrow keys to reach the place in the Label Format Container where you want it to appear, then press F3 until On-File highlights the Template Container area you want.
4. Press F4 to paste the area onto the Format Label Container.
5. To paste another area on the same line, press the space bar until the cursor reaches the new area's starting point (On-File shades the spaces), then repeat steps 3 and 4.
6. To make On-File print "boilerplate" text on every label, enter it on the Label Format Container. You can do this to put a comma be-

tween the city and state or to include, say, *Renew!* on a mailing label for a magazine.

7. Repeat steps 3 through 6 until you have pasted all the print areas on the Label Format Container.

8. On-File indicates the print format by displaying *FIXED* or *FLOAT* at the top of the screen. To switch formats, press F5 or F6.

9. When you finish defining the label format, press F1 to make On-File save it.

Pressing F1 makes the Print Selected Cards menu reappear. Now you can print the labels or envelopes.

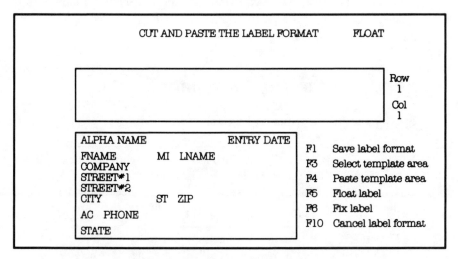

Figure 12-3. Cut and Paste the Label Format screen.
Courtesy of Multimate International Corp.

Print Procedure

To print labels or envelopes, you must first tell On-File what kind of set-up you have. That is, you must tell it whether to assume continuous or hand-fed stock and, for continuous stock, how many lines separate labels.

To begin, choose "Print labels" from the Print Selected Cards screen. On-File displays the *Print Labels* screen we show in Figure 12-4.

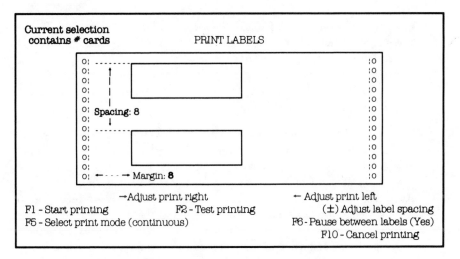

Current selection
contains # cards   PRINT LABELS

Spacing: 8

Margin: **8**

→Adjust print right   ← Adjust print left
F1 - Start printing   F2 - Test printing   (±) Adjust label spacing
F5 - Select print mode (continuous)   F6 - Pause between labels (Yes)
                                                           F10 - Cancel printing

Figure 12-4. Print Labels screen.
Courtesy of Multimate International Corp.

The Print Labels screen is similar to the Print On-File Cards screen in Chapter 11 (see Figure 11-13 in the "Printing Cards" section), except it has a *Spacing* parameter that indicates the number of lines between the tops of labels. To increase or decrease the spacing, press the + or − key on the numeric keypad. You may also adjust the left-hand margin, by pressing the left or right arrow key, and select continuous or hand-fed stock by pressing the F5 key.

Before committing to a print job, do a test printing by pressing F2. On-File shows how it will print each label by producing a series of Xs. If the margin or spacing is not what you want, adjust it and test-print again.

When you are satisfied with the spacing, press F1 to start printing. On-File displays a *Start Printing* screen that lets you:

- Start/Resume printing (F1)
- Readjust (F9). That is, return to the Print Labels screen.
- Cancel printing (F10) and return to the Print Selected Cards screen.

When printing finishes, press Esc to return to the Main Menu.

Questions and Answers

Question: I'm using On-File cards to keep track of appointments. The date area specifies the day and the text area gives the details. How can I sort them with the earliest date first?

Answer: Select all the cards and start the sort procedure. Next, select your template and specify the date area for sorting, in ascending order. Finally, press F1 to start sorting.

Question: I have a template that makes On-File ask for a person's first and last name, and now I want to make it to ask for a middle initial as well. However, there is only one space between the first and name areas. How can I insert a data area for the middle initial?

Answer: On-File doesn't let you insert an area directly. Instead, you must delete the last name area and then add the middle initial area. Finally, enter the last name area again. Because On-File views the middle initial and last name areas as new, it puts them last in the sequence. Thus, you must resequence the template so that On-File asks for the first name, middle initial, and last name, in that order.

Question: When On-File prints my labels, it jams all the data together. For example, it prints a name as "JohnJ.Smith." I put spaces between the data areas in the Label Format Container, so what's going on?

Answer: To enter space between areas, you pressed the right-arrow key instead of the space bar. The space bar creates what the manual calls "space holders," while the right-arrow key simply moves the cursor.

Hints

1. To sort cards by date, you must first define the date area as you would any other area. The date area starts at column 39 of row 1 and is 11 characters long.
2. You can make a template area any length you want, but the lengths shown in Table 12-1 work well for most applications. That is, company names and street addresses are 30 characters long, city names and last names of people are 20 characters long, and first names are 15 characters long.

3. When you add a new area to an existing template, On-File always gives it the next letter in the alphabet, which means you will be asked for its data last. To change the area's entry position, you must resequence the template.

Key Point Summary

Table 12-2 summarizes the On-File keys and commands we introduced in this chapter. For a complete list, see Appendix B.

Table 12-2. Keys and commands introduced in Chapter 12.

Create and Add a Card menu (F1 from Main Menu)
F3—Template Selection

Display of Current Card Selection menu (F3 from Main Menu)
F3—Sort cards
    F3—Select sort template (then F1)
        Define the Sort Criteria menu
     F1—Perform the sort
     F3—Ascending sort order
     F5—Descending sort order
     F7—Color (ascending order only)
     F10—Cancel the sort
    F10—Cancel sort
F4—Top Card Options
    F4—Edit card
        F3—Template selection
        F9—Template area names (switch between data and names)

Print Selected Cards menu (F4 from Main Menu)
F1—Print using a template
    F1—Print cards
    F4—Select template
    F9—Select vertical spacing (1)
    F10—Cancel printing
F3—Create label format
    F1—Create using this template
        Cut and Paste the Label Format screen
        F1—Save label format
        F3—Select template area (to be pasted)
        F4—Paste template area (on Label Format Container)
        F5—Float label (omit empty space)
        F6—Fix label (print per Label Format Container)
        F10—Cancel label format

    F3—Select template
    F10—Finished with create
F4—Print labels
    F1—Start printing
        F1—Start/Resume printing
            F5—Skip this label
            F6—Pause (stop printing and show next label)
            F9—Readjust (return to Print Labels menu)
            F10—Cancel printing
    F2—Test printing
    F5—Select print mode (hand-fed or continuous)
    F6—Pause between labels (Yes or No)
    F10—Cancel printing

Use Special Features menu (F5 from Main Menu)
F3—Create and edit templates
    F1—Create a new template
    F2—Delete an existing template
    F3—Edit an existing template
        F1—Add or edit template areas
        F2—Rename template or area names
        F3—Delete or resequence template areas
            Return—Move between areas
            Del—Delete area
            Home—Select sequence order
        F9—Select template
        F10—Finished editing templates
    F4—Copy an existing template
    F10—Return to Use Special Features

---

1. A template is a form that makes On-File prompt for data when you
   create a new card. A template also lets you specify the sequence in
   which On-File is to ask for the data, and lets you sort cards based on
   the data they contain.
2. To create a template, choose "Use Special Features" from the Main
   Menu, then press F3. When the Create and Edit Templates menu
   appears, press F1 for "Create a new template."
3. To define a data area on a template, you must indicate where it starts
   and how long it is, then give it a name. To reach the starting point,
   move the cursor there using the Return and arrow keys. To specify
   the length of an area, press any letter key once for each character
   position you want. A *Length* counter at the right keeps track of the
   length.

4. On-File substitutes a sequence letter for each length character you enter; it substitutes A for the first area, B for the second, and so on. The letter indicates the order in which On-File will ask for data when you create cards.

5. To name a data area, press the F1 key, enter the name, and press Return.

6. To edit or rename a template, choose "Create and edit templates" from the Use Special Features menu, then "Edit an existing template." You can now change the length of an area or add new areas (F1), rename the template or an area on it (F2), or delete areas or resequence the template (F3).

7. To change the length of an area, use the arrow keys to reach it, then press + to make it longer or − to make it shorter.

8. To use a template to create cards, choose "Create and Add a Card" from the Main Menu. Then select a template by pressing F3 until its name appears.

9. When creating cards with a template, On-File prompts for data area-by-area. For each area, enter the data and press Return. When you finish, press F1 to add the card to the box.

10. On-File lets you sort a selected deck on up to three areas (data areas or the color). To sort, choose "Display, Sort and Edit Selected Cards" from the Main Menu, then press F3 to obtain the "Sort Cards" screen. For each area you want to sort, select ascending or descending order (colors only sort alphabetically).

11. To create a template similar to one you already have, copy the existing template, then edit the copy. To copy a template, choose "Use Special Features" from the Main Menu, then "Create and edit templates" and "Copy an existing template."

12. To produce a summary of the data on a deck of cards, print using a template. The template tells On-File which areas to print and what order to list them. To produce the summary, choose "Print Selected Cards" from the Main Menu, then select "Print under template."

13. On-File can also use templates to print labels and envelopes on either continuous or hand-fed stock. This involves creating a label format, and then printing.

14. To create a label format, choose "Print Selected Cards" from the Main Menu and "Create label format" from the Print Selected Cards menu. When On-File shows its "Create Label Format" screen, select the template, then press F1 to "Create using this template."

15. When On-File displays the "Cut and Paste Label" screen, use the Return and arrow keys to reach the Label Format Container position where you want an area to appear, then press F3 to select the template area and F4 to paste it. To paste another data area or enter

"boilerplate" material on the same line, press the space bar (*not* the right-arrow key) to reach its starting position.

16. To select a print format for labels or envelopes, tell On-File to use either *Fixed* (print data as shown on the template) or *Float* (omits blanks).

17. When you finish defining a label format, press F1 to save it.

18. To print labels or envelopes, choose "Print labels" from the "Print Selected Cards" screen. Press the + or − key to increase or decrease the spacing between labels, the left or right arrow key to adjust the margin, and F5 to select continuous or hand-fed stock. To start printing, press F1 twice.

13

Using On-File with Advantage and Other Programs

On-File provides a variety of ways for you to transfer information between cards and other programs. For example, it can convert the data on cards to a Merge Data File, the kind described in Chapter 8. You can then produce form letters by using Advantage's Merge Print Utility to combine the Data File with a Primary Document (that is, a generalized letter). Conversely, you can convert the entries in a Merge Data File to On-File Cards.

On-File also lets you create cards from the Document Summary Screens of Advantage documents. This is helpful for keeping track of the documents on a disk, especially if you are using a hard disk.

Further, On-File provides ways to convert the information on cards to a text, or *ASCII*, file that can be used by a spreadsheet, database, or other non-Advantage program. Conversely, it can convert an ASCII file that has been generated by another program to a set of On-File cards.

Finally, On-File can copy templates from one card box to another. This saves you from redefining them in the second box.

Except for producing a Merge Data File from On-File cards, each of these jobs require you to use the facilities of the MultiMate On-File Utilities disk.

Starting the On-File Utilities

The On-File Utilities disk holds a variety of programs that provide additional card-related functions. To use it, obtain the DOS prompt (and, if you have a hard disk, get into the correct subdirectory), type **ofut**, and then press Return. When the On-File Utility copyright screen appears, press the space bar to obtain the *MultiMate On-File Utilities* menu (see Figure 13-1).

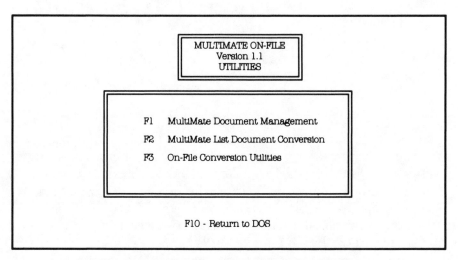

MULTIMATE ON-FILE
Version 1.1
UTILITIES

F1   MultiMate Document Management

F2   MultiMate List Document Conversion

F3   On-File Conversion Utilities

F10 - Return to DOS

Figure 13-1. MultiMate On-File Utilities menu.
Courtesy of Multimate International Corp.

Using On-File with Advantage

This section describes how to create Advantage Merge Data Files from On-File cards, and vice versa, and how to convert Document Summary Screens to cards.

Converting Cards to Merge Data Files

To create a Merge Data File for form letters, start On-File as usual and open the box that contains the cards you want. Then select the cards that are to be converted and set up a template for them. The template must, of course, include the areas that are named as data fields in the Primary Document. Further, the area names cannot be more than 12 characters long.

Once you have your card deck and template, do the following:

1. From the Main Menu, press F5 to "Use Special Features."
2. When the Use Special Features menu appears, press F5 to "Transfer cards to/from files," then F3 to "Write selected cards to a MultiMate Merge Data file." On-File displays a *Write MultiMate Merge Data File* screen.
3. Press F3 until the name of the template you want appears, then press F1 to begin the conversion.
4. When On-File asks for the Merge Data File, enter its name and press Return.

Pressing Return here starts the conversion operation. When it finishes, the bottom on the screen shows a message of the form:

```
File write complete...# cards had template information
Press any key to continue
```

Press Esc to return to the Main Menu.

Merging Key Account Data

Suppose you want to produce a memorandum that lists your company's key accounts and the sales reps who service them. By no coincidence, this is the same data we needed in the "Summarizing the Key Account Cards" section. Thus, we can use the print template, *prtaccts*, here.

To produce the Data File, follow the procedure we just gave, and select the *prtaccts* template in step 3. For step 4, you could name the Data File *keydata*. What On-File generates is a standard Data File with each account's data on a separate page ready for merging. To summarize the accounts, your Primary Document must contain a *REPEAT: 5* instruction, because there are five key accounts.

Converting Merge Data Files to Cards

To convert a Merge Data File to cards, you must first create a box that is to receive the cards and a template that specifies the card format. The template must have a data area for each item you want to read from the Data File; the areas must, of course, be named the same as fields in the Data File.

The conversion operation consists of two parts: writing the Data File to a temporary "output file" on disk (using the On-File Utilities), then reading the contents of the output file into a card box (using a standard On-File function).

To begin, start the On-File Utilities program. That is, enter **ofut** and, when the copyright screen appears, press Return. Then do the following:

1. Choose "MultiMate List Document Conversion" from the Utilities menu.
2. If the Merge Data File and the card box are on the same disk, put it in drive B and press Return. Otherwise, if they are on different disks, put the Merge Data File disk in drive A and the card box disk in drive B and press Return.
3. On-File displays six prompts in succession, for which you must enter:

   a) The disk drive (*A*, *B*, or *C*) that is to receive files; that is, the drive that has the card box disk.
   b) The On-File box name that is to receive files (cards).
   c) The drive that contains the List Document (Merge Data File).
   d) The name of the List Document.
   e) The drive that is to receive the output file. Generally you enter the name of the drive that has the card box disk.
   f) The name of the output file. If your Data File has 250 records (pages) or less, enter the card box name. If it has more than 250 records, enter a file name that ends in "1"; for example, *FILE1* or *TEMP1*.

Pressing Return the final time makes the *MultiMate List Document Conversion* screen appear. Figure 13-2 shows what this screen looks like if the Data File contains information from a Document Summary screen.

```
┌──────────────────────────────────────────────────────────────────────┐
│                 MULTIMATE LIST DOCUMENT CONVERSION                     │
│                                                                        │
│        ┌──────────────────────────── BLUE ─────────┐  MERGE ITEM       │
│        │ DOCUMENT                          CHANGE DATE │ DOCUMENT       │
│        │                                             │ CHANGE DATE     │
│        │ AUTHOR           DISK-TITLE                 │ AUTHOR          │
│        │ ADDRESSEE        CREATION DATE              │ DISK-TITLE      │
│        │ OPERATOR         KEY LAST    KEY TOTAL   PAGES │ ADDRESSEE     │
│        │                                             │ CREATION        │
│        │                                             │ KEY LAST        │
│        │                                             │ KEY TOTAL       │
│        │                                             │ PAGES           │
│        │ KEYWORDS                                    │ KEYWORDS        │
│        └─────────────────────────────────────────────┘                │
│                      DOCUMENT MANAGEMENT                               │
│                  F1    Start the conversion                            │
│                  F3    Select different template                       │
│                  F4    Change card color                               │
│                  F10   Cancel the conversion                           │
└──────────────────────────────────────────────────────────────────────┘
```

Figure 13-2. MultiMate List Document Conversion screen.
Courtesy of Multimate International Corp.

4. Select the template you want by pressing F4 and select the card color by pressing F4.
5. Press F1 to "Start the conversion."
6. On-File now lets you enter descriptions for template areas (see the On-File manual for details). When you finish, press F9.
7. On-File does the conversion, then tells you how many cards it converted. Press F10 to get back to the Utilities menu and press F10 again to return to DOS.

At this point, On-File is holding the card information in an output file on the disk. To create the actual cards, and put them in the card box:

1. Put your On-File System disk in drive A and the card box disk in drive B, then start On-File.
2. Open the box that is to contain the converted cards and press Return.
3. Choose "Use Special Features" from the Main Menu, "Transfer cards to/from files" from the Use Special Features menu, and "Read cards from a File into a Box" from the Transfer Cards to/from Files menu.
4. For *File Name:*, enter the name of your output file and press Return.
5. When On-File finishes reading cards, press Esc to return to the Main Menu.

Since the conversion is over, you no longer need the output file. As we mentioned in Chapter 11, you can delete it by entering a DOS Erase command of the form:

erase *outfile***.mof**

If you don't remember the name of the output file, get a list by entering:

dir *.mof

Keeping Track of Documents

You can also use On-File to keep track of Advantage documents. This involves maintaining a box whose cards contain the data from Document Summary Screens. We won't go into the details here; the On-File manual fully describes them under "MultiMate Document Management." The manual tells you how to:

- Create a card box and tailor it for document management. This involves copying a set of *MLIBRARY* files into the box.
- Set up templates for reading data from Document Summary Screens.
- Convert Document Summary Screens to cards, using the "MultiMate Document Management" (F1) option on the On-File Utilities menu.
- Update and delete cards.

Using On-File with Other Programs

As we mentioned earlier, On-File lets you transfer data between a card box and a spreadsheet, database, or any other program that can work with ASCII text.

Converting Cards to ASCII Files

To convert cards to an ASCII file, you must write them to a temporary "output file" (using On-File), then read the contents of the output file into an ASCII file (using the On-File Utilities). To create the output file:

1. Start On-File and select the cards you want to convert.
2. Choose "Use Special Features" from the Main Menu and "Transfer cards to/from files" from the Use Special Features menu.
3. When the Transfer Cards to/from Files menu appears, choose "Write selected cards to a file."
4. Enter the name of the output file. Since the file is temporary, its name is unimportant; you could enter the box name, for example.
5. When On-File finishes writing the cards, press Return to get back to the Transfer Cards to/from Files menu and Esc to get back to the Main Menu.
6. Exit to DOS and replace the On-File System disk with the On-File Utilities disk.

Now you must convert the temporary output file to ASCII. Do this as follows:

1. Start the On-File Utilities program and choose "On-File Conversion Utilities" from the Utilities menu. This makes the *On-File Conversion Utilities* menu appear (see Figure 13-3).

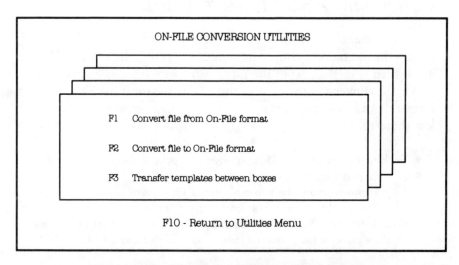

Figure 13-3. On-File Conversion Utilities menu.
Courtesy of Multimate International Corp.

2. Choose "Convert file from On-File format."
3. On-File displays four prompts, for which you must enter:

   a) The name of the "source On-File drive"; that is, the drive that has the output file.
   b) The "source On-File filename" (the name of the output file).
   c) The name of the "target drive" (the drive that is to receive the ASCII file).
   d) The "target filename" (the name and extension of the ASCII file). Most programs require ASCII files to have an extension of either *.ASC* or *.TXT*. If you were converting our key accounts cards, you might enter **keyaccts.asc.**

4. Pressing Return the final time makes On-File start the conversion. When it finishes, press Return to get back to the On-File Conversion Utilities menu, then press F10 to get back to the Utilities menu.

The resulting ASCII file contains 25 lines for each card, one line for the color and 12 lines each for the front and back. Every line starts and ends with a quotation mark. For example, a color line might appear as "BLUE". On-File separates each set of card data or *record* with a blank line.

Converting ASCII Files to Cards

On-File can also convert an ASCII file to cards. To do this, you must write the file to a temporary output file (using the On-File Utilities), then read the output file into a card box (using On-File).

For the conversion to succeed, the ASCII file must have the same format that On-File produces; see the preceding section. It must follow these rules:

- Each record must have 25 lines, even if they are blank.
- No line may be longer than 50 characters.
- Line 1 must contain the name of one of On-File's eight colors.
- Line 2, the subject line, must be 50 characters long. Character positions 1 through 35 may contain a subject (it is optional), but positions 39 through 49 must contain a date in On-File's format (e.g., 11 JUN 1986).
- Lines 3 through 12 may contain text for the front of the card.
- Line 13, the index line, may contain index words.

- Lines 15 through 25 may contain text for the back of the card.
- Each line must start and end with a quotation mark (").
- Records must be single-spaced.
- There must be one blank line between records.

These are very specific requirements, of course, and not many programs other than word processors can produce records in this format directly. However, you can easily use Advantage to modify whatever your program produces, to put it in On-File's format. Simply convert the ASCII file to an Advantage DOC file (see the "File Conversion" section in Chapter 10), make your changes (e.g., insert quotation marks), and convert the document back to ASCII.

Once you have generated the ASCII file and changed it as necessary, use On-File to set up a box for the cards. To convert data produced by dBASE II, you could call the box DBASDATA. Now, to generate the temporary output file, do the following:

1. Start the On-File Utilities program and choose "On-File Conversion Utilities" from the Utilities menu, then "Convert file to On-File format" from the On-File Conversion Utilities menu.
2. On-File displays four prompts, for which you must enter:

   a) The name of the "source drive"; that is, the drive that has the ASCII file.
   b) The "source filename" (the name of the ASCII file).
   c) The name of the "target On-File drive" (the drive that has the card box).
   d) The "target On-File filename" (the name of the output file). The card box name is as good as any, so you could enter, say, **dbasdata.**

3. Pressing Return the final time makes On-File start the conversion. When it finishes, press Return to get back to the On-File Conversion Utilities menu, then press F10 again to get back to the Utilities menu.

Now you must convert the temporary output file to cards. Do this as follows:

1. Start On-File and create or open a box for the cards.
2. Choose "Use Special Features" and "Transfer cards to/from files" from the Use Special Features menu.

3. When the Transfer Cards to/from Files menu appears, choose "Read cards from a file into a box."
4. Enter the name of the temporary output file and press Return.
5. When On-File finishes creating the cards, press Return to get back to the Transfer Cards to/from Files menu and Esc to get back to the Main Menu.

Converting Cards to ASCII under a Template

The procedure in the "Converting Cards to ASCII Files" section produces a file that contains 25 lines of data in each record—the 24 lines on the card, plus the color. In most cases, however, you want to convert only certain areas on the card, not everything. To do this, you can specify the areas using a template.

To begin, start On-File and unlock the box that contains the conversion cards. Then set up the template that specifies the areas you want to transfer and the order they should appear in the ASCII file. Finally, select the applicable cards. You can make the conversion as follows:

1. Choose "Use Special Features" from the Main Menu and "Transfer cards to/from files" from the Use Special Features menu.
2. When the Transfer Cards to/from Files menu appears, choose "Write selected cards under template to an ASCII file." On-File reports the number of selected cards at the top left-hand corner of the screen.
3. Select the conversion template by pressing F4 until its name appears, then press F1 to "Write ASCII template file."
4. Enter the name of the ASCII file (up to eight characters) in the *File Name:* field and press Return.
5. When On-File finishes writing (i.e., creating) the file, press Esc to return to the Main Menu.

On-File always adds the extension *DAT* to the name of the ASCII file. Entering **accts** in step 4 produces a file named *ACCTS.DAT*. If your program requires a different extension, rename the file using the DOS Rename command. For example, to change *ACCTS.DAT* to *ACCTS.ASC*, enter

ren b:accts.dat *.asc

When On-File creates the ASCII file, it converts the data on each card to a *record*. Within each record, it encloses data items with quotation marks and separates them with a comma. Recall from Chapter 10 that this a format dBASE II can use directly.

For example, to convert our key accounts cards to an ASCII file, you can design a template that will transfer the buyer's name, area code, telephone number, and affiliation—in that order. Two records in the ASCII file will look like this:

```
"Paul","Wilkinson","212","555-3589","Wilburg Sons"
"Wayne","Beck","404","783-8832","Symtech"
```

Copying Templates between Boxes

The On-File Utilities program also lets you copy templates from one card box to another. If the box you're copying to does not exist, On-File creates it, and gives it the template(s) you have specified. Otherwise, if you copy templates to an existing box, On-File *replaces* its templates with the copies.

To copy templates between boxes:

1. Start the On-File Utilities program and choose "On-File Conversion Utilities" from the Utilities menu, then "Transfer templates between boxes" from the On-File Conversion Utilities menu.
2. On-File displays four prompts, for which you must enter:
   a) The name of the "target drive for transfer"; that is, the drive that has the box that is to receive the templates.
   b) The "target filename for transfer" (the name of the box that is to receive the templates). Here, you may specify an existing box or a new one. Specifying an existing box makes On-File warn that it will replace the box's templates with the copies. It displays:

   ```
   There is already a file with
   that name. Replace? (y/n)
   ```

   Type **y** to proceed or **n** to get back to the Conversion Utilities menu.
   c) The name of the "1st template drive" (the drive that has the card box containing the templates).

d) The "1st template filename" (the name of the card box that contains the templates).

3. Pressing Return the final time puts three new options on the screen.
Press F7 to select the template you want to copy, F8 to perform the
copy operation, or F10 to exit. Once On-File has copied a template, it
displays:

```
Transfer of tempname complete
Press any key
```

4. To copy another template from this box, press F7 to select it and F8
to copy it. Otherwise, press F10.
5. Pressing F10 makes On-File ask

```
Would you like to transfer another template
box? (y/n)
```

Type **y** to copy templates from another box (On-File returns to step
2.c, but this time asks for the name of the "2nd template drive") or **n**
to get back to the Conversion Utilities menu.

Hints and Warnings

1. When preparing a template that selects areas to merge with an Advantage document, don't worry about the sequence. Advantage's merge
operation will select the data it needs, regardless of their order.
2. For merge operations, be sure the area names on your template are no
longer than 12 characters.
3. Remember that copying templates to an existing card box makes On-
File *replace* the templates that are already in the box. To retain existing templates, you must recreate the template you want to add.
4. Like the main On-File program, the Utilities program uses F1 to complete an operation, F10 to cancel it and return to the preceding menu,
and Esc to cancel and return to the Utilities menu.

Key Point Summary

Tables 13-1 and 13-2 summarize the On-File and On-File Utilities
commands we introduced in this chapter.

Table 13-1. On-File commands introduced in Chapter 13.

Use Special Features menu (F5 from Main Menu)
F5—Transfer cards to/from files
    F3—Write selected cards to a MultiMate Merge Data file
    F4—Write selected cards to a template under an ASCII file

---

Table 13-2. On-File Utilities commands introduced in Chapter 13.

On-File Utilities menu
F1—MultiMate Document Management
F2—MultiMate List Document Conversion
F3—On-File Conversion Utilities
F10—Return to DOS

MultiMate Document Management menu (F1 from Utilities menu)
F1—Perform Document Management for MultiMate diskette or
    subdirectory
F2—Perform Document Management for selected MultiMate file(s)
F3—List available MultiMate documents
F4—List available On-File boxes
F5—Select new document color
F6—Select update document color
F10—Return to Utilities Menu

MultiMate List Document Conversion screen (F2 from Utilities
    menu)
F1—Start the conversion
    F9—Bypass rest of template
    F10—Cancel processing
F3—Select different template
F4—Change card color
F10—Cancel the conversion

On-File Conversion Utilities menu (F3 from Utilities menu)
F1—Convert file from On-File format
F2—Convert file to On-File format
F3—Transfer templates between boxes
    F7—Select template
    F8—Transfer template
    F10—Finished transferring templates
F10—Return to utilities menu

---

1. On-File can convert the data on a deck of cards into an Advantage
   Merge Data File. Then you can produce form letters by using Advantage's Merge Print Utility to combine the Data File with a Primary Document (that is, a generalized letter).

2. To produce a Merge Data File from a card deck, choose "Use Special Features" from the Main Menu, then "Transfer cards to/from files" and "Write selected cards to a MultiMate Merge Data file." Select the template, enter the name of the Data File, and press Return.

3. On-File can transfer the information on Document Summary Screens to cards. This is helpful for keeping track of your documents.

4. On-File lets you transfer data between a card box and a spreadsheet, database, or any other program that can work with ASCII text.

5. To convert cards to an ASCII file, write them to a temporary "output file" (using On-File), then read the contents of the output file into an ASCII file (using the On-File Utilities).

6. To create the output file, choose "Use Special Features" from On-File's Main Menu, "Transfer cards to/from files" from the Use Special Features menu, and "Write selected cards to a file" from the Transfer Cards to/from Files menu.

7. To convert the output file to ASCII, choose "Convert file from On-File format" for the On-File Utilities menu, then specify the drive and filename of the output ("source") file and the ASCII ("target") file.

8. To convert an ASCII file to cards, you must write the file to a temporary "output file" (using the On-File Utilities), then read the output file into a card box (using On-File).

9. To create the output file, choose "On-File Conversion Utilities" from the On-File Utilities menu and "Convert file to On-File format" from the On-File Conversion Utilities menu, then specify the drive and filename of the ASCII ("source") file and the output ("target") file.

10. To convert the output file to cards, choose "Use Special Features" from On-File's Main Menu, "Transfer cards to/from files" from the Use Special Features menu, and "Read cards from a file into a box" from the Transfer Cards to/form Files menu.

11. You can also convert specific data areas on cards to an ASCII file, by using a template. To do this, choose "Use Special Features" from the On-File's Main Menu, "Transfer cards to/from files" from the Use Special Features menu, and "Write selected cards under template to an ASCII file" from the Transfer Cards to/from Files menu. Select the conversion template by pressing F4 until its name appears, then press F1 to "Write ASCII template file."

12. The On-File Utilities program also lets you copy templates from one card box to another. If the box you're copying to does not exist, On-File creates it, and gives it the template(s) you have specified. Other-

wise, if you copy templates to an existing box, On-File *replaces* those in the box with the copied templates.

13. To copy templates between card boxes, choose "On-File Conversion Utilities" from the Utilities menu and "Transfer templates between boxes" from the On-File Conversion Utilities menu, then specify the drive and filename of the box that is to receive the templates (the "target") and the box that contains them (the "1st template" file).

14. After copying a template, On-File lets you copy others from this box or a different one.

Appendix A

Advantage Commands

Table A-1. Function key combinations.

Function key	Key only	Shift + key	Alt + key	Ctrl + key
F1	Go to page	*Help*	*Set place mark*	*Go to next place mark*
F2	Page break	Combine pages	*Page length*	Repaginate
F3	Center	Column mode	*Scroll left*	Add row
F4	Indent	Decimal tab	*Scroll right*	Add column
F5	Use library entry	Attach library	*Highlight word*	Build key procedure
F6	Search	Replace	Highlight line	Pause command
F7	Move text or column	*Soft hyphen*	*Highlight sentence*	Prompt command
F8	Copy text or column	External copy	*Highlight paragraph*	Execute key procedure
F9	Change format	Current format line	Page format line	System format line
F10	Save/exit	Save page	Spell edit	Spell check

Note: The combinations printed in italics are not described in this book. Refer to your *Advantage Reference Manual* for details.

Other Function Key Operations

Alt-F1   *From within a Data File:* Select or deselect a record
F2   *From within a Data file:* Start a new record
Shift-F2   *From within a Data File:* Delete a record
F5   *From within a Data File:* Sort the records based on the field where the cursor is
            From a Document Summary Screen: Create a library
F7   *In move, copy, or external copy mode:* Move or copy the format as well as the text
Shift-F10   *From a Document Summary Screen:* Create a Data File

Table A-2. Control key combinations.

Key(s)	Function
Cursor-moving operations	
Up-arrow	Previous line
Down-arrow	Next line
Left-arrow	Previous character
Right-arrow	Next character
Home	Beginning of screen
Ctrl-Home	Beginning of page
End	End of screen
Ctrl-End	End of page
PgUp	Previous screen
Ctrl-PgUp	Previous page
PgDn	Next screen
Ctrl-PgDn	Next page
Text operations	
− (minus)	Delete character (use − on numeric keypad)
+	Insert character (use + on numeric keypad)
Backspace	Delete previous character
Del	*In edit mode:* Delete text
	In column mode: Delete column
	In search or replace mode: Delete string character
Ins	*In edit mode:* Insert text
	In column mode: Insert column
Return	New paragraph (≪)
Print-related operations	
Alt-+	Underline, but skip spaces and punctuation (use + on top row of keyboard)
Alt-underscore	Underline everything
Ctrl-underscore	Double underscore (⥯)
Shift-underscore	Underline or de-underline character at cursor position

Table A-2. Control key combinations (continued).

Key(s)	Function
Alt-E	Draw a line or box
Alt-F	Footer (f)
Alt-H	Header (╫)
Alt-O	Strikeout (+)
Alt-Q	Start superscript or end subscript (↑)
Alt-W	Start subscript or end superscript (↓)
Alt-Z	Bold print (▌)
Ctrl-Break	Stop print operation
Ctrl-PrtSc	Hot print (print the current page)

Miscellaneous operations

Key(s)	Function
Esc	Cancel current operation
Alt-B	Required page break (⊥)
Alt-G	Reverse CASE setting in search or replace mode
Alt-M	Merge code (⊦)
Alt-R	Replay the last key procedure
Alt-S	Hard space (∅)
Alt-T	Thesaurus
Alt-U	Section numbering (∘)
Alt-V	Footnote (♫)
Alt-Y	*From within a document:* Clear all place marks
	From within a Data File: Select or deselect a record.
Ctrl-M	Change modes while editing a key procedure

Appendix B

MultiMate On-File Commands

Main Menu
F1—Create and Add a Card
F2—Search and Select Cards
F3—Display, Sort and Edit Selected Cards
F4—Print Selected Cards
F5—Use Special Features
F9—Finished using this box
F10—Exit On-File (return to DOS)

Create and Add a Card menu (F1 from Main Menu)
F1—Add card (to box)
F2—Review before adding
F3—Template Selection
F4—Color (change the color)
F5—Index (use current text word as index word)
F6—Flip
F7—Center (current text line)
F8—Automatic Indexing (choose from previous index words)
F10—Cancel card

Search and Select Cards menu (F2 from Main Menu)
F1—Search cards by SUBJECT
F2—Search cards by INDEX (word)
F3—Search cards by COLOR
F4—Search cards by DATE(S)
    Create and Edit Card Selection menu (after F1, F2, F3, or F4)
      F1—Select these cards—release prior selection
      F2—Add these cards to prior selection

        F3—Remove duplicate cards from prior selection
        F4—Keep any of these cards that are also in prior selection
        F5—Display these new cards
        F10—Cancel this search—leave prior selection alone
    F5—Select all the cards (without searching)
    F6—Match selected cards for word or phrase (appears when cards have
        been selected)
        F1—Start scan
        F6—Flip card
        F10—Cancel scan
    F10—Return to Main Menu

Display of Current Card Selection menu (F3 from Main Menu)
F1—Forward (next card)
F2—Backward (preceding card)
F3—Sort cards
    F3—Select sort template (then F1)
        Define the Sort Criteria menu
        F1—Perform the sort
        F3—Ascending sort order
        F5—Descending sort order
        F7—Color (ascending order only)
        F10—Cancel the sort
    F10—Cancel sort
F4—Top Card Options
    F1—Display both sides
    F2—Print card
    F3—View under template
        F3—Display next available template
        F4—Template Area Names (switch between data and names)
        F6—Flip card
        F10—Return to Top Card Options
    F4—Edit card
        F1—Perform the above change
        F3—Template Selection
        F8—Automatic Indexing
        F9—Template Area Names (switch between data and names)
        F10—Cancel the above change
    F5—Delete card
    F6—Flip card
    F10—Resume display
F6—Flip card
F10—Finished (return to Main Menu)

Print Selected Cards menu (F4 from Main Menu)
F1—Print using a template
    F1—Print cards
    F4—Select template
    F9—Select vertical spacing (1)
    F10—Cancel printing
F2—Print cards
F3—Create label format
    F1—Create using this template
        Cut and Paste Label Format screen
        F1—Save label format
        F3—Select template area (to be pasted)
        F4—Paste template area (on Label Format Container)
        F5—Float label (omit empty space)
        F6—Fix label (print per Label Format Container)
        F10—Cancel label format
    F3—Select template
    F10—Finished with create
F4—Print labels
    F1—Start printing
        F1—Start/Resume printing
            F5—Skip this label
            F6—Pause (stop printing and show next label)
        F9—Readjust (return to Print Labels menu)
        F10—Cancel printing
    F2—Test printing
    F5—Select print mode (hand-fed or continuous)
    F6—Pause between labels (Yes or No)
    F10—Cancel printing
F10—Exit to Main Menu

Use Special Features menu (F5 from Main Menu)
F1—Display calendar cards (starting with current month)
    F1—Ahead one month
    F2—Back one month
    F3—Ahead one year
    F4—Back one year
    F10—Return to Use Special Features
F2—Assign color identification
F3—Create and edit templates
    F1—Create a new template
    F2—Delete an existing template
    F3—Edit an existing template
        F1—Add or edit template areas

F2—Rename template or area names
F3—Delete or resequence template areas
    Return—Move between areas
    Del—Delete area
    Home—Select sequence order
F9—Select template
F10—Finished editing templates
F4—Copy an existing template
F10—Return to Use Special Features
F4—Delete selected cards
F5—Transfer cards to/from files
    F1—Write selected cards to a file
    F2—Read cards from a file into a box
    F3—Write selected cards to a MultiMate Merge Data file
    F4—Write selected cards under template to an ASCII file
    F10—Return to Use Special Features
F9—Turn sound on (or off)
F10—Return to Main Menu

Index

About the Author

Leo Scanlon, a native of Pittsburgh, Pennsylvania, received his B.S. degree in Aeronautical Engineering from St. Louis University. He also studied Electrical Engineering and Computer Science at the University of California at Berkeley.

Leo's experience includes technical writing in the minicomputer and microcomputer industries. He served as Technical Publications Manager with Computer Automation, Inc. in Irvine, CA, and Rockwell International Corp. in Anaheim, CA. He is the author of 16 microcomputer books.

A freelance writer in Inverness, Florida, he enjoys listening to jazz and boating with his wife, Pat, and sons Roger and Ryan.